ANNIE K. KOSHI

The City College of New York
City University of New York

DISCOVERIES

READING, THINKING, WRITING

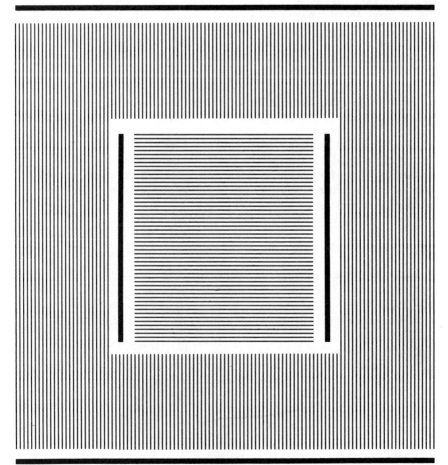

Heinle & Heinle Publishers
A Division of Wadsworth, Inc.
Boston, Massachusetts 02116 U.S.A.

Photo credits: **2**, Nino Mascardi, The Image Bank; **23**, W. H. Hodge, Peter Arnold, Inc.; **45**, The Bettmann Archive; **77**, Arthur W. Ambler, Photo Researchers, Inc.; **112** (left), Van Bucher, Photo Researchers, Inc.; **112** (right), Bob Klein, Black Star; **133**, Spencer Grant, Photo Researchers, Inc.; **167**, Jim Anderson, Woodfin Camp & Associates, Inc.; **195** (top), Culver Pictures; **195** (bottom), Springer/Bettman Film Archive; **222**, Renee Lynn, Photo Researchers, Inc.

Vice President and Publisher: Stanley J. Galek
Editorial Director: David C. Lee
Assistant Editor: Kenneth Mattsson
Project Management: Hockett Editorial Service
Production Supervisor: Patricia Jalbert
Manufacturing Coordinator: Lisa McLaughlin
Text and Cover Design: Marsha Cohen, Parallelogram
Illustrations: David Weisman

Discoveries: Reading, Thinking, Writing

Manufactured in the United States of America

Library of Congress Cataloging-in-Publication Data

Koshi, Annie K.
    Discoveries—reading, thinking, writing / Annie K. Koshi.
       p. cm.
    ISBN 0-8384-2386-8
    1. English language—Rhetoric. 2. English language-
    -Grammar—1950-   3. College readers. I. Title
    PE1408.K698 1992
    808'.042—dc20   91-43289
                                                                CIP

ISBN 0-8384-2386-8

10 9 8 7 6 5 4 3 2 1

CONTENTS

U N I T · 1
C H A P T E R · 1

C H A P T E R · 2

C H A P T E R · 3

C H A P T E R • 4

UNIT·2

CHAPTER·5

CHAPTER•6

CHAPTER•7

CHAPTER•8

CHAPTER•9

UNIT•3
CHAPTER•10

PREFACE

This book, *Discoveries: Reading, Thinking, Writing*, invites the users to discover the processes of writing by "reflective" reading. The philosophy underlying this approach is that students write best when their writing activities follow "reflective" reading of sample written pieces (professional, amateur, academic, and journalistic), requiring them to arrive inductively at the lexical, syntactical, grammatical, and rhetorical "conventions" the writers follow for effective communication to their readers.

The specific technique used in this book is the explicit analysis of authentic, unedited selections. By answering problem-posing and problem-solving questions, learners are guided to discover the meanings expressed by different discourse elements. Thus, even the discussions on grammar are meaning oriented and contextual. The discovery and description of textual structure help students become mature readers.

The book employs neither the process approach nor the product approach, but integrates both. The philosophical sources are current trends in cognitive psychology, which include schema theory, cognitive learning strategies, and critical thinking.

The book comprehensively covers the important elements needed to develop good writing, namely, (1) specific content, (2) organization of content material, (3) vocabulary, (4) cohesion, (5) coherence, (6) culture-specific (relating to Western thinking) rhetorical patterns, (7) sentence structure, and (8) grammatical accuracy. Since the order of importance these elements bear to the acquisition process is controversial, the book does not follow any specific order in discussing them.

Discoveries is an innovative writing text. It is not a "how-to" textbook, but a "how-is-it-being-done" textbook. It teaches students to rely on both content schemata and formal schemata by asking "metareading" and "metawriting" questions on the content, structure, and rhetorical genres used in the sample reading materials. The idea is to help students recognize these schemata as a "reading–prewriting" skill to be transferred into their own writing. The cognitive and metacognitive strategies of organizing new information and consciously relating it to existing knowledge encourage students to become mentally active learners of the devices "discovered" by text analysis. Once students become accustomed to using learning strategies in this way, they will become cognitively adept in *applying* them to their free writing.

The contextualized, text-oriented discussions invite students to monitor their own learning. These discussions and writing activities also lend themselves to group and collaborative learning, with students taking the responsibility for their own learning.

Flexibility and adaptability are the keys to using this book. Since the reading and discussions cover a wide range of materials adaptable to the needs of low intermediate to advanced learners, both learners and teachers can freely select from the contents.

The book is primarily aimed at college-bound ESL students whose background knowledge of the conventions and rhetorical genres, syntax, grammar, and vocabulary needs to be supplemented by exposure to sample mature writing. However, the book is also adaptable to the following groups:

1. Career-bound ESL students who need extensive practice in applying their background knowledge of discourse elements
2. Remedial English-speaking students who cannot function in academic courses because they are deficient in grammatical accuracy, syntactic maturity, and other discourse elements
3. Students enrolled in tutorial courses (both remedial and ESL) who need to review and apply their background knowledge of discourse elements
4. Students enrolled in writing laboratories to supplement the instruction received in regular courses

Finally, the author presents this "handy handbook" with the hope that both learners and teachers will have the same kind of rewarding experience that she has had for about three years in applying the cognitive and metacognitive teaching/learning approach used in this book.

TO FACILITATORS AND LEARNERS

This book is meant for learners who have attained at least an intermediate level of language and writing proficiency, that is, those who have some idea of expository writing, rules of syntax and grammar, vocabulary, and word forms. The lessons aim at helping them make a smooth transition from "sheltered" English (if they have been taught through mechanically driven, carefully controlled reading and writing exercises) or from extensive reading and writing of stretches of unstructured pieces (if they have been taught through the whole-language approach) to intensive reading of sample pieces of authentic writing, followed by writing. The purpose of this intensive reading is to acquire skills in expository writing characterized by syntactic maturity, coherence, cohesion, and appropriate rhetorical style.

THE ORGANIZATION OF THE BOOK

The book comprises ten chapters followed by an Answer Key. It is broadly divided into three units—Unit 1 (Chapters 1–4), Unit 2 (Chapters 5–9), and Unit 3 (Chapter 10).

Unit 1 discusses the general structure and logical/chronological organization of expository paragraphs and essays. The readings are meant as models to be read intensively. Chapter 4 provides an extensive reinforcement/review of the various discourse components of an expository essay in general. This is meant as a "bridge" to mastering the conventions involved in using rhetorical genres.

The emphasis in Unit 2 is on the rhetorical genres of comparison and contrast, classification, process analysis, cause and effect, and argumentation. Each chapter in this unit begins with a model reading passage and ends with a variety of supplementary reading passages—all samples of the specific rhetorical genre discussed.

The following sections appear in Units 1 and 2.

- Reading
- Grammar
- Sentence Combining
- Sentence Relating
- Vocabulary, Word Forms, and Idioms
- Writing
- Writing Activities

Unit 3 is meant as an editing guide for use in the last step of the writing process—to check on grammatical accuracy and idiomatic usage.

Reading

The reading passages provide an anthology of essays covering differing areas such as industry, biology, sociology, psychology, linguistics, and feminism. Even though some of these essays have been abridged to a certain extent, none is simplified or adapted to suit the teaching objectives specific to the discussion. Since the philosophy underlying the book is that reading provides second-language learners with language schemata, the reading selections are used as the source materials for teaching grammar, syntax, sentence variety, vocabulary, cohesion, and patterns of expository writing—the elements that make up textual discourse.

Even though these reading selections provide models for the specific discourse elements and rhetorical genre discussed, they are in no way meant to be imitated, reproduced, or manipulated. This would only encourage the production of artificial writing. The analytical discussions, contextual exercises, and writing assignments that follow each reading selection are meant to raise students' awareness of how the product has been put together, and of how the inclusion of each particular feature (lexical, syntactic, organizational, and so on) contributes to the appeal of the piece. Learners may want to adapt these features to produce acceptable compositions.

Each reading selection is preceded by a prereading activity, requiring students to check on their background knowledge of the content of the passage. The postreading activities help students evaluate the new information received from their reading, comparing it with their background knowledge. These postreading activities are meant not to test students' factual knowledge of what they read, but to develop higher order thinking skills built on factual knowledge.

Unit 2 provides a variety of readings for learners to choose from, with both prereading and postreading activities.

Grammar

Since the simplest syntactic features chosen by a writer to give a unified form to the text are tense and voice, these are given the primary emphasis. Other grammatical items like modal verbs, conditionals, prepositions, articles, participles, gerunds, and infinitives are also discussed.

The discussion of each grammatical item is oriented more to meaning and use in communicative writing than to abstract rules. The reading passages are analyzed in such a way as to make students understand *how* and *why* native English writers choose a certain grammatical item to convey their meaning. Gradually, learners will be able to start with thought, not with rules.

The formative rules discussed are presented in the logical form of mathematical formulas.

Chapter 10, The Editing Process, covers most grammatical points not included in the contextual discussions in the other nine chapters.

Punctuation

Using the reading passage as the basic source material, a contextual analysis of the use of different punctuation marks is given in Chapter 3, followed by a comprehensive discussion.

Sentence Combining

Here the purpose is to show how mature writers write sentences of varying length and complexity to effect a "flow" of writing style, to hold the sentences together, and to make the writing piece cohesive.

The discussions on coordination, subordination, and embedding—all in the context of the reading selections analyzed—are rather comprehensive. As in the grammar section, learners are shown *how* and *why* writers employ specific sentence-combining techniques.

The extensive content-related and grammar-free sentence-combining practice is intended to motivate learners to *use* their already learned grammatical ability with confidence. These text-based sentence-combining exercises will help learners self-monitor and evaluate their performance by checking their answers against the sentences in the text. These exercises also help learners use their cognitive ability to store longer "chunks" of discourse in their memory for transference to the writing activities provided in the Application, Writing Assignments, and Writing Activity sections.

Sentence Relating

This section mainly discusses the transition words used in the models as a discourse technique to relate one idea to another through agreement, addition, contrast, concession, and the like.

The most commonly used transition words are discussed in the context of the reading passages. Here again, the explanations are meaning oriented, with the purpose of making learners understand *why* mature writers use specific transition words and *how* these structures help hold the piece together.

Vocabulary, Word Forms, and Idioms

One of the biggest hurdles second-language learners experience in their writing is the application of the vocabulary learned from reading to their writing. Although they might get the meaning of a specific word from the context and/or the dictionary, they cannot be considered to have mastered the item unless they reach the productive stage of using the new lexical item in all different syntactic contexts. Therefore, the primary emphasis in this section is on *word forms*. Reading passages are followed by fill-in exercises requiring students to use vocabulary words in the same textual context and meaning but mostly in different word forms, with the syntax altered. This section also encourages learners to find synonyms of the vocabulary words they learn.

Writing

With the reading passages displayed as models, the textbook gives extensive discussions of:

- Paraphrasing
- Summarizing
- Paragraph writing
- Writing an expository essay (structure and rhetorical patterns)
- Process writing (prewriting, organizing, writing, revising, editing)

The discussions are followed by writing assignments, which provide a multiplicity of writing activities like writing summaries, critiques, reviews, short essays, and long expository essays.

Writing Activities

This has four parts: (1) Learning Log, (2) Reaction Journal, (3) Writing Assignment, and in some chapters (4) Alternate Writing Assignment.

The Learning Log is meant to be done after each chapter has been discussed and studied in detail. The purpose is to have learners monitor and self-evaluate their learning and decide on the kind and amount of further learning or improvement needed. The facilitators may decide to read this log to evaluate themselves and the learners.

The Reaction Journal requires learners to apply their critical thinking skills to what they learn from each chapter.

The Writing Assignments require learners to summarize, recall, organize, and interpret their learning, drawn from individual chapters, their wide reading, and world experience (by interviewing, talking to people, and so on).

How to Use This Book

Advanced-level learners might need a total of 90 semester hours to complete this book. The readings may be done as an out-of-class activity. However, the pre- and postreading activities should be done in class and in small groups. Grammar, Sentence Combining, Sentence Relating, Punctuation, and Vocabulary sections may be done as homework. Using the Answer Key and textual readings, students will be able to monitor their answers. With the help of the facilitator, learners can follow up on these in their group work by cognitively sharing and discussing how and why they chose the particular answers they did. The facilitator may want to add further discussions as necessary.

Learners may want to select from the various supplementary readings. Along with the main reading selections, these provide models for the specific rhetorical genre discussed in each chapter. Learners are expected to relate the reading of these essays to their writing. An effective way to do this is as follows.

Having done the exercises following the main reading selection in each chapter and read the two expository writing sections, learners may be assigned to write essays on topics selected from the supplementary readings. Before starting their essays, they may go over the prereading activity for the sample professional essay, which can serve as a brainstorming activity. However, they should not be encouraged to read the sample essays before writing their own essays. After writing the essays, learners may conduct group discussions, and, with the help of the facilitator, compare and contrast their work with the professional samples given in the textbook and make suggestions to one another for improving on their drafts.

Pick and Choose

Finally, flexibility is the key to using this textbook. This is not just a textbook, but a handbook and a resource book, too. Each learner and facilitator may want to adapt the materials to his or her needs. For example, advanced learners may not need to begin with Unit 1, which is an introduction to expository writing. All they need might be a quick review. Similarly, some intermediate learners may find Unit 2 above their interlanguage learning level and need extensive help from their facilitators.

Most of the exercises and activities are adaptable to either individual or group work. They are mostly learner centered. The textual readings, the note sections, and the Answer·Key are meant to promote independent growth.

On the whole, most reading materials (both the main reading selections and the supplementary readings) are on a higher level than the other sections, since most learners' reading comprehension is a little higher than their writing ability. Some of the supplementary readings are very advanced. Learners are advised to match their interests and reading levels with these readings.

The author hopes that this book will meet the needs of learners of varied interests and learning levels.

ACKNOWLEDGMENTS

I am grateful to the editorial staff of Heinle and Heinle Publishers, in particular to Dave Lee, Editorial Director, Academic ESL, who has always been available for any kind of help. Thanks are also due to Chris Foley who made my first contact with Heinle and Heinle possible and successful, and to Anne Sokolsky.

I am grateful to my colleagues at City College, City University of New York, who proofread portions of this book and made suggestions; they are Carole Riedler-Berger, Dominic Pietrosimone, and Barry Antokoletz. Grateful acknowledgment is also made to Betty Jane Doocey, my colleague at St. John's University, Jamaica, New York, who read some portions of the manuscript and made suggestions.

Special thanks are needed for the reviewers whose comments were critical in the development of this book: J.D. Brown, University of Hawaii; Maria Cantarero-Schipull, Miami-Dade Community College; Duane Ratzlaff, Christ College Irvine; Duane Roen, University of Arizona; Matt Stowell, College of Insurance; and Julia Yobst, University of Miami.

I am thankful to Rachel Youngman and Carol Schardt of Hockett Editorial Service for overseeing the production of the book, to Amy Rose for her careful copyediting, and to David Weisman for the production of the artwork.

And finally, this book would not have been possible without the help of Mathew, my husband, also a teacher, whose encouragement and moral support have been the driving force throughout the life of this project. I also credit the cooperation and patience of my children, Sarita, Anita, and Jomo, who had to take over household chores whenever I was busy with my writing.

Annie K. Koshi

UNIT · 1

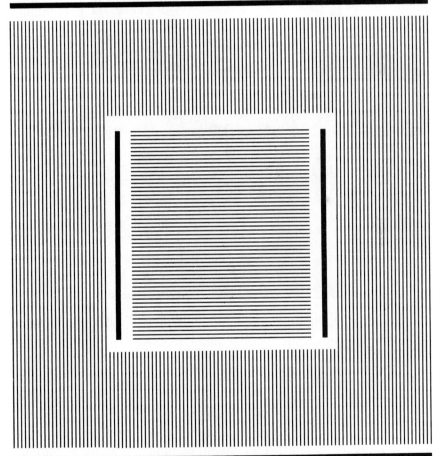

C H A P T E R · 1

Part 1: READING

PREREADING ACTIVITIES

Test your background knowledge about soda by answering the following questions.

1. Do you know of *soda* by any other name?
2. What is the basic chemical principle underlying the production of soda?
3. Who discovered this principle?
4. Where in the United States was the manufacturing of soda first started?
5. How were soda bottles stoppered during the early manufacturing period?
6. How are they being stoppered now?
7. What are the different phases in the manufacturing of soda?
8. Name five leading soft drink companies which make soda.
9. Is drinking soda healthy?
10. Tourists to many developing countries are advised to drink soda rather than tap water. Why?

Reading: SODA

1. Soda has been known by different names. It used to be called "tonic" by some people. Depending on where you live today, you may know it as "pop," "soda pop," or just plain "soda." We are all familiar with the stuff. Soda — that sweet, bubbling, sinfully-delicious drink — is available in every color of the rainbow and is found in nearly every restaurant and bar-n-grill, not to mention the shelves of supermarkets and most probably your kitchen cabinets!

2. Although the name "soda" was born in the early nineteenth century, the product's true beginnings go back several centuries. As early as biblical times, man enjoyed the pleasures of bubbling waters that spouted from natural springs. For centuries thereafter, scientists, especially in Europe, attempted to reproduce the effervescent quality found in naturally carbonated waters. In 1767, an English scientist named Joseph Priestly began experiments to simu-

Excerpted from Joan Murray, "Soda Industry," *Privilege* (Spring 1983) : 33–36, 52, 54.

late the "fixed air" found in natural waters. At a brewery, Priestly used a primitive apparatus to pour water from one vessel to another while holding the contraption close to the fermenting vats. He found that the water in the vessels easily absorbed the gas (later identified as carbon dioxide) from the vats. Priestly published his findings in a paper entitled, "Directions for impregnating water with fixed air." For the rest of the eighteenth century and early into the next century, scientists in England and abroad worked at perfecting Priestly's apparatus.

3.   Across the Atlantic, researchers in the U.S. followed Priestly's example and began devising their own methods for making carbonated drinks. Philadelphia is recognized as the locale of the earliest attempt to bottle soda in America. In 1809, Joseph Hawkins was granted the first U.S. patent to bottle soda water. Shortly thereafter, he opened a small bottling plant on Chestnut Street. Profits increased slowly but steadily and word spread. By 1849 there were 64 bottling plants in the U.S. and twenty years later that number had more than quadrupled, with 387 plants reportedly bottling soda water in 1870. Today there are more than 3,000 plants involved in the manufacturing of soda with more than 200 brands on the market.

4.   Compared to today's methods of bottling soda, early manufacturing was simple and unsophisticated. Water was filtered by using such crude materials as sand, animal charcoal and sponge. Bottle filling was a manual operation and required an employee to literally fill bottles with syrup and carbonated water by hand and then do his or her best to prevent gas from escaping while the stoppers were put in place.

5.   In 1892, William Painter introduced the Crown Cap which was an effective method for stoppering bottles. Prior to his invention, more than 1,500 stoppering devices had been tried with little success. Shortly after the Crown Cap's advent, the Saratoga Springs Company of New York began using machine-made bottles for their soda water.

6.   Machine-made bottles meant equipment could be standardized and this, in conjunction with the Crown Cap, ultimately meant soda could be produced more quickly and efficiently. The soda industry was on its way to becoming an international phenomenon.

7.   The modern soft drink plant is a highly mechanized, sophisticated operation that can turn out units of soda at a rate of about 2,000 per minute, in contrast to the average speed of 150 units per minute in 1950. Depending on the soda plant, the phases of production include compounding ingredients to make simple syrup; water treatment; carbonation; container filling; packaging and inspection.

8.   Simple syrup is made by dissolving sugar in purified water, adding flavorings and sometimes food coloring. Approximately six pounds of sugar are used per gallon of water. Most modern plants do not make their own syrup on the premises but rather purchase it from wholesalers, who deliver it in large containers. The syrup used in soda does more than act as a sweetening agent. Its properties help to blend ingredients while intensifying flavor.

9. More than eighty-five percent of the total volume of soda is water. The water must be highly purified to avoid alteration of taste and appearance in the final product. Filters, especially those made of carbon, are used to remove foreign substances from the water. Most plants have extensive water purification systems for meeting their needs.

10. Soda contains carbonation ranging from one to five volumes — a volume being equal to fifteen pounds per square inch pressure at sea level and sixty-degrees fahrenheit. Soda plants obtain their carbon dioxide in pressurized containers. The gas is released into a device known as carbonator. The purified water mixed with syrup is then exposed to the gas and taken under pressure to filling machines where it is packaged and inspected. The amount of gas dissolved varies directly with the temperature of the water and carbon dioxide under pressure. The lower the temperature of the water, the less gas pressure needed to carbonate the soda.

11. Thirty years ago, about three-fourths of all soda containers were in returnable bottles. Consumer trends forced manufacturers to come up with convenient disposable one-way containers. Aluminum cans first appeared on supermarket shelves in the early 1950's. Shatterproof plastic containers were perfected in the 1970's. Today, about three-quarters of all soda is packaged in plastic containers.

12. Most carbonated drinks manufactured today are under franchise agreements with companies that own the rights to formulas and trademarks. The five leading parent soft drink companies are : Coca-Cola, Pepsi, Dr. Pepper, Seven-Up, and Royal Crown, in that order.

13. In recent years, there has been much controversy over the place of soda in the diet, especially in regard to its water content. A review of the drink's contents reveals that it is comprised of anywhere from 86 to 93 percent water, 7 to 14 percent sugar plus fruit flavorings and colorings approved by the Food and Drug Administration. Some nutritionists claim that 7 to 14 percent sugar (equivalent of approximately 10 teaspoons in a 12 ounce can) is too much.

14. Despite the numerous controversies surrounding soda, there is one aspect of the drink which most will agree is positive : a beverage that contains ninety-percent water can't be all bad. Water is necessary to maintain normal bodily functions. It has long been known that man can exist sixty days without food, but without some type of moisture, he would not last more than five days. Moreover, the water in soda is highly purified and in many respects surpasses ordinary tap water which can contain pollutants, bacteria and other impurities. Doctors often recommend soda for patients with upset stomach and others who cannot tolerate food or liquids. Most importantly, the soda industry has set up standards world-wide to insure that the water used for soft drinks internationally is just as pure as that used in the U.S.

POSTREADING ACTIVITIES

1. Your Science Club is convening a Science Fair. The members are supposed to talk about the scientific principle underlying one of the manufacturing products of their choice. Your choice is soda. Write down your speech, explaining the chemical activity underlying the manufacturing of soda.
2. You have to give a talk to your speech class on how the machine age has conquered time. Taking the soda industry as an example, explain to the class how machines are helping to speed production. (Here you are required to compare and contrast the early, simple methods of soda production with the sophisticated methods of mechanical manufacturing).
3. You have a job interview for the position of Assistant Production Manager of the Pepsi Cola branch in your hometown. A friend of the manager of the company has told you that you might be tested on your background information on the process of soda manufacturing. Prepare your answer in advance, explaining the different phases of production. (You are not going to be given more than two minutes to talk.)
4. Recently, your aunt has been advised by her doctor to drink soda two times a day because of a stomach ulcer. However, she refuses to follow the doctor's advice because, according to her, soda is machine-made water, high in sugar content, and full of chemicals. Write a letter to her explaining the composition of soda with special reference to its water content.

Part 2: GRAMMAR

VERB TENSES

Simple Present vs. Simple Past Tense

For Your Critical Thinking

1. Why is Paragraph 1 (Par. 1) written in the simple present tense and Paragraph 2, in the simple past tense?
2. What tense does the writer use in sentence 2 (S2), Par. 1? Why?

3. What tense is used in the following sentences taken from Paragraph 3?

    S1. Philadelphia is recognized as the locale of the earliest attempt to bottle soda in America.

    S2. Today there are more than 3,000 plants involved in the manufacturing of soda with more than 200 brands on the market.

4. Why is the tense used in these two sentences (S1 and S2, above) different from that used in the other sentences in Paragraph 3?
5. Find other paragraphs in the reading passage, in which the writer uses both simple present and simple past tenses.

Present Perfect vs. Simple Present Tense

For Your Critical Thinking

1. What difference in meaning would it make if you changed the underlined verbs in the following sentences into simple present tense?
2. Analyze the form of the underlined verbs and make out a formula for the present perfect tense verb form.

    S1. In recent years there has been much controversy over the place of soda in the diet. (Par. 13)

    S2. It has long been known that man can exist sixty days without food. (Par. 14)

    S3. Most importantly, the soda industry has set up standards worldwide to insure that the water used for soft drink internationally is just as pure as that used in the United States. (Par. 14)

Note

The simple present tense is used in the following contexts:

1. To express "eternal truths" or generally accepted facts.

    Ex. 1. The earth is round.
    Ex. 2. Big cities are crowded.

2. To express repeated or habitual action.

    Ex. 1. Whenever I visit my mother, who lives in Florida, I go swimming.
    Ex. 2. I work three days a week.

The formulas for the simple present tense verb form are:

sing. n. subj. + base v. + <u>s</u> = simple pres. tense

<u>he</u>/<u>she</u>/<u>it</u> + base v. + <u>s</u> = simple pres. tense

pl. n. subj. + base v. = simple pres. tense

<u>I</u>/<u>you</u>/<u>we</u>/<u>they</u> + base v. = simple pres. tense

The present perfect is used in the following contexts:

1. To express an action or state which began some time in the past and continues into the present. Usually, this use is accompanied by time words like *since, so for, up to now, up to the present, up to this moment,* etc.

    Ex. 1. *I have been trying* to find a job since I graduated.
    Ex. 2. *So far* I *have* not *had* any luck.

2. To express an action or state which was repeated in the past and which will, in all probability, be repeated in the future.

    Ex. 1. Since I came to this school, I *have* never *gotten* any grade higher than a B.
    Ex. 2. I *have watched* that movie several times.

3. To express an action that occurred at an unspecified or indefinite time in the past. For this reason the present perfect tense is sometimes called the indefinite past tense. You can use this tense whenever you are not sure exactly when the action took place or when the exact time of the action is not important. Since words like *already, at last, recently, never, ever, finally, yet, just,* etc. do not necessarily indicate an exact time, they often accompany verbs in the present perfect tense.

    Ex. 1. I *have already studied* the present perfect tense.
    Ex. 2. However, I *have* not *yet used* it in my writing because I could never figure out when to use it, and I *have always used* the simple past tense instead.
    Ex. 3. *Finally,* after reading this *Note,* I *have gained* confidence in how to use it.

The formula for the present perfect tense is:

<u>have</u>/<u>has</u> + past participle = present perfect tense

Application

Write a paragraph (about ten sentences) on:

1. The new places you have visited since you came to this country
2. The new friends you have made in your new job or in your new school

Simple Past vs. Past Perfect Tense

For Your Critical Thinking

1. What are the two periods of time expressed in the following sentence?
2. Change the underlined phrase into a clause (beginning your sentence with *Before*) and compare the time of action indicated by the two verbs in your sentence.

    S1. <u>Prior to his invention</u>, more than 1,500 stoppering devices had been tried with little success.

Note

The simple past, also called the past definite to distinguish it from the indefinite past (that is, the present perfect) tense, is used to express a completed action that occurred at a specified time in the past. This specified time should be indicated by the time word *ago*, time expressions like *yesterday, last month*, etc., or any word, phrase, or dependent clause denoting or implying a definite time in the past.

    Ex. 1. I *studied* the simple past tense last semester.
    Ex. 2. I *visited* London two years ago.
    Ex. 3. My grandfather *was* born before the first world war.
    Ex. 4. The Crusades *took* place in the Middle Ages.

The following formula applies to the simple past verb form:

simple (base) verb form + (e)d/t/n = simple past tense

The past perfect is used to describe an action which was completed before another action or time in the past or which continued up to another time in the past. For this reason, the past perfect tense is also called the earlier past tense.

Ex. 1. The train *had left* when I reached the station.
Ex. 2. Until two days ago I *had read* only one book.
Ex. 3. By 8 o'clock last night I *had finished* doing all my homework.

The formula for the past perfect verb form is:

had + past participle = past perfect tense

Usually, with the words *before* and *after*, the simple past tense, not the past perfect, is used, since these words indicate earlier or later time. However, it is not wrong to use the past perfect in these two contexts.

Ex. 1. The train *left* before we reached the station.
Ex. 2. The train *had left* before we reached the station.

Application

You happened to witness a fight between two teenagers, one of whom got wounded in the process. Make up a report of the event, describing chronologically what happened.

PASSIVE VOICE

Problems for You to Solve

1. Find all the passive voice verbs in the reading passage and underline them. Explain how you identified them and why you think the writer preferred the passive voice to the active voice in the specific contexts. (Notice that there are about 20 passive voice verbs — about a quarter of the total number of verbs — used in this passage.)
2. Why do you think there are so many passive voice verbs used in this passage?

For Your Critical Thinking

Answer the questions with reference to the following sentences.

S1.   It used to be called "tonic" by some people.

Q1.   Why didn't the writer begin the sentence with "Some people"?

S2.   Philadelphia is recognized as the locale of the earliest attempt to bottle soda in America.

Q1.   Who recognized Philadelphia as the locale of the earliest attempt to bottle soda in America?

Q2.   Why didn't the writer make this the subject of the sentence?

S3.   Joseph Hawkins was granted the first U.S. patent to bottle soda water.

Q1.   Do you think the writer knows who granted Hawkins the patent?

Note

The passive verb form is used when the actor or performer (the grammatical subject of the verb) is either unknown or when we do not want to mention the actor or performer. It is also used when we want to give importance to the receiver, not to the actor or performer. The passive form of the verb has the following formula.

form of <u>to be</u> + past participle = passive verb form

Scientific essays require the use of the passive voice a lot. Why? As stated above, the passive voice is used when the doer of the action (the subject of the verb) is either not known or is unimportant. To put it in another way, you use the passive voice when you want to make the receiver of the action (the object of the verb) important. This is the situation in activities related to scientific inventions.

Ex. 1.   Electricity was discovered by Edison.

This sentence means that the topic the writer is talking about is *electricity*, not Edison (the doer of the action). Even though Edison is the one who invented electricity, the writer of this sentence has decided to give importance to *electricity* and not to *Edison*.

Ex. 2. Einstein developed the theory of relativity.

Here the topic of the sentence is Einstein, not the theory of relativity. Hence the active voice.

Application

1. Write a short paragraph on your last birthday celebration, giving importance to you and the celebration, not to those who gave you the party, gifts, etc.
2. Describe the history and development of one of the following:

   • The automobile industry
   • The aircraft industry

(Note: You will have to use many verbs in the passive voice to do these assignments.)

3. Suppose you are one of the lab supervisors. Give directions to a newly appointed employee on how to:

   • Make syrup (Par. 8) or
   • Carbonate water (Par. 10)

(Remember, to do this exercise you have to use the active voice.)

ADJECTIVES: DEGREES OF COMPARISON — POSITIVE DEGREE

For Your Critical Thinking

What are the things compared in the following sentence?

S1. Water used for soft drinks internationally is just as pure as that used in the U.S. (Par. 14)

Note

The positive degree, like the comparative degree, is used when there are only two things or people or sets of things or people to compare. The positive degree, in contrast to the comparative degree, expresses equality — the two people or things are equally good or bad. The formula for the form of positive degree is:

$$\underline{as} + adj. + \underline{as} = positive \ degree$$

Application

Write sentences to express the following situations:

1. Yesterday you and your friend bought a VCR from a local store. You found the two equally expensive.
2. You are taking two courses in ESL this semester. You have found both the courses equally difficult.

Part 3: SENTENCE COMBINING

Problems for You to Solve

Combine the following sets of sentences into one sentence each. After combining the sentences, check your sentences against the ones in the textbook and discuss your answers with your group members and then with your instructor. The paragraph numbers are indicated after each pair.

1a. You may know it as "pop," "soda pop," or just plain "soda."
 b. It depends on the place you live. (Par. 1)

2a. The name "soda" was born in the early nineteenth century.
 b. However, the product's true beginning goes back several centuries. (Par. 2)

3a. At a brewery, Priestly used a primitive apparatus to pour water from one vessel to another.
 b. At the same time, he was holding the contraption close to the fermenting vats. (Par. 2)

4a. William Painter introduced the Crown Cap.
 b. It was an effective method for stoppering bottles. (Par. 5)

5a. The modern soft drink plant is a highly mechanized, sophisticated operation.
 b. It can turn out units of soda at a rate of 2,000 per minute. (Par. 7)

6a. The phases of production include compounding ingredients to make simple syrup, water treatment, etc.
 b. The phases of production depend on the soda plant. (Par. 7)

7a. The purified water is mixed with syrup.
 b. This is then exposed to the gas.
 c. This is taken under pressure to filling machines.
 d. There it is packaged.
 e. There it is inspected. (Par. 10)

8a. There are numerous controversies surrounding soda.
 b. However, there is one aspect of the drink.
 c. Most (people) will agree this is positive. (Par. 14)

9a. A beverage contains 90% water.
 b. This cannot be all bad. (Par. 14)

10a. The water in the soda is highly purified.
 b. In many respects this water surpasses ordinary tap water.
 c. Tap water can contain pollutants, bacteria, and other impurities. (Par. 14)

11a. Doctors often recommend soda for patients with upset stomachs.
 b. Doctors often recommend soda for other patients.
 c. These patients cannot tolerate food or liquids. (Par. 14)

CLAUSE MARKERS

Who, Which, That

All three clause markers above introduce adjective clauses. *Who* replaces persons and sometimes animals. For example, in combining sentences 11a, 11b, and 11c, *these patients* and *other patients* are replaced by *who*. *Which* replaces animals and things. For example, in combining 10a, 10b, and 10c, *tap water* is replaced by *which*. *That* can be used for humans and both animate and nonanimate objects. In the examples above *that* replaces only things. You will see examples of *that* replacing people later.

For Your Critical Thinking

What is the difference in the uses of *that* in the following pairs of sentences?

1a. Soda—*that* sweet, bubbling, sinfully-delicious drink—is available in every color of the rainbow and found in nearly every restaurant... (Par. 1)
 b. He found *that* the water in the vessels easily absorbed the gas. (Par. 2)

2a. Some nutritionists claim *that* 7 to 14 percent sugar is too much. (Par. 13)
 b. Most carbonated drinks manufactured today are under franchise agreements with companies *that* own the rights to formulas and trademarks. (Par. 12)

While, Where

While and *where* are clause markers that introduce adverbial clauses. *While* replaces time phrases, and *where* replaces locative phrases. Unlike adjective markers, they do not replace nouns or pronouns.

Although, Even Though, Even If

Although, like *while* and *where*, is an adverbial clause marker, but it does not indicate time. The clause introduced by *although* conveys a meaning contradictory to that conveyed by the main clause. Synonyms of *although* are *even though*, *even if* and *though* (informal). Another synonym is *despite*. However, bear in mind that *despite* is a phrase marker, not a clause marker, and is followed by a noun or noun phrase. See, for example, the first sentence of Par. 14. See also 8a, b, and c above.

PARTICIPIAL PHRASES

Sentences can also be combined using participial phrases. As you know, a participle is the *-ing* (present participle) or an *-(e)d/-(e)n* (past participle) form of a verb. Examples are : *a loving mother, a smiling boy, a pampered child, overdone work.* Two sentences can be combined with a participle or participial phrase, provided the subject of the two sentences is the same. The sentence that is made into a participial phrase becomes a half sentence in the combining process. An example is the last sentence of Par. 7 and the second sentence in Par. 1. See 1a and b and 6a and b, pp. 13–14.

Part 4: SENTENCE STRUCTURE

PHRASE MARKERS

Not to Mention

Paragraph 1 ends with the following phrase: "not to mention the shelves of supermarkets and most probably, your kitchen cabinets." This is a rhetorical statement, negative in form, but positive in meaning. The statement means: There is no need to mention supermarkets and your kitchen cabinets. Obviously, all supermarkets and kitchen cabinets have soda on their shelves.

Especially

For Your Critical Thinking

Can you split the following sentences into two complete sentences each?

S1. For centuries thereafter, scientists, *especially* in Europe, attempted to reproduce the effervescent quality found in naturally carbonated waters. (Par. 2)
S2. Filters, *especially* those made of carbon, are used to remove foreign substances from the water. (Par. 9)
S3. In recent years, there has been much controversy over the place of soda in the diet, *especially* in regard to its sugar content. (Par. 13)

Note

Especially is not a clause marker like *who, when, because,* etc. It introduces a phrase, not a clause. However, in word order, the phrase introduced by *especially* functions almost like a clause, either following the main part of the sentence and separated by a comma as in #3 above, or placed in the middle of a sentence and separated by a pair of commas as in #1 and 2. Remember, the phrase that *especially* introduces cannot stand by itself, so never put a period after the phrase.

Part 5: VOCABULARY, WORD FORMS, AND IDIOMS

FILL-INS

Paragraph **b** in each of the following pairs is a paraphrase of **a**. Using synonyms and antonyms (which need not be exact), changing sentence structure, and changing word forms are some of the devices used in making the paraphrase.

Your task : Fill in the blanks with appropriate words or phrases. Each blank line indicates one word. The underlined words in the original may give you the clues.

1a. The product's true beginnings go back several centuries. (Par. 1)

b. Soda (1) _____ to be (2) _____ several centuries (3) _____ .

2a. As early as biblical times, man enjoyed the pleasures of bubbling waters that spouted from natural springs. (Par. 2)

b. From (4) _____ times man has found (5) _____ in the (6) _____ that (7) _____ _____ from natural springs.

3a. Scientists attempted to reproduce the effervescent quality found in naturally carbonated waters. (Par. 2)

b. Scientists made several (8) _____ to make (9) _____ of the (10) _____ found in naturally carbonated waters.

4a. Joseph Priestly began <u>experiments</u> to <u>simulate</u> the "fixed air" found in natural waters. (Par. 2)

b. Joseph Priestly began (11) _____ on (12) _____ the "fixed air" found in carbonated water.

5a. Twenty years later the number of bottling plants had more than <u>quadrupled</u>, with 387 plants <u>reportedly</u> bottling soda in 1870. (Par. 3)

b. It is (13) _____ that there were 387 bottling plants in 1870, (14) _____ _____ the number that existed twenty years earlier.

6a. Water was <u>filtered</u> by using such <u>crude</u> materials as sand, animal charcoal, and sponge. (Par. 4)

b. The (15) _____ of water was done by using such (16) _____ materials as sand, animal charcoal, and sponge.

7a. In 1892, William Painter <u>introduced</u> the Crown Cap which was an <u>effective method</u> for <u>stoppering</u> bottles. (Par. 5)

b. The (17) _____ of the Crown Cap by William Painter, in 1892, brought about good (18) _____ in the (19) _____ bottles were (20) _____.

8a. <u>Prior to</u> his invention, more than 1,500 stoppering <u>devices</u> had been tried with <u>little success</u>. (Par. 5)

b. (21) _____ this invention, many manufacturers tried to (22) _____ several stoppering methods, but they (23) _____ _____. _____

9a. Machine-made bottles meant equipment could be <u>standardized</u> and this, <u>in conjunction</u> with the Crown Cap, <u>ultimately</u> meant soda could be <u>produced</u> more <u>quickly</u> and <u>efficiently</u>. (Par. 6)

  b. Machine-made bottles led to the (24) _____ of equipment and this, (25) _____ with the Crown Cap, (26) _____ made soda (27) _____ (28) _____ and more (29) _____ .

10a. The modern soft drink plant is a highly mechanized, sophisticated <u>operation</u> that can <u>turn out</u> units of soda at a rate of about 2,000 per minute, <u>in contrast to</u> the average speed of 150 units per minute in 1950. (Par. 7)

  b. The modern soft drink plant, which (30) _____ on a highly mechanized and sophisticated level, (31) _____ units of soda at a rate of about 2,000 per minute, (32) _____ in 1950, the average speed was 150 units per minute.

11a. <u>In recent years,</u> there has been much <u>controversy</u> over the place of soda in the diet, especially <u>in regard</u> to its sugar content. (Par. 13)

  b. (33) _____ , there has been much (34) _____ about the place of soda in the diet, especially (35) _____ _____ to its sugar content.

12a. Water is <u>necessary</u> to maintain normal <u>bodily</u> functions. (Par. 14)

  b. Water is (36) _____ the most important element for a human being to keep up the normal (37) _____ functions.

Part 6: WRITING

PARAPHRASING

Discussion

Reading comprehension involves skill in restating the writer's ideas in the reader's own words (borrowing the writer's ideas, but not his/her words and style of writing). What students often do in answer to comprehension questions is just to copy the relevant sentence(s) from the reading passage. Even though this shows reading comprehension, it does not demonstrate the skill of paraphrasing.

Paraphrasing is also a necessary skill in writing term papers. "Lifting" stretches of sentences from published works and calling them your own is plagiarism — a "sin" that many researchers, especially students, commit. Practice in paraphrasing will help students avoid this kind of "temptation." You can borrow ideas, but do not put these ideas in the author's exact words.

In restating the author's words in one's own words, you may omit some details, but you should retain the basic ideas. However, unlike summarizing, paraphrasing does not involve condensing the passage into a shorter one. Reporting direct quotations, using synonyms and different word forms, and varying sentence structure are some of the devices which can be used in paraphrasing. Also note that it is unacceptable simply to paraphrase an author's words when writing a term paper.

Paragraph 3 from "Soda" is paraphrased below as an example.

Following Priestly's example, researchers in the U.S. started making carbonated drinks in their own ways. Philadelphia is said to be the first city which bottled soda in America. The opening of the small bottling plant on Chestnut Street in 1809 by Joseph Hawkins, the first one which was granted the U.S. patent to bottle soda water, marked the beginning of the industry. Increase in profit was slow, but steady. Gradually, the news spread to other cities, and more businessmen came into the field. Soon, soda manufacturing became a thriving industry, and the number of plants began to multiply. Today, we have more than 3,000 plants with more than 200 brands, while there were only 64 plants in 1849.

Problems for You to Solve

Critically examine each paraphrased sentence above; compare it to the original paragraph in the textbook; find the devices used in paraphrasing the writer's ideas.

WRITING ACTIVITIES

Reaction Journal

Write in your journal:

- What you like and do not like about this chapter, giving reasons
- What you can contribute to the chapter
- What changes you would like to make
- If there is anything in the reading passage that you disagree with, and why

Learning Log

Write in your learning log:

- What you already knew about soda and soda industry
- What new information you have received from your reading
- How you can apply the new information to your life
- What additional information you would like to get
- If you have anything more to add to the content (from your extra reading and/or personal experience)
- If your reading of this article has changed any of your concepts about soda
- Five to ten new words you have learned from your reading, which you feel confident to use in your writing
- How helpful/not helpful the discussions in Part 2 have been (Explain with examples.)

Writing Assignment

Overview

Scan through the pages of this book or of any book, magazine, or newspaper. Paraphrase a key idea from one of the articles you found interesting and informative. You will do this assignment in a group. After you write down the paraphrase, you will present it to the class.

Purpose of Assignment: To make a presentation to the class
Audience: Your class members

Procedure

INDIVIDUAL WORK

Scan through the pages of this book, or of any book, magazine, or newspaper. Find an article, news item, or editorial, the topic of which you find interesting or informative. Read this piece. Do not stop reading for any reason (for example, to look up words in the dictionary, to check with friends or instructors on the meaning of words, etc.). The purpose of this reading is to find what the writer says about the topic. After you have finished reading, pick out the key idea that you found most informative. Identify the paragraphs where the writer explains this one idea. Paraphrase these paragraphs.

GROUP WORK

Purpose of Group Work: To get feedback from your peers
Material: Photocopies of the original and your written work

1.   Each group discusses the following:

   • The problems each member had in paraphrasing
   • What each member did to solve this problem

2.   Group members exchange photocopies.
3.   Members read each other's work (originals first, paraphrase next) and then discuss:

   • If the paraphrased work expresses the same idea, but in different ways
   • How many of the devices used in the sample paraphrased paragraph above have been applied by members
   • What device(s) the members found the easiest, and most difficult, and why

4.   Based on peer feedback, members rewrite their written pieces and make oral presentations to the entire class.

C H A P T E R · 2

Part 1: READING

PREREADING ACTIVITIES

Test your background knowledge about the poppy by discussing the following questions with your group members.

1. What does opium look like?
2. Is it made from chemicals, or does it come from plants?
3. What is the origin of the name *morphine*?
4. Are opium, morphine, and heroin related? How?
5. Do you think these three are useful to humanity in any way?
6. What evil effects do these drugs have on humans?
7. Do you think that the use of drugs should be legalized? Give your reasons.
8. What are some of the measures that governmental and community agencies take to counteract the illegal use of these drugs?
9. Why do some people get addicted to drugs?
10. Do you know of any kind of treatment given to drug addicts? Describe it.

Reading: THE POPPY

1. Papaver somniferum — that pretty little poppy — is unique in its capacity to effect both good and evil. Opium, morphine, and heroin — products from the poppy — if used properly, have marvelous medicinal effects. In fact, they have been used largely in the pharmaceutical industry for a long time. For example, the drug codeine in pill form relieves pain after operations or tooth extractions. But from *papaver somniferum* also comes the drug heroin. Smuggled into the U.S., it reaches nearly every community and every level of society, bringing addiction and misery to hundreds of thousands. Theft committed for money to buy heroin is a major cause of crime in American cities.

Excerpted and adapted from Peter T. White, "The Poppy," *National Geographic* (February 1985): 143–88. Used with permission.

2. What gives the opium poppy its power for good or evil? Let us examine the plant's chemistry. Day and night certain nitrogen-containing compounds, or alkaloids, are produced by the plant and stored in its cells. After the petals fall, the seed capsule swells. If the capsule is shallowly incised while still green and unripe, a milky, alkaloid-rich sap seeps from the tiny tubes in the capsule wall. It dries, darkens, and turns gummy. That is opium — a dark, shiny substance which looks like chocolate icing.

3. From prehistoric times opium has been used in various ways — in magic, in religious rituals, as a sedative and sleeping potion, etc. It has even been speculated that the "vinegar mingled with gall" offered to Christ on the Cross must have contained opium.

4. Opium dissolved in alcohol, known as laudanum, is said to have been an essential item in most medicine chests during the Middle Ages. India, the biggest poppy grower, has a long recorded history of opium use — all for good purposes. Opium was given to war elephants of the Mogul Empire and to Indian soldiers under the British to make them brave and feel less pain if hurt. Inside the Taj Mahal, built by Emperor Shah Jahan as a tomb for his favorite wife, his marble cenotaph is inlaid with carnelian poppies. It is said he used to drink opium in his wine. Today, opium is legally available to India's Ayurvedic doctors for treating sprue, asthma, scorpion bites, etc. However, these indigenous doctors are very careful in handling it. Some practitioners mix herbal juices with opium medicine to counteract bad effects, such as constipation. They also adjust the dosage downward without telling the patient, so that when the treatment ends, there will be no withdrawal sickness or addiction.

5. In 1815, a German pharmacist, F. Serturner, isolated the principal opium alkaloid — $c_{17}H_{19}NO_3$ — and named it for Morpheus, the Greek god of dreams. Morphine is the modern world's standard against which all pain medicines are measured. For example, the prescription for cancer patients suffering from severe pain could be morphine, given orally and carefully tailored to the patient's needs. Daily doses of codeine, taken through a stomach tube, are given to cancer patients suffering from intense pain. Codeine is to cancer patients what insulin is to diabetic patients. It controls recurring attacks of severe pain. Doctors and relatives get a feeling of joy, not because the patients are high, but because they are without pain and depression. Thus, in addition to its power to relieve cancer patients from severe pain, codeine serves the humanitarian purpose of allowing the patients to enjoy their families, resolve problems, and bring about family reconciliation during their last days.

6. When the morphine base is treated with the chemical, acetic anhydride, increasing its strength as an analgesic, or pain killer, about two and a half times, we get heroin. Introduced in Germany in 1898 as a remedy for cough and diarrhea, heroin was also proposed as a morphine substitute less likely to lead to addiction.

7. Heroin has become a social problem, especially since the invention of the hypodermic needle in 1893. A worldwide notion for a long time was that heroin is mainly an American problem. But that has been changing. Now it is a known fact that addiction is rising in all parts of the world.

8. There is disagreement over the best ways to help addicts. It is reported that the spectacular treatment of addicts at Tham Krabok Monastery north of Bangkok results in a 70 percent success rate, according to its records. The ten-day free treatment begins with a vow to the Buddha never to use narcotics again. Then patients are given herbal medicine that makes them vomit immediately. The monks, who have treated 80,000 since 1959, say the medicine "clears poisonous drug residue from the body and helps eliminate the physical desire for drugs." Herbal steam baths, milder tonics, and herbal pills, along with continuous counseling, are part of the regimen. Another country where a religious approach is used to cure addicts is Malaysia, where drug addiction has become an increasing problem. Religious healers called bomohs report a 60% cure rate.

9. Governments are up against drug addiction and are trying to adopt measures to control the drug problem. By the worldwide treaty now in force, 116 parties have agreed to call for international cooperation against drug abuse.

10. Opinions differ as to what exact measures have to be adopted to counteract illegal drug use. Some insist that we should give top priority to the eradication of illicit poppies. Some others urge that we should make people stop wanting heroin, through psychiatric treatment of addiction. Many seem to think that we should stop anti-drug propaganda because it only arouses more interest in drugs.

11. In spite of all the anti-drug movements sponsored by agencies, governments, and religious organizations, the problem is still with us as a social evil. After all, the fight between good and evil is as real as life itself. We must have been taught in religion classes, what most of us learn by just living — that the fight between good and evil has no end. It is a part of our existence. And when seen in that light, isn't *Papaver somniferum,* bringing both good and evil, another symbol of life?

POSTREADING ACTIVITIES

Compare your background knowledge about the poppy with the new information you received from reading this passage. Write down all the new ideas.

Part 2: GRAMMAR

VERB TENSES

Present Perfect: Reinforcement

For Your Critical Thinking

1. According to the following sentence, are the monks still treating the drug addicts? How do you know that?

   S1. The monks, who have treated over 80,000 drug addicts since 1959, say that the medicine clears poisonous drug residue from the body. (Par. 8)

2. Why did the writer use the present perfect tense in the following sentence?

   S1. By the worldwide treaty now in force, 116 parties *have agreed* to call for international cooperation against drug abuse. (Par. 9)

Present Continuous vs. Present Perfect Continuous

For Your Critical Thinking

How would you explain the difference in the time of action between the two *-ing* verbs underlined in the following sentences?

S1. The worldwide notion that heroin is mainly an American problem has been <u>changing</u>. (Par. 7)
S2. Governments are up against drug addiction and are <u>trying</u> to adopt measures to control the drug problem. (Par. 9)

Note

The present continuous tense is used to express an action in progress at the moment of speaking or writing. It implies: *in the act of or in the process of.* The formula for the present continuous tense is:

form of <u>to be</u> + base v. + <u>-ing</u> = present continuous tense

The present perfect continuous tense is used in almost the same way as the present perfect except that it emphasizes the duration of time which began in the past and continues into the present.

PASSIVE VOICE: REVIEW

For Your Critical Thinking

1. Why are most of the verbs in this article used in passive voice?
2. Separate each of the following sentences into as many complete sentences as possible and change them into the active voice to see why the writer preferred to use the passive voice.

   S1. Opium dissolved in alcohol, known as laudanum, is said to have been an essential item in most medicine chests during the Middle Ages. (Par. 4)

(Split the sentence into three complete sentences before you try the active voice.)

   S2. It is reported that the spectacular treatment of addicts at Tham Krabok Monastery results in a 70 percent success rate. (Par. 8)

See Chapter 1, pp. 11-12 on the use of the passive voice.

MODAL VERBS: *SHOULD, MUST HAVE*

For Your Critical Thinking

What meaning is conveyed by *should* and *must have* in the following sentences?

S1. The "vinegar mingled with gall" offered to Christ on the Cross must have contained opium. (Par. 3)
S2. We should give top priority to the eradication of illicit poppies. (Par. 10)
S3. We should make people stop wanting heroin. (Par. 10)
S4. We must have been taught in religious classes that the fight between good and evil has no end. (Par. 11)

Note

Should is used as a modal verb to express obligation or advisability. *Must have* is always used with a past participle and expresses a guess or logical deduction.

THE *-ING* FORMS OF VERBS

For Your Critical Thinking

In the following sentences, *writing* has the same *-ing* form. How do they differ in use? Check your answers against the "Note" below.

S1. I am writing a book now.
S2. Writing a book, I learned many new things.
S3. Writing a book is not easy.
S4. I hope to finish writing this book in a month.

Note

There are three uses an *-ing* verb can serve: (1) to form the continuous tense, Ex. S1 above; (2) to form present participles, Ex. S2 above; and (3) to form gerunds, Ex. S3 and S4 above. (See Chapter 2, pp 27-28 for the present continuous tense, and Chapter 1, p. 15 and Chapter 3, pp. 55-56 for present participles.)

A participle is used as an adjective, and also to form half sentences. Gerunds are used as nouns, so they can function as subjects and objects.

In S3 above, *writing* is a gerund, used as part of the subject of the sentence. Together with the rest of the subject, it makes a gerund phrase. In S4, *writing this book* (gerund phrase) is the object of the verb *finish*.

Application

Underline the gerunds and gerund phrases in the following sentences and find if they are used as subjects or objects.

S1. Taking drugs for kicks and taking them to control pain are entirely different things.
S2. Giving drug addicts inexpensive daily doses of the synthetic drug methadone is widely favored now in the U.S.
S3. Numerous therapists say that it is just substituting one addiction for another.

DEGREES OF COMPARISON: POSITIVE DEGREE (REVIEW)

For Your Critical Thinking

What degree of comparison is used in the following sentence? Check your answer against the "Note."

S1.   The fight between good and evil is as real as life itself. (Par. 11)

See Chapter 1, pp. 12-13, for a note on the positive degree of comparison.

Part 3: SENTENCE COMBINING

CLAUSE MARKERS

Problems for You to Solve

Combine each set of sentences given below into one sentence. Check your sentences against the sentences in the reading passage. Discuss your answers with your group members and then with your instructor. Paragraph numbers are indicated in parentheses.

Who, Which, That (Review); *Where, Because*

1a.   Morphine is the modern world's standard.
 b.   All pain medicines are measured against it. (Par. 5)

2a.   Doctors and relatives get a feeling of joy.
 b.   The reason is not that the patients are high.
 c.   The reason is the patients are without pain and depression. (Par. 5)

3a.   Patients are given the herbal medicine.
 b.   The herbal medicine makes them vomit immediately. (Par. 8)

4a. The monks have treated 80,000 drug addicts since 1959.
 b. They say the medicine clears poisonous drug residue from the body.
 c. It helps eliminate the physical desire for drugs. (Par. 8)

5a. Another country is Malaysia.
 b. In this country drug addiction has become an increasing problem.
 c. Here a religious approach is used to cure addicts. (Par. 8)

Whose

For Your Critical Thinking

What noun or pronoun does *whose* substitute for in the following sentence ?

S1. The pretty little poppy — *whose* petals may be white, red, mauve, or purple — is unique in its profound and far-reaching effects on humanity. (Par. 1)

Note

Like *who, which,* and *that, whose* also introduces an adjective clause. However, the noun or pronoun it replaces should be in the possessive case. For example, *whose* in the above sentences replaces the possessive pronoun *its* as shown below.

1a. The little poppy is unique in its far-reaching effects on humanity.
 b. *Its* petals may be white, red, or mauve.

Application

Compose five sentences using *whose.*

PAST AND PRESENT PARTICIPIAL PHRASES

Problems for You to Solve

Combine each of the following sets of sentences into one complete sentence.

1a. It is smuggled into the U.S.
 b. It reaches nearly every community and every level of society.
 c. It brings addiction and misery to hundreds of thousands. (Par. 1)

2a. Heroin was introduced in Germany in 1898 as a remedy for cough and diarrhea.
  b. It was also proposed as a morphine substitute less likely to lead to addiction. (Par. 6)

Note

Like present participles, past participles also can combine sentences, provided the subjects of the sentences combined are the same.

Application

Complete the following sentences:

1. Written _____, this book _____.
2. Printed _____, this magazine _____.
3. Sung _____, this opera _____.
4. Watching _____, I _____.
5. Crying _____, the baby _____.

REDUCTION OF ADJECTIVE CLAUSES

For Your Critical Thinking

Examine the process of clause reduction involved in the following sentences.

S1. Theft (which is) committed for money to buy heroin is a major cause of crime in American cities. (Par. 1)
S2. The vinegar (which was) mingled with gall (and which was) offered to Christ on the Cross must have contained opium. (Par. 3)
S3. Opium (which was) dissolved in alcohol and (which was) known as laudanum is said to have been an essential item in most medicine chests during the Middle Ages. (Par. 4)

Note

1. Adjective clauses which define the nouns which the clause markers stand for (restrictive clauses) can be reduced as above.

2. Usually, for this kind of reduction to be possible, the clause should contain a "to be" verb.
3. If there is no form of "to be," the action verb may be reduced to participles.
4. Only adjective clauses introduced by *who, which,* and *that* can be reduced to form adjective phrases.

Application

Combine each of the following sets into one sentence, reducing the adjective clause to an adjective phrase.

1a. Students are waiting in line for registration.
 b. They are getting tired.

2a. The teenager got a ticket for speeding.
 b. He was driving a blue car.

3a. My friends take Professor Carlton's class.
 b. They have a hard time getting good grades.

4a. Many foreigners tour New York during the summer time.
 b. They have to stand in long lines to see the Statue of Liberty.

5a. The news about student strikes was published in the newspaper.
 b. It was exaggerated.

Part 4: SENTENCE RELATING

IN FACT, HOWEVER, FOR EXAMPLE, BUT

For Your Critical Thinking

How are the sentences in each of the following groups related to one another?

S1. Opium, morphine, and heroin — products from poppy — if used properly, have marvelous medicinal effects. In fact, they have been used largely in the pharmaceutical industry for a long time. For example, the drug codeine in pill form relieves pain after operations or tooth extractions. (Par. 1)

S2. Opium is also legally available to India's Ayurvedic doctors for treating sprue, asthma, scorpion bites, etc. However, these indigenous doctors are very careful in handling it. (Par. 4)

S3. A worldwide notion for a long time was that heroin is mainly an American problem. But that has been changing. Now it is a known fact that addiction is rising in all parts of the world. (Par. 7)

Application

Complete the following sentences:

1. My writing has improved a lot recently. In fact, _____.

2. The computer industry has revolutionized the life of modern people. In fact, _____.

3. English is very difficult to learn. However, _____.

4. Yesterday's test was very difficult. However, _____.

Part 5: VOCABULARY, WORD FORMS, AND IDIOMS

FILL-INS

Paragraph b in each of the following pairs is a paraphrase of a. Using synonyms and antonyms (which need not be exact), changing sentence structure, and changing word forms are some of the devices used in making the paraphrase.

Your task: Fill in the blanks with appropriate words or phrases. Each blank line indicates one word. The underlined words in the original may give you the clues.

1a. Smuggled into the U.S., it reaches nearly every community and every level of society, bringing addiction and misery to hundreds of thousands. (Par. 1)

b. (1) _____ heroin is a crime prevalent in
(2) _____ every (3) _____ of the United States,
and many people get (4) _____ to it, making themselves
and their families (5) _____ .

2a. <u>What</u> gives the opium poppy its power for good or evil? Let us
<u>examine</u> the plant's chemistry. <u>Day and night certain</u> nitrogen-
<u>containing</u> compounds, or alkaloids, are <u>produced</u> by the plant and
<u>stored</u> in its cells. After the petals fall, the seed capsule <u>swells.</u> If the
capsule is <u>shallowly incised</u> while still green and unripe, a milky,
alkaloid-rich sap <u>seeps</u> from the tiny tubes in the capsule wall. It
<u>dries,</u> darkens, and turns gummy. That is opium — a dark, shiny
substance which <u>looks like</u> chocolate icing. (Par. 1)

b. By (6) _____ the plant's chemistry, we may be able to find
the (7) _____ for its power for both good and evil.
(8) _____ , the plant produces (9) _____ compounds which (10) _____ nitrogen, or alkaloids, and
(11) _____ them in its cells. The seed capsule gets
(12) _____ when the petals fall. A (13) _____
(14) _____ on the green, unripe capsule causes a milky,
alkaloid-rich sap to (15) _____ _____ from the
tiny tubes in the capsule wall, which, when (16) _____ ,
becomes opium — a dark, shiny, and gummy substance,
(17) _____ chocolate icing.

3a. Opium <u>dissolved</u> in alcohol, known as laudanum, is said to have
been an <u>essential</u> item in most medicine chests during the Middle
Ages. (Par. 4)

b.   During the Middle Ages, laudanum, made by (18) _____
     opium in alcohol, was one of the (19) _____ items in most
     medicine chests.

4a. Opium is legally available to India's Ayurvedic doctors for <u>treating</u>
     sprue, asthma, scorpion bites, etc. <u>However,</u> these indigenous <u>doc-</u>
     <u>tors</u> are very <u>careful</u> in handling it. Some practitioners <u>mix</u> herbal
     juices with opium medicine to <u>counteract</u> bad effects, <u>such as</u> con-
     stipation. They also <u>adjust</u> the dosage <u>downward</u> without <u>telling</u> the
     patient, so that when the treatment ends, there will be no with-
     drawal sickness or <u>addiction</u> (Par. 4)

b.   (20) _____ _____ it is legal for the Ayurvedic
     doctors in India to use opium for the (21) _____ of certain
     diseases, they handle it very (22) _____. Bad effects,
     (23) _____ constipation, are (24) _____ by hav-
     ing the opium medicine (25) _____ with herbal juices.
     Also, by (26) _____ (27) _____ the dosage
     without letting the patient become (28) _____ of it, they
     help the patient not to have any withdrawal sickness. Neither does
     the patient get (29) _____.

5a. The <u>prescription</u> for cancer patients <u>suffering</u> from <u>severe</u> pain
     could be morphine, given orally and <u>carefully tailored</u> to the
     patient's needs. Daily doses of codeine, taken through a stomach
     tube, are given to cancer patients suffering from <u>intense</u> pain.
     Codeine is to cancer patients what insulin is to <u>diabetic patients</u>. It
     controls recurring attacks of <u>severe</u> pain. Doctors and relatives get a
     <u>feeling</u> of joy, not because the patients are high, but because they
     are without pain and depression. Thus, <u>in addition to</u> its power to
     <u>relieve</u> cancer patients from severe pain, codeine serves the human-

itarian purpose of allowing the patient to enjoy their families, resolve problems, bring about family reconciliation, etc., during their last days. (Par. 5)

b. Doctors (30) _____ daily doses of morphine for cancer patients who (31) _____ from (32) _____ pain, to be given orally and (33) _____ (34) _____ to their needs. Acting like insulin, which controls (35) _____ , codeine not only (36) _____ the (37) _____ of pain in cancer patients, but (38) _____ effects (39) _____ from pain. Seeing the patients without pain and depression, their doctors and relatives (40) _____ joy. The relief from pain might give some patients enough time to become (41) _____ to their family members by having problems (42) _____ . Finally, they can have a (43) _____ _____ .

6a. It is reported that the spectacular treatment of addicts at Tham Krabok Monastery north of Bangkok results in a 70 percent success rate, according to its records. The ten-day free treatment begins with a vow to the Buddha never to use narcotics again. Then patients are given herbal medicine that makes them vomit immediately. The monks, who have treated 80,000 since 1959, say the medicine "clears poisonous drug residue from the body and helps eliminate the physical desire for drugs." Herbal steam baths, milder tonics, and herbal pills, along with continuous counseling, are part of the regimen. (Par 8)

b. The monks at Tham Krabok Monastery north of Bangkok, who have treated 80,000 drug addicts since 1959, (44) _____ that 70 percent of the patients get cured during the ten-day free treatment, which is (45) _____ with a vow to the Buddha that they will (46) _____ from (47) _____ narcotics. The herbal medicine with which these patients are treated (48) _____ (49) _____ (50) _____, making the body (51) _____ of all poisonous residue and (52) _____ the patient in (53) _____ the physical desire for drugs. The regimen (54) _____ steam baths, milder tonics, and herbal pills. In addition, the patients are being (55) _____ (56) _____.

Application

You are offered a job as an assistant to the director of a rehabilitation center. On your first day of work you are asked to make a case study of one of the ex–drug addicts at the center. Write up the report, using appropriate vocabulary words. In addition to the vocabulary words you used in the above exercise, the following vocabulary words from the reading passage may help you do this exercise.

- speculate
- isolate
- measure
- congestive
- nauseate
- consumption
- substitute
- eradication
- reduction

Part 6: WRITING

SUMMARIZATION

In Chapter 1, you learned how to state the author's ideas in your own words (paraphrasing). In this chapter, you will learn how to summarize the writer's ideas in as few words as possible — another skill you need to have, especially when you are reading extensively with the purpose of writing term papers.

Summarizing means reporting in your own words and in a condensed form the information you received from your reading. Here, you are borrowing the author's ideas, but not necessarily his or her words. This does not mean that the summary should not contain any words from the original. Key words, around which the whole article's argument revolve, cannot be altered. Except for these words, summarization should be done as much as possible in your own words. Lifting the key statements from the original and putting them together does not make a summary.

The best way to approach this task is to imagine this: Your mother, father, husband, or wife did not have time to read the article. After dinner you are sitting with him or her for a casual conversation. Since you have found the information you received from your reading very interesting, you want to share it with him or her. However, you are not sure if he or she is also interested in the information, so you make a special effort not to bore him or her by condensing the information as much as possible. Also, because you are doing this during a casual conversation, you have to put it in as simple words as possible too. However, no significant information can be left out.

If you are a beginner, you may want to answer some questions about the article before you write down the summary. For example, answers to the following questions may help you in summarizing "The Poppy."

1. What effects does the poppy have on human beings?
2. What are the three different forms in which it is being used?
3. How are these three made from the poppy?
4. How does each of the three affect human lives?
5. Are drugs a threat to humanity?
6. What are some measures taken by governments and social workers to counteract the drug problem?
7. Does the author think that the drug problem can be completely remedied?

Application

1. Visit a drug rehabilitation center in your area. Interview a social worker on the different kinds of help given to different drug addicts. Take down notes. Summarize the interview by going over your notes. Report to class.
2. Write a summary of the main ideas in "The Poppy" in about 200 words (one quarter of its length).

THE PARAGRAPH: STRUCTURE

For Your Critical Thinking

1. Find the sentence in Par. 1 that gives you the topic of the whole paragraph.
2. Find one sentence in Par. 3 that summarizes the thought development of the whole paragraph.
3. What specific aspect does the writer talk about in Par. 4?
4. How many examples does the writer give in Par. 8 of "ways to help addicts"?
5. What idea does the example of cancer patients support in Par. 5?

Note

An expository paragraph is marked by both physical and structural characteristics. The physical characteristics consist of an indented initial sentence, followed by other unindented sentences. Structurally, a paragraph should have (1) unity, and (2) coherence.

A paragraph has *unity* when it talks about one topic or, if it is part of an essay, one aspect of the topic. Usually, this central idea is introduced in the beginning of the paragraph in what is called the *topic sentence.* A topic sentence has two structural parts: the *topic* and the *controlling idea.* The topic part of the topic sentence introduces the reader to the topic of the paragraph. The controlling idea tells the reader what specific aspect of the central idea is going to be discussed in the paragraph.

A paragraph has *coherence* when all the sentences are directly related to the controlling idea given in the topic sentence and no irrelevant ideas are conveyed by any sentence. Giving supporting details, arranging these details systematically (according to the order of importance or chronologically), moving from the general to the particular or vice versa, giving examples, and quoting data or statistics are some of the devices you can use to develop the controlling idea.

Some writers summarize the paragraph by giving a concluding sentence. However, leaving out the conclusion does not affect the structure of the paragraph.

In Paragraph 1 of "The Poppy", the first sentence is the topic sentence, which has two parts: (1) the topic, namely, *papaver somniferum,* and (2) the poppy's unique capacity to effect both good and evil. The controlling idea — the good and bad effects — are explained by giving examples. Notice the use of *in fact* and *for example* to relate sentences.

Exercise: Analyze the structure of Par. 4.

Application

Write a paragraph on the topic : "How People Get Addicted to Drugs."

THE PARAGRAPH: PROCESS

Prewriting

The Note and the analysis of Paragraph 1 given above have given you an idea about the structure of a paragraph. However, *you should first have ideas* before structuring a paragraph. Where do you get the ideas from ? One way of doing this is to do some research on the topic. However, if you are asked to write a composition in class, you do not have time to do the research. The alternative is to get ideas out of your background knowledge, which has already been stored in your memory, gathered from your reading, from observation of the world around you, etc. The process of getting ideas out of your memory is called brainstorming.

One way of brainstorming is to ask yourself questions about the topic. Another way is to write down whatever comes to your mind until you exhaust all the information stored in your brain about the topic.

The next step in prewriting is to *narrow your ideas to the specific.* The brainstorming might give you many ideas about the topic. However, you cannot write about all of them in your paragraph. Pick the one you are most comfortable with and that will be the central idea of your paragraph.

The third step is to *decide on the topic sentence.* Remember, the topic sentence should have a controlling idea. The idea which you find the easiest to develop could be made into a topic sentence.

The fourth step is *organizing the ideas* you got during brainstorming to suit your controlling idea. At this stage, you may want to make an outline of your ideas, which consists of the controlling idea and the supporting details. You have to decide what device you want to use to develop the controlling idea. Giving examples is the easiest way for beginners.

For example, for your writing assignment given above, "Drugs taken for nonmedicinal purposes can lead to addiction," could be made the topic. However, you have to find a controlling idea to make it a topic sentence. You can find it by brainstorming. You may want to ask questions like :

- Why are drugs harmful ?
- How does taking these drugs lead to physical dependence ?
- Do drug abusers start with large doses or small doses ?
- Why do they take these drugs ?
- What initial pleasure do they get out of it ?

- How does this sensation make them want more and eventually make them dependent ?
- What kind of physical problems do they experience if they do not continue taking the drugs ?

Stay with the questions you are most comfortable with and find answers to them. Pick your controlling idea from among these answers. From the brainstormed ideas, find the ones that most relate to the controlling idea and organize them systematically. With this step you are finished with prewriting and are ready for *writing,* by phrasing your ideas into sentence form (composing) and, finally, into paragraph form.

WRITING ACTIVITIES

Reaction Journal

Write in your journal :

- How factual or nonfactual you found the information given in the reading passage
- The changes you would make if *you* wrote the article
- What information in the passage makes you angry or sympathetic, and why

Learning Log

Write in your learning log :

- What you expected to learn from this chapter and how your expectation was or was not realized
- Three new things you learned from the chapter
- Three things discussed in the chapter which you already knew
- Any items that confuse you and why they are confusing
- Three situations in which you can apply some of the learning
- Three things you want to learn more about
- Ten to fifteen vocabulary words you learned and sentences using them

Writing Assignment

Overview

Interview a social worker, counselor, teacher, or an agent at an institution on a social issue. Make a written summary of the responses from the interviewee and present it to the class.

Real-life Purpose of Assignment: To present to an audience the report of an interview on a social issue
Academic Purpose of Assignment: To practice :

- Brainstorming for ideas
- Narrowing down the brainstormed ideas to the specifics
- Summarizing
- Paragraph structure

Audience: Class members.

Procedure

IN-CLASS GROUP WORK

Purpose of Group Work: To prepare a questionnaire for the interview
Group Size: Five

1. After discussion among the members, the group chooses a topic for the interview. The topic should relate to a modern technological, scientific, or medical invention, which, in spite of its positive contributions, has been abused a lot (like the poppy).
2. Each member individually reflects on the topic (five minutes).
3. Members write (without stopping even to think) whatever questions come to their mind about the topic (five to ten minutes).
4. Members share their questions and find the one(s) which relate to a specific aspect of the topic.
5. Members free-write whatever questions come to their minds on this one specific topic (five to ten minutes).
6. Members compare their questions and pick five to ten questions which most of the members wrote on this one specific topic (ten minutes).
7. The recordkeeper of the group writes down these questions for other members to copy (five minutes).
8. The group agrees on the kind of agency, institution, or individual to approach for the interview.

(Remember, do not approach anybody for an interview without making an appointment. It is also advisable to inform the interviewee about the topic and give him or her the questions in advance.)

OUT-OF-CLASS ACTIVITY

1. Individual members interview different agencies, institutions, social workers, counselors, or teachers as agreed upon by the group members.
2. Tape record the interview.
3. Review the tape. Write a paragraph summarizing the answers. (See Chapter 2, pp. 38-39 for a discussion on summarization.)

IN-CLASS GROUP DISCUSSION

Purpose of In-Class Group Discussion: To make a summary of the five reports the five members have made.

Group members exchange their papers to be read by every member of the group. While reading each other's papers, members individually take down notes on commonly expressed ideas in each report. Led by the group leader, members discuss these ideas and make a summary of their report in one paragraph. When all the groups have finished writing the summary, each group leader presents it to the class for feedback on:

- Clarity of expression
- Staying on the same topic from beginning to end with no unrelated ideas
- No repetition of ideas
- Explaining the topic with enough details and examples (See Chapter 2, pp. 40-41 for a discussion on paragraph structure.)

OUT-OF-CLASS WRITING

Based on the feedback received by the class members, revise and rewrite the piece.

CHAPTER · 3

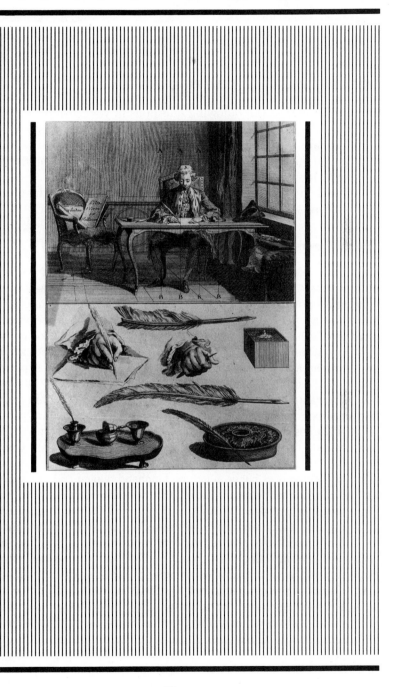

Part 1: READING

PREREADING ACTIVITIES

Discuss answers to the following questions in your group.

1. Compare writing longhand, typing, and word processing.
2. Do you think word processing has brought about a revolution in writing? How?
3. What is your biggest problem when you are asked to write an essay?
4. What is writer's block?

Reading: FROM QUILL TO COMPUTER

1. Every advance in technology manages somehow to transform the creative process. Improved fabrication of steel forms stimulated a new vision of architecture's possibilities. Developments in electronics gave musicians unimagined creative freedom and artistic control. Now, a relatively new technology, word processing, may be transforming the art of writing. It is too early to predict all the ways in which writing will change, but we can get some clues by looking at research in cognitive psychology and by studying the experiences of people who use word processors.

2. The range of available word processors is large. They vary in size from one small box weighing less than four pounds to a deskload of heavy equipment; their costs are similarly variable — from about $1,000 up to $20,000. But, basically, they are all the same: electronic devices that allow you to type, store, modify and print text.

3. The differences between writing longhand, typing and word processing are obvious even to the most reluctant first-time user of a word processor. Writing with paper and pencil is slow, laborious, and downright painful in time. Composing on a typewriter helps with speed and physical comfort, but correcting a typo, inserting a new sentence or repositioning a paragraph requires messy erasure, fumbling with correction fluid or "cutting and pasting" — physically relocating a misplaced paragraph with scissors and tape.

4. The word processor accomplishes these and several other tasks electronically, and consequently can transform writing in three distinct ways: It can ease the mechanical drudgery of writing; it can enhance our motivation and willing-

Excerpted from Robert Sekuler, "From Quill to Computer," *Psychology Today* (February 1985): 37–42.

ness to spend time going through the entire process of writing ; and it can bring about qualitative changes in the writing product, helping writers in their thinking process.

Drudgery

5. Nearly all books on writing emphasize the importance of revision, typically advising "revise, revise, and then revise some more." Many writers treasure the tools of revision — erasers, scissors, tape, correction fluid and wastebasket — almost as much as they value the implements of production — pencils, pens, and typewriters. But while teaching freshman composition a few years ago, I rediscovered what teachers of English have long known : Most writers have a strong aversion to revision. Teachers may deplore this reluctance to revise, but it is easily understood. Ordinarily, revision is both difficult and tedious.

6. A word processor certainly can make cleaning up typos, misspellings, and punctuation errors easy to do. But good prose, of course, is not just a collection of neatly displayed and properly constructed sentences : To lead the reader from one idea to the next, naturally and without hesitation, the writer must provide appropriate road signs — clear transitions and connections between sentences, paragraphs, and larger sections.

7. Though these transitions are often as hard to produce as the elements themselves, research has shown that readers (and writers) pay a price when writing does not flow smoothly. Marcel Just and Patricia Carpenter, cognitive psychologists at Carnegie-Mellon University, presented readers with two sentences — either adequately or inadequately linked — as in the following pairs: 1. A) It was dark and stormy the night the millionaire died. B) The killer left no clues for the police to trace. 2. A) It was dark and stormy the night the millionaire was murdered. B) The killer left no clues for the police to trace.

8. As the participants read, Just and Carpenter tracked their eye movements and found that on average, readers spent half a second less on the second pair of sentences than on the first pair. Why? In the second pair, the transition is clear: The writer uses the phrase "was murdered" in the first sentence to set the reader up for "The killer" in the second sentence. When transitions are missing, you must stop and mentally create them yourself — a distracting and time-consuming task. If you can imagine reading an entire article with sloppy connections not only between sentences but between paragraphs and collections of paragraphs, you can see why good transitions are so important.

9. How would a word processor help? As Peter Wason, a psychologist at University College, London, observes, "Writing is difficult for some people because they try to do two incompatible things at the same time: say something, and say it in the most acceptable way." In *Writing With A Word Processor,* William Zinsser suggests that you forget links and transitions initially. Concentrate instead on "letting your creative motor run the full course at full speed; repairs can always be made later." Following Zinsser's advice, you can mark each place where a transition word might be needed (say, with an "XXX"). Later, you can instruct the word processor to locate each "XXX" and display the surrounding text, and then develop and insert the needed transitions. Many people, in fact, do the same thing when composing with pen, pencil, or typewriter, but the whole process is less convenient than it is with a word processor and therefore, less likely to get done. The same thing can be done with other aspects of revision.

10. Word processors are also helpful because they make it easy to get a clean printed copy of your latest revision. Andrew Fluegelman and Jeremy Hewes, authors of *Writing in the Computer Age,* argue that getting clean copies on demand offers positive psychological benefits. The copy's attractive, professional appearance provides reinforcement: When you have been really struggling with the text, the clean copy holds out a promise of better times ahead. Also, the clean copy makes it easier for you to review the material as any other reader would, without interruptions from complex marginal notes, messy insertions and deletions.

Motivation

11. Word processors make an important contribution, improving motivation not only during revision but also during the entire writing process. Once beginners overcome their fear and awe of word processors, they realize that these imposing gadgets can make writing more bearable for several reasons. For one, word processors eliminate one of the more perplexing obstacles for many writers — the blank sheet of paper that seems to stare back reprovingly. Some people claim that a blank word-processor screen actually evokes less terror than does a blank piece of paper. Since few word-processor screens display the equivalent of an entire 8½-by-11-inch page, Fluegelman and Hewes say you can fill a screen faster than you can a sheet of paper, in effect dividing the chore into smaller, more manageable subtasks.

12. One friend of mine, however, is bothered less by a blank page or screen than by another common problem — writer's block. When he is stuck on one part of an article he must write, he quickly detours to another part that will be easier to complete. Not only does the detour give his writer's block sufficient time to work itself out, but when he has finally gotten all the parts completed and in place, the word processor can remove all telltale marks of the chaos from which his article emerged. Many people take similar detours when writing longhand or on a typewriter, but both methods tend to promote thinking in one direction — from a document's beginning to a document's end. Inserting materials into something you have already written is possible, but again, not convenient.

How We Write

13. Even though the mechanical and motivational effects of the word processor are powerful in their own right, they may prove minor compared to one potential effect of this new technology : changing the way they think about the writing process itself. To appreciate this fully, we will have to consider what creative writing is.

14. Many textbooks and teachers describe creative writing as a series of clearly defined steps. According to this view, you pick a manageable topic, do the required research, compose an outline, flesh out that outline and, finally, polish what you have written. Although this view encourages the idea that writing can be taught and learned in simple and convenient chunks, many cognitive psychologists — and successful writers — have a different understanding of the writing process. The novelist E. M. Forster put it well, asking : "How do I know what I think until I see what I say ?" Kurt Vonnegut makes the same point when he observes that when writing, he feels like someone who is "watching a teletype machine in a newspaper office to see what comes out." Fine, for the creative genius, you might say, but what about the average person ?

15. Psychologists Linda Flower and John Hayes of Carnegie-Mellon University asked college students to write essays on women's rights or abortion and, at the same time, describe aloud what they were doing. Their research suggests that good writers do not do as much detailed mental planning as we might think. In fact, Flower and Hayes found that writers often did not know precisely what they would write until they had written it.

16. Though these findings are somewhat discomforting, suppose that they are true. What are the implications of this new view of creative writing for writing on a word processor ? Because a word processor makes it easier both to produce and to modify our writing, a word processor may also make it easier to find out what we think.

17. One way to understand this is to consider what Susan Horton, a professor of English at the University of Massachusetts, calls reformulation. In *Thinking Through Writing,* Horton likens revision to tinkering and reserves the term "reformulation" for significant changes in organization, structure, and clarity. Reformulation, then, is a form of creative play, requiring intuition and experimentation. Reviewing the text, the writer may feel that a change is needed at a particular place without knowing precisely what that change should be.

18. One way of resolving this dilemma is to ask a series of "what if" questions. This type of question has been popularized by computer programs, such as VisiCalc, used for financial planning. In such programs the user enters all the relevant data and assumptions — for example, interest rates. The program then projects an outcome based on those data and assumptions. You can then ask a "what if" question by telling the computer to recalculate its projections based on some changed assumptions : what if interest rates rise, for example.

19. These programs encourage the same kind of playful, creative experimentation that an experienced word processor user comes to depend on. You simply examine what you have already written and then try various "what ifs" — "What if I invert this sentence. ... move this paragraph. ... delete this phrase ?" and so on. If you have made an improvement, it can be retained ; if not, you can try again. By making alternative reorganizations more accessible, a word processor encourages you to experiment where you probably would not bother on a page of typed manuscript.

20. A word processor can certainly help an individual to write, but often writing involves collaboration with others. Though there haven't been any formal studies, in my experience a word processor can prove equally helpful when collaborating with another author.

21. When Randy Blake, a colleague at Northwestern, and I collaborated on a textbook, we divided the chapters between us and worked separately to prepare very rough first drafts. When a rough draft was ready, we sat down together at one word processor, using one keyboard but two display screens so that each of us had an unimpeded view of the action. Then we took turns reading aloud, revising and reorganizing the text in tandem. The idea was to encourage joint work before the text had become too polished and therefore resistant to change. Working together in this way, we generated far more "what if" questions than we would have singly. The result is a text that not only reads well (we're told) but appears to be seamless ; reviewers say they can't tell who wrote what.

22.   There is little doubt that, when used properly, a word processor can be a valuable tool for writing. But like all stories, this one has another side that should not be ignored. Some writers become so entranced by these devices that the new-found power to revise turns into an obsession. When that happens, the word processor tends to resemble its counterpart in the kitchen — the food processor. Perhaps you know cooks who can not resist using their marvelous toy, so that everything they create is sure to be very well sliced, diced or pureed.

23.   There is a lesson here, not just for cooks and writers, but for all of us. No matter how powerful the technology we may have to help us, we still need good judgment and self-control.

POSTREADING ACTIVITIES

1. Compare the new information you received from reading the passage with the background knowledge you had on word processors before reading it.
2. What are the different ways a word processor can help in the writing process ?

Part 2: GRAMMAR

VERB TENSES: REVIEW

For Your Critical Thinking

1. How many tenses are used in Par. 1 ? What are they ?
2. Why does the writer shift to the simple present tense in the third sentence of Par. 1 ?
3. What tense is mostly used in this essay ? Why ?

MODAL VERBS: *CAN, MIGHT, MUST*

For Your Critical Thinking

1. What do *can, must* and *might* mean in the following sentences?
2. What time of action do they indicate — present, past, or future?

> S1. A word processor *can* transform writing in three distinct ways. (Par. 4)
> S2. The writer *must* provide appropriate road signs. (Par. 6)
> S3. You *can* mark each place where a transition *might* be needed. (Par. 9)

Note

Can expresses ability in the present and future. *Might* expresses probability or possibility in the present and future. *Must* expresses a guess or a logical deduction based on the information supplied previously or implied in the context. It can also express necessity, in which case it can be substituted for *have to* (past: *had to*). In S2 above *must* expresses necessity.

COMPARISON: COMPARATIVE DEGREE

For Your Critical Thinking

Find the points of comparison and the vocabulary used to express comparison, in the following sentences.

S1. The whole process of composing with pen, pencil, and typewriter is less convenient than it is with a word processor. (Par. 9)
S2. A word processor screen actually evokes less terror than does a blank piece of paper. (Par. 11)
S3. Since few word processor screens display the equivalent of an entire 8½-by-11-inch page, you can fill a screen faster than you can fill a sheet of paper. (Par. 11)
S4. Because a word processor makes it easier both to produce and to modify our writing, a word processor may also make it easier to find out what we think. (Par. 16)

Note

Comparisons can be made using adjectives, adverbs, and nouns. There are three degrees of comparison:

1. positive
2. comparative
3. superlative

The following are examples of comparative degree. Only the comparative degree is discussed in this chapter. (See Chapter 1, pp. 13-14 on the positive degree.)

> Ex. 1.   My father is older than my mother. (adjective)
> Ex. 2.   I find mathematics more difficult than chemistry. (adjective)
> Ex. 3.   This bottle has more water than the other one. (noun)
> Ex. 4.   I run faster than my sister. (adverb)
> Ex. 5.   My father drives more carefully than my brother. (adverb)

Problems for You to Solve

1. When would you use -er ... than ? When would you use more ... than ?
2. Find the following vocabulary words used in this article, which express similarities and differences and study the contexts in which they are used.

> **Vocabulary Expressing Similarity :**   same, similar
> **Vocabulary Expressing Difference :**   but, differences, even if, less, compared to, easier

Application

Write a paragraph comparing one of the following :

- Radio and television
- Traveling by train and traveling by bus
- Renting an apartment and buying a house

For Your Critical Thinking

1. How many times does the writer use but in this article ?
2. Why is but repeatedly used ?

Note

In the expository essay, "From Quill to Computer," the writer has employed the rhetorical device of comparison and contrast to explain his point that word processors afford many conveniences to writers. In comparing and contrasting word processors with other tools of writing, the writer has to explain both similarities and differences. *But* is a handy word to explain points of differences. Some synonyms of *but*, often used in writing, are *however, on the other hand, on the contrary,* and *however.*

APPOSITIVES

An appositive is a restatement, explanation, or description of a word or group of words. They are of two kinds : restrictive and nonrestrictive. They both give additional information about the word or group of words to which they are in apposition. The difference is that the restrictive appositive limits the meaning of the word it stands for, whereas the nonrestrictive appositive does not.

> Ex. 1. My brother John runs a business. (means, I have only one brother.)
> Ex. 2. My brother, John, runs a business. (means, I have more than one brother and that the one named John runs a business.)

(For punctuation of appositives see Part VI, pp. 66-69.)

Problems for You to Solve

Find the appositives used in the reading passage and underline them. Separate them into restrictive and nonrestrictive.

GERUNDS AND PARTICIPLES

Problems for You to Solve

1. The underlined groups of words in Groups A, B, and C below have one point of similarity in form. What is this point of similarity ?
2. Do they also function the same way grammatically ? What is the difference ?

GROUP A

S1. Inserting materials into something you have already written is possible, but again, not convenient. (Par. 3)
S2. Writing with paper and pencil is slow, laborious, and downright painful in time. (Par. 3)
S3. Correcting a typo, inserting a new sentence or re-positioning a paragraph requires messy erasure, fumbling with correction fluid or "cutting and pasting." (Par. 3)

S4. A word processor is a big help in <u>writing an essay, an article, or term paper,</u> using transition words.
S5. Beginning writers in a second language, even if they revise, are interested only in <u>correcting basic mistakes.</u>
S6. Word processors are also helpful in <u>getting a clean, printed copy.</u>
S7. This gives the effect of <u>dividing the chore</u> into smaller, more manageable subtasks. (Par. 11)

GROUP B

S1. <u>Reviewing the text,</u> the writer may feel that a change is needed at a particular place. (Par. 17)
S2. <u>By making alternative reorganizations more accessible,</u> a word processor encourages writers to experiment where they probably would not bother on a page of typed manuscript. (Par. 19)

GROUP C

S1. Now, a relatively new technology, word processing, may <u>be transforming</u> the art of writing. (Par. 1)
S2. We <u>are trying</u> to find the similarities and differences among the three groups of underlined words given above.
S3. My telephone <u>was ringing</u> when you rang the door bell.
S4. I <u>have been studying</u> English for two years.

Note

There are three kinds of *-ing* forms we can derive from an English verb : (See Chapter 1, p. 15 and Chapter 2, p. 29, Note.)

- Continuous tenses (present, past, present perfect, etc.). Together with *to be* verb forms, these *-ing* verb forms make complete verbs (See Chapter 2, pp. 27-28), which the participles and gerunds cannot do. The sentences in Group C above are examples.
- Participles. Group B above provides examples.
- Gerunds. Group A above provides examples.

Even though participles and gerunds are both derived from verbs, only gerunds can function as nouns. As nouns, they can make either the subjects or the objects of sentences.

Ex. 1. *Swimming* is a good exercise. (subj.)
Ex. 2. You can learn *writing* only by *writing*. (obj. of verb and of preposition)

Since both participles and gerunds are derived from verbs, they can take objects after them. For example, in Group B, S1, *the text* is the object of the participle *reviewing*. Similarly, in Group A, S3, *a typo, a new sentence,* and *a paragraph* are objects of the gerunds *correcting, inserting,* and *repositioning,* respectively. Other examples are S4, S5, S6, and S7 in Group A above. Together with these objects they make phrases. Gerunds can also be followed by prepositional phrases. Examples are S1, S2, and S3 (*fumbling with mistakes*) in Group A above.

A *gerund phrase*, like a gerund, can make either the subject or object of a sentence. For example, in Group A, S1, S2, and S3 (*correcting a typo, inserting a new sentence,* or *repositioning a paragraph*), the gerund phrases are the subjects of the sentences. In the rest of the examples the gerund phrases are objects of verbs or prepositions, or complements.

Since a gerund is derived from a verb, it can also have its own subject. When the subject of the gerund is expressed, it is put in the possessive case.

Ex. 1.   *His* witnessing against me was a proof of his insincerity.
Ex. 2.   I enjoy *Kathy's* singing.

A sure test to distinguish the gerund (or a gerund phrase) from a participle (or participial phrase) is to substitute the word or word group for *it*. If the resulting sentence is grammatically correct, it means the phrase replaced by *it* is a gerund, not a participle.

For Your Critical Analysis

Apply the substitution test, explained above, to the underlined phrases in Groups A and B above and differentiate the gerunds from the participles. (Neither participles nor gerunds can function as main verbs of sentences, so they cannot make complete sentences like the continuous verbs in Group C above.)

Application

Suppose you recently moved out of your parents' house and started staying in the dormitory. Your parents are very concerned about how you spend your time. Write a letter to them describing your daily activities. Write two to three sentences explaining each activity.

Some verbs you may want to use are :

- sing
- play
- read
- type
- watch
- listen
- clean
- swim
- write
- review

Part 3: SENTENCE COMBINING

CLAUSE MARKERS

Who, Which, That, Where, Because, Since, Even If, Even Though, Although, But (Review)

Problems for You to Solve

Separate each of the following sentences into as many complete sentences as possible and analyze the composing process. Find how and why the underlined word or group of words in each sentence happen to be in the sentence.

S1. The differences between writing longhand, typing and word processing are obvious even to those <u>who</u> are inexperienced in the word processor. (Par. 3)

S2. Beginning writers in a second language, <u>even if</u> they revise, merely correct basic mistakes.

S3. You can mark each place <u>where</u> a transition might be needed. (Par. 9)

S4. Many people do the same thing <u>when</u> composing with pen, pencil, or typewriter, <u>but</u> the whole process is less convenient than it is with a word processor and <u>therefore</u>, less likely to get done. (Par. 9)

S5. Clean copies offer positive psychological benefits <u>because</u> they prompt the writer into reviewing the material. (Par. 10)

S6. Word processors eliminate one of the more perplexing obstacles for many writers—the blank sheet of paper <u>that</u> seems to stare back reprovingly. (Par. 11)

S7. <u>Since</u> few word processor screens display the equivalent of an entire 8½-by-11-inch page, the writer can fill a screen faster than s/he can fill a sheet of paper. (Par. 11)

S8. A word processor helps writers to detour to another part <u>that</u> will be easier to complete. (Par. 12)

S9. <u>Though</u> the mechanical and motivational effects of the word processor are powerful, they may prove minor compared to one potential effect of this new technology. (Par. 13)

S10. <u>Even though</u> this view encourages the idea <u>that</u> writing can be taught and learned in simple and convenient chunks, many writers have a different understanding of the writing process. (Par. 14)

S11. Reviewing the text, the writer may feel <u>that</u> a change is needed at a particular place without knowing precisely what that change should be. (Par. 17)

Note on Adjective Clauses

There are two kinds of adjective clause: restrictive and nonrestrictive, depending on whether the writer wants to restrict the meaning of the noun or pronoun which the clause marker stands for. Both kinds add information about the noun or pronoun. However, a *restrictive adjective clause defines* the noun or pronoun which the clause marker stands for and *distinguishes* the specific meaning the word has in the sentence from all other meanings of the word. Since a *nonrestrictive clause* describes the noun or pronoun, and does not define but *describes,* it is marked off by commas. Usually the clause marker *that* is not used with nonrestrictive clauses.

Ex. 1. Mothers who abuse their children do not deserve respect from the society. (restrictive)

Ex. 2. Mothers, who are usually busy with their housework, find very little time to watch TV. (nonrestrictive)

Problems for You to Solve

1. Find the adjective clauses in S1-S11 above.
2. How many of these adjective clauses are restrictive? List them.
3. How many are nonrestrictive? List them.

WHEN, ONCE, SO THAT

Problems for You to Solve

Combine each of the following sets of sentences into one. Check your answers against the writer's own sentences given in the textbook. Discuss your answers with your group members and then with your instructor.

1a. The initial copy is made.
 b. Then writers can concentrate on the content.

2a. Beginners overcome their fear and awe of word processors.
 b. At that moment they realize one thing.
 c. These imposing gadgets can make writing more bearable in several ways. (Par. 11)

3a. Some cooks cannot resist using their marvelous toy.
 b. The result is everything they create will be well sliced, diced, or pureed. (Par. 22)

Note

When and *once* introduce time clauses (adverbial), so they replace time phrases as in the examples above. (*When* can also introduce adjective clauses.)

So that is an adverbial clause marker introducing a clause expressing purpose/result.

NOT ONLY ... BUT ALSO

For Your Critical Thinking

Critically examine the composing process involved in the following sentence:

S1. The word processor improves motivation not only during revision but also during the entire writing process.

Note

The above sentence can be split into the following two sentences:

1a. The word processor improves motivation during revision.
 b. It also improves revision during the entire process.

Application 1

Combine the following pairs of sentences using *not only ... but also.*

1a. This book helps me improve my writing.
 b. It also helps me improve my reading.

2a. My father works during the day.
 b. He also works during the night.

3a. I had to pick up my brother from the airport.
 b. I had to take my mother to the hospital, too.

Application 2

Make up sentences of your own using *not only ... but also.*

REDUCTION OF ADVERBIAL CLAUSES

For Your Critical Thinking

1. What do the following underlined groups of words have in common ?
2. Are they all clauses ?

   S1. Many people do the same <u>when composing with pen,</u> pencil, or typewriter. (Par. 9)
   S2. Many people take similar detours <u>when writing longhand or with a typewriter.</u> (Par. 12)
   S3. <u>When used properly,</u> a word processor can be a valuable tool for writing. (Par. 22)

Note

Each underlined part of the three sentences above is derived from adverbial clauses as shown below :

- When we compose with pen
- When we write longhand or with a typewriter
- When it is used properly

When any two sentences combined have the same subject, one sentence can be made into a half sentence by cutting off the subject and changing the verb to an *-ing* form (participle) and leaving out the "to be" verb if there is one. This half sentence can be used with adverbial conjunctions (showing time) like *when, while, after, etc.*, as in the above examples. For this kind of sentence combining to be possible, the two sentences should have the same subject.

Ex. 1a. I am doing the exercises in this textbook.
Ex. 1b. I am thinking too.
Combined sentence : While doing the exercises in this textbook, I am thinking too.

Ex. 2a. Betsy was walking to the corner grocery store.
Ex. 2b. She was bitten by a stray dog.
Combined sentence : While walking to the corner grocery store, Betsy was bitten by a stray dog.

The same process of composing explains the construction of the following sentence, the only difference being that the half sentence is introduced by a preposition, not by a time adverbial.

S1. By making alternative reorganizations more accessible, a word processor encourages the writer to experiment where he or she would not bother on a page of typed manuscript. (Par. 12)

Application

Reduce the following adverbial clauses by changing the verb into its *-ing* form.

1. While I was watching the movie, I fell asleep.
2. After I handed in the test, I discovered that two of my answers were wrong.

Part 4: SENTENCE RELATING

TRANSITION MARKERS

Problems for You to Solve

Read the following groups of sentences and find what device the writer uses to relate the sentences.

1. Improved fabrication of steel forms stimulated a new vision of the possibilities of architecture. Developments in electronics gave musicians unimagined creative freedom and artistic control. Now, a relatively new technology, word processing, may be transforming the art of writing. (Par. 1)
2. Nearly all books on writing emphasize the importance of revision. Many writers and some advanced writers, too, treasure the tools of revision, such as scissors, erasers, etc. But most writers have a strong aversion to revising. (Par. 5)
3. A word processor certainly can make cleaning up typos, misspellings, and punctuation errors easy to do. But good prose is not just a collection of neatly displayed and properly constructed sentences. (Par. 6)
4. To lead the reader from one idea to the next naturally and without hesitation, the writer must provide appropriate road signs. For example, good writers use appropriate transition words to have the ideas expressed flow smoothly.
5. Once beginners overcome their fear and awe of word processors, they realize that these imposing gadgets can make writing more bearable in several ways. For one, word processors eliminate one of the very perplexing obstacles for many writers—the blank sheet of paper. (Par. 11)

Note

Any expository paragraph should have two rhetorical characteristics:

- Coherence
- Cohesiveness

(See Chapter 2, p. 40 for a discussion of the structure of a paragraph.)

A paragraph is coherent if the writer stays with one topic and all the sentences talk about the same topic. In addition to the unity of the topic expressed in the different sentences (*cohesion*), each sentence should flow smoothly from one to the other (*coherence*). One of the devices used to obtain the effect of cohesiveness is the use of transition words.

In the five groups of sentences above, *now, but, for example*, and *for one* (meaning "for instance") are transition words. In Group 1 above, *now* effects a smooth "time" transition between the earlier and later periods of technological development. In Groups 2 and 3 *but* introduces the readers to the points of difference between the two things compared. In the last two groups, *for example* and *for one* serve to illustrate the points discussed.

Application

Relate the sentences in each pair below by using appropriate transition words:

1. Professor Peters' classes are very interesting. His homework assignments are very demanding.
2. Writing in English is very difficult for me. I am getting good grades in my writing class.
3. Textbooks are very expensive. My chemistry textbook cost me $40.00.

Part 5: VOCABULARY, WORD FORMS, AND IDIOMS

FILL-INS

Paragraph **b** in each of the following pairs is a paraphrase of **a**. Using synonyms and antonyms (which need not be exact), changing sentence structure, and changing word forms are some of the devices used in making the paraphrase.

Your task: Fill in the blanks with appropriate words or phrases. Each blank line indicates one word. The underlined words in the original may give you the clues.

1a. The <u>differences</u> between writing longhand, typing and word processing are <u>obvious</u> even to those who are <u>inexperienced</u> in the word processor. (Par. 3)

b. How word processing (1) _____ from writing longhand and typing is (2) _____ even to those who

(3) _____ _____ _____ much about word processing.

2a. Nearly all books on writing <u>stress</u> the <u>importance</u> of <u>revising</u>. (Par. 5)

b. Nearly all books give (4) _____ to the fact that (5) _____ is (6) _____.

3a. <u>But</u> most writers, <u>especially</u> students, have a <u>strong aversion</u> to revision.

b. (7) _____, most writers, (8) _____ students, (9) _____ (10) _____ the idea of revision.

4a. To <u>lead</u> the reader from one idea to <u>the next</u> naturally and <u>without</u> hesitation, the writer must <u>provide</u> appropriate road signs. (Par. 6)

b. Appropriate road signs must be (11) _____ by the writer so that the reader is (12) _____ from one idea to (13) _____ naturally and (14) _____ _____ hesitation.

5a. Composing with pen, pencil, or typewriter is <u>less convenient</u> than it is with a word processor. (Par. 9)

b. It is (15) _____ _____ to compose with pen, pencil, or typewriter than with a word processor.

6a. Word Processors are <u>also helpful</u> in getting a <u>clean</u> printed copy. (Par. 10)

b. (16) _____, word processors (17) _____ writers in getting (18) _____ printed copies.

7a. A blank word processor screen evokes <u>less terror</u> than does a blank piece of paper. (Par. 11)

b. A blank piece of paper is (19) _____ _____ than a blank word processor screen.

8a. <u>Even though</u> the mechanical and motivational effects of the word processor are powerful in their own right, these may prove <u>minor</u> <u>compared to</u> one <u>potential</u> effect of this new technology : <u>helping</u> writers <u>modify</u> the text in accordance with their thinking. (Par. 13)

b. The mechanical and motivational effects of the word processor are powerful in their own right. (20) _____, these may be of much (21) _____ importance in (22) _____ _____ its (23) _____ to help writers in (24) _____ the text in accordance with their thinking.

9a. <u>Reviewing</u> the text, the writer may feel that a change is needed at a <u>particular</u> place <u>without knowing</u> <u>precisely</u> what that change should be. (Par. 17)

b. When the writers (25) _____ the text, they may feel that a change is needed at a (26) _____ place, but they may (27) _____ _____ what (28) _____ that change should be.

10a. Some writers become so <u>entranced</u> by these devices that the new-found power to revise <u>turns into</u> an <u>obsession.</u> (Par. 22)

b. These devices (29) _____ some writers so much that they become (30) _____ with the new-found power to revise.

SENTENCE COMPOSING

Suppose one of your friends or relatives is obese because of overeating. Write a letter advising him or her how to reduce his or her intake. Some vocabulary words you may want to choose from are:

1. transform (Par. 1)   stimulate (Par. 1)   consequently (Par. 4) enhance (Par. 4)   interruption (Par. 10)   contribution (Par. 11) overcome (Par. 11)   resist (Par. 22)
2. bring about (Par. 4)   compared to (Par. 13)   according to (Par. 14) turn into (Par. 22) thereby   in accordance with

Part 6: PUNCTUATION

COMMA (,)

For Your Critical Thinking

Find out why the following sentences are punctuated with commas.

S1. Now, a relatively new technology, word processing, may be transforming the art of writing. (Par. 1)
S2. Writing with paper and pencil is slow, laborious, and downright painful in time. (Par. 3)
S3. Composing on a typewriter helps with speed and physical comfort, but correcting a typo, inserting a new sentence, or re-positioning a paragraph is very messy. (Par. 3)
S4. The word processor accomplishes all these and several other tasks electronically, and consequently, it can transform writing in three distinct ways. (Par. 4)
S5. A word processor certainly can make cleaning up typos, misspellings, and punctuation errors easy to do. (Par. 6)
S6. For example, the writer must provide appropriate road signs. (Par. 6)
S7. Many people, in fact, do the same thing when composing with pen, pencil, or typewriter, but the whole process is less convenient than it is with a word processor and therefore, less likely to get done. (Par. 9)

S8.   When the initial copy is made, the writer can concentrate on the content.

S9.   According to this view, you pick a manageable topic, do the required research, compose an outline, flesh out the outline, and finally, polish what has been written. (Par. 14)

S10. Reviewing the text, the writer may feel that a change is needed at a particular place without knowing precisely what that change should be. (Par. 17)

S11. There is little doubt that, when used properly, a word processor can be a valuable tool for writing. (Par. 22)

Note

1.   Use a comma to join a list of items. (The last item on the list is joined to the rest by the conjunction *and*, preceded by a comma.)

2.   Use a comma before :

   * The abbreviation *etc.*
   * The coordinating conjunctions *and, but, for, or,* and *nor.*

3.   Use a comma after :

   * Transition words
   * Adverbials and -ly adverbs, adverbial clauses, and adverbial phrases
   * Frequency adverbs like *usually, recently,* etc.
   * Opinion-expressing phrases like *according to this view, in my opinion,* etc.
   * "Generalizing" or "summarizing" expressions like *in brief, in general, on the whole,* etc.
   * Participial phrases, if these begin the sentence or clause
   * Nonrestrictive adjective clauses and appositives (those that describe, but do not define the nouns they stand for)

4.   Use a pair of commas if any of the words or phrases in 3 above comes in the middle of a sentence. (Set it off with a pair of commas.)

Application

Find examples in the reading passage of the rules given above.

COLON (:)

Problems for You to Solve

Why did the writer use a colon after *ways* in the following sentence?

S1. The word processor can transform writing in three distinct ways : It can motivate us to better writing by easing the mechanical drudgery involved in revising ; it can enhance our motivation and willingness to spend time going through the entire process of writing ; it can bring about qualitative changes in the writing product. (Par. 4)

Note

Since a colon indicates elucidation, explanation, or enumeration, a list may be introduced by a colon.

SEMICOLON (;)

Problems for You to Solve

Find why the writer uses semicolons (not commas) in the following sentence.

S1. The word processor can ease the mechanical drudgery of writing ; it can enhance our motivation and willingness to spend time going through the entire process of writing ; it can bring about qualitative changes in the writing product. (Par. 4)

Note

A semicolon is required between two independent clauses which are not, but could be, joined by *and, but, or,* or *nor.*

Application

Find examples of the use of the semicolon from your general reading and copy five of them.

DASH (—)

For Your Critical Thinking

Explain the use of dashes in the following sentences.

S1. Correcting a typo, inserting a new sentence or re-positioning a paragraph requires messy erasure, fumbling with correction fluid or "cutting and pasting" — physically relocating a misplaced paragraph with scissors and tape. (Par. 3)

S2. Many writers and some advanced writers, too, treasure the tools of revision — erasers, scissors, tape, correction fluid, and wastebasket — almost as much as they value the implements of writing — pencils, pens, and typewriters. (Par. 5)

Note

A dash (—) is used with nonrestrictive appositives, if the appositive is long, or if it has internal punctuation. (See Chapter 3, p. 54 for appositives.)

Ex. Mr. Daxter — the most friendly social worker, according to my father's opinion — should be recognized by being given an award.

In this sentence, the appositive has internal punctuation (comma).

Application

Find other examples of the use of dash from the reading passage.

Part 7: WRITING

THE EXPOSITORY ESSAY: FORM

Like anything in nature which is orderly, an expository essay should have an organization and structure. The physical shape of an essay resembles that of a robotic human body; it has four parts:

1. A head — the introduction
2. A neck, namely the thesis statement — connecting the head to:
    3. The main body parts, namely the developmental paragraphs
    4. The conclusion (which may be considered a passport size photo of the whole body)

This structure of the essay may be shown diagrammatically as follows:

```
                  INTRODUCTION

                     Thesis
                    statement
 ┌──────────────────────────────────────┐
 │            paragraph #1               │
 ├──────────────────────────────────────┤
 │            paragraph #2               │
 ├──────────────────────────────────────┤
 │            paragraph #3               │
 ├──────────────────────────────────────┤
 │            paragraph #4               │
 └──────────────────────────────────────┘
                   Conclusion
```

The funnel shaped Head, namely the introduction, as shown in the diagram, begins with a broad statement relating to the topic (the wide mouth of the funnel) and narrows down gradually to specifics (the neck that connects the head to the body), namely the thesis of the whole essay.

A well written *introduction* serves two purposes:

1. It introduces the topic so that the reader can check into his or her background experiences and make some predictions about the information, and
2. It arouses the curiosity of the reader in such a way that he or she is encouraged to read all the way through with interest.

The *thesis statement* introduces the main idea of the essay. This is the proposition — an announcement to the reader about what exactly the writer is going to discuss about the topic. This should be written in very specific terms and with a view to what is going to be discussed in the developmental paragraphs.

The *developmental paragraphs* elaborate on the thesis statement, explaining the writer's point of view. Each paragraph should be cohesive and coherent. To maintain coherence, writers should confine themselves to the topic and subtopics given in the thesis statement. In other words, each developmental paragraph should discuss only one subtopic given in the thesis statement. Sentences should be related to one another using pronouns, transition words, and similar devices to maintain coherence.

The *conclusion* can be a summary of the introduction and/or the developmental paragraphs, to help readers leave the essay with a condensed message — a "passport-size photocopy" of the whole essay. Some writers end an essay with rhetorical questions, some reflections about the topic discussed, some suggestions, etc.

For Your Critical Thinking

With the short discussion above on the structure and organization of an expository essay in mind, answer the following questions on "From Quill to Computer."

1. How many paragraphs does the writer take for the introduction?
2. Draw the funnel-shaped introduction of this essay, indicating the flow of ideas from the broad to the narrow.
3. What prediction can you make about the rhetorical pattern of the essay from the third paragraph?
4. What role does Par. 4 play in the whole essay?
5. What are the controlling ideas or subpoints in the proposition or thesis statement?
6. How many paragraphs does the writer take to explain each of the subpoints mentioned in the thesis statement?
7. What key words are repeated in Par. 5–10 as a device to keep these paragraphs tied together and within the limit of one subpoint? What substitutes are used for these words?
8. Pick the words in Par. 10 which relate Par. 10 to Par. 5–9?
9. How does the writer relate Par. 9 to the first subtopic given in the thesis statement?
10. What device does the writer employ to relate Par. 11 to the previous paragraphs?
11. What does "For one" mean in Par. 11? What purpose does it serve in the paragraph?
12. Do Par. 11 and 12 talk about the same subtopic or two different subtopics? Why is Par. 12 written as a separate paragraph?
13. What subtopic does the writer discuss in Par. 13?
14. How does the writer relate this subtopic to the other two subtopics already discussed?
15. How does the writer conclude his essay? summarizing? speculating? suggesting? advising?

Application

1. Suppose with constant help from your tutor you have learned how to use the word processor to do your writing assignments. Pleased with your success, he/she has asked you to write an article for the ESL Department Newsletter. Write this article. You may want to use the information you received from reading "From Quill to Computer." You can also add your own personal experience (if you have any) in using word processors.

(Review paraphrasing and summarizing, and discussions on the structure and oganization of an expository essay: Chapter 1, p. 20, Chapter 2, pp. 38-39, and Chapter 3, pp. 69-71.)

2. Write a four to five paragraph essay on one of the following:

    -   Microwave ovens have helped modern housewives to ease the drudgery of cooking. Discuss the advantages of microwave cooking, comparing it to old-fashioned ways of cooking by charcoal or gas.
    -   Power steering has been a big boon to modern drivers, especially in long-distance driving. Compare and contrast driving a modern car with driving an old-fashioned one.
    -   Modern cities are equipped with many conveniences of life. Discuss the advantages and disadvantages of living in a modern city, in comparison with those of living in a rural town.

THE EXPOSITORY ESSAY: PROCESS

Prewriting: Brainstorming

As in paragraph writing (See Chapter 2, p. 40), the first thing you need for writing an expository essay is *ideas.* You can get ideas from different sources: from your reading, from your research, from your discussion with peers, from observing the world, etc. You can also get ideas onto paper by recalling the information you have already stored in your brain about the topic — by *brainstorming.*

There are several ways you can do this brainstorming. We will discuss two techniques to help you write the above assignment.

Free Writing

Free writing means writing whatever comes to your mind on the topic, until you find enough relevant ideas to write about. You do not have to write in sentences or in any specific order. You should be writing without stopping — not stopping even to think. You can do this in chunks of ten to fifteen minutes each. After each break you read what you have written and underline the relevant material.

Questioning

Asking yourself appropriate questions about the topic can open the door to a wealth of ideas you have already stored in your brain. These questions come broadly under "what," "when," "where," "why," and "how," types.

For example, if you choose the first topic in the assignment above, you may want to ask yourself questions, such as:

- What is a microwave oven?
- What are its physical characteristics?
- How does it do the cooking?
- When did the "microwave age" in cooking begin?
- In what ways does it help housewives?
- For what kind of cooking are microwave ovens helpful?
- What are some kinds of cooking for which they are not useful?
- How expensive or inexpensive is microwave cooking?
- How does it compare with gas cooking with respect to speed, expense, taste and flavor of cooked products, etc.?
- What is gas cooking?
- Who uses it?
- How popular is it?
- How economical is it?
- How long does it take to cook by gas?
- What are the dangers of gas cooking?
- Why do people want to cook by gas?
- What are the advantages and disadvantages of gas cooking?

You do not have to use any specific order to generate these questions. They can be in any order. After you have generated all the questions you can think of and answered them (it is not necessary at this stage to answer the questions in complete sentences), stay with the ones about which you have the most information.

WRITING ACTIVITIES

Reaction Journal

Write in your journal:

- If there are any ideas expressed in the reading passage that are confusing to you, what they are, and why they are confusing
- What you like or do not like about the different sections (Part 2, 3, etc.) in this chapter (give reasons)
- How you react to the following statements by the writer and if and how they apply to your writing experiences:

  - Many writers have a strong aversion to revision. Teachers may deplore this reluctance to revise. Ordinarily, revision is both difficult and tedious. (Par. 5)
  - Word processors eliminate one of the more perplexing obstacles for many writers — the blank sheet of paper that seems to stare back reprovingly. (Par. 11)
  - Flower and Hayes found that writers often did not know precisely what they would write until they had written it. (Par. 15)
  - No matter how powerful the technology is, we still need good judgment and self-control. (Par. 23)

- Your reaction to any other statements made in the reading passage
- What you found the easiest and most difficult learning item in the chapter and why

Learning Log

Write in your learning log:

- If you received any new information from reading "From Quill to Computer" and what it is
- If, how, and where you can apply this new information
- If any of the information given in the article has changed your views on the writing process and how
- Five to ten vocabulary words you have learned and sentences using them

Writing Assignment

Overview

Imagine that you are a student representative to a college-wide curriculum committee organized by the College Faculty Council. At one of the meetings you were asked to state your point of view on the kind of writing required in most courses in your college. The Committee members were very impressed with your response, and they asked you to write a position paper, to be presented at the next meeting. Write this position paper.

> *Real-life Purpose of Assignment:* To state your point of view about writing requirements in content areas (for example, Social science, biology, etc.)
>
> *Academic Purpose of Assignment:* To practice brainstorming for ideas, free writing, expository writing
>
> *Real-life Audience:* Curriculum Committee members of the College Faculty Council (comprised of five professors, one dean, and two student representatives.)
>
> *Classroom Audience:* Your class members and instructor

Procedure

OUT-OF-CLASS ACTIVITY

1. Review the three chapters discussed so far, the journals, and the learning log.
2. Reflect for fifteen to thirty minutes on what you have learned and how you learned it.
3. Free-write all your thoughts about your learning for thirty to fifty minutes in chunks of ten minutes.
4. Read to yourself what you wrote.
5. Make conclusions about the kind of learning that did or did not take place.
6. Write down your conclusions.

IN-CLASS DISCUSSION : WORK IN PAIRS

1. Share your conclusions with your classmates.
2. Find one class member who has almost the same conclusions as yours.
3. Work with this class member, and together pick one conclusion which is specific enough and about which you both have good ideas. (This is your position statement.)
4. Share the ideas and take down notes.

Sample position statement : "Keeping a learning log should be required in all courses because it helps students analyze and synthesize their learning experience."

OUT-OF-CLASS WRITING

Write the position paper :

- Begin with an introductory paragraph where you state your position.
- Develop this statement, stating the "whys" and "hows."

For example, in developing the sample position statement above, you can explain how a learning log helps students analyze and synthesize their learning experience. You can give yours and your classmates' experience as examples.

IN-CLASS PEER WORK

Exchange your paper with a classmate (not the one you worked with at the previous classmeeting). Get feedback on :

- Whether the introduction clearly states your position and tells him or her specifically what you are going to talk about in the rest of the essay
- Whether each of the developmental paragraphs talks about one specific aspect of your position statement
- Whether you have clearly explained these specifics with no repetition and without too many language errors

(See Chapter 3, pp. 69-71 for an explanation on the general structure of an expository essay.)

CHAPTER · 4

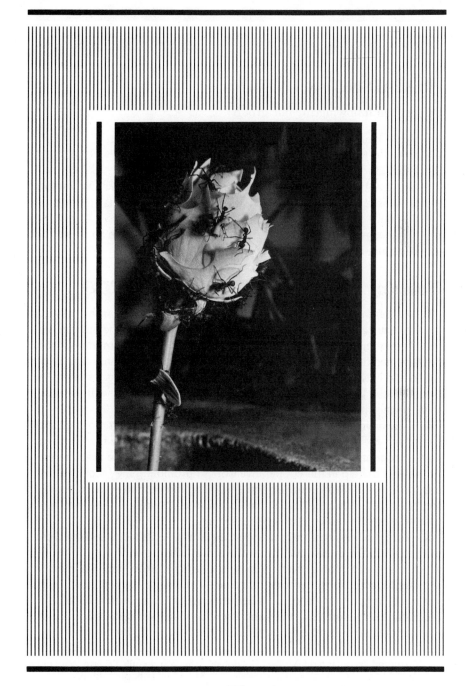

Part 1: READING

PREREADING ACTIVITIES

Discuss the following in your group:

1. What kind of species do ants belong to?
2. How do they "increase and multiply"?
3. What do you know about ant behavior?
4. Being as tiny as they are, how do they survive on earth? Do you think they have any defense system, like the military systems human societies have?
5. What communication system do you think they have to meet their basic needs like food and shelter?

Reading: THE ANT AND HER WORLD

1. As premier social insects, ants share a lot with human beings. Even though they belong to an utterly different species, they, like the humans, have met, throughout their long evolution, many of the same problems human societies have had to face. These problems involve both war — intense competition within and between species — and peace — coping with hunger and environmental stress. We humans are but mere neophytes, compared with the ants, in solving these problems.

2. The hallmark of ants is their highly developed social behavior. Ant societies, which are exclusively female, can have a million or more members, each rigidly programmed to a division of labor and to behave in the best interest of her sisters. To help in this cooperative work of promoting the "society's" interest, they have evolved complex and subtle communication systems based on scents and body language. Yet all their behavior is dominated by instinct, not by such human traits as emotions or reasoning.

3. An ant colony resembles an extended family. All its members have a common mother, the queen, and often the same father, one of the drones with which the queen mated. Each colony is a self-contained unit, the members working together for a common purpose — to ensure the reproduction and survival of its common genes. This demands not only cooperation but altruism. For instance, the female worker ants sacrifice their own fertility because it is more efficient to help raise the eggs of a single, continually laying queen than to

---

Excerpted and adapted from Bert Hölldobler, "The Wonderfully Diverse Ways of the Ant," *National Geographic* (June 1984): 779–813. Used with permission.

lay and rear their own eggs. Likewise, soldier ants automatically risk their own lives to defend a territory needed to feed their colony's brood.

4. The colony also has a division of labor, often a caste system that assigns specific tasks to specialized workers. For example, among the weaver ants, the minors lick the scales to clean them, collect the discharge, and regurgitate it on demand. The majors divide into age groups, charged with particular duties. Young majors tend the queen, larvae, and pupae. The middle-aged forage, while oldsters serve as protectors, recognizable by worn mandibles and missing legs. These soldiers live in barrack nests at the edge of the colony's territory. Having sharp eyesight and sense of smell, they act as guards and scouts.

5. The construction of the tentlike nest which the weaver ants literally weave from leaves and which has given them their name, is another example of the kind of cooperation and division of labor that they have evolved. First, a swarm of weavers form living chains. One ant grasps another's waist and so on, until their chain of bodies reaches a leaf needed for a new nest. Then the living chain contracts, pulling or rolling the leaf into the desired position. Next, members of the swarm scurry back to the home nest. Minutes later they return, each ant carrying a white larva in her mandibles. They then move the larvae back and forth across the leaves they want to join together. As they do, the workers stroke the larvae in a way that provokes them to secrete silk. This silk glues, or weaves, the leaf into position.

6. The ultimate and most important division of labor in any ant colony is sexual. To the queens and drones fall the colony's paramount mission — spreading the genes. The queen carries the primary burden, which puts her understandably at the center of the ant colony's attentions. Moreover, she fosters her daughters' devotion. Chemical excretion makes the weaver queen, for instance, so attractive to her worker offspring that a crowd of workers literally covers her at all times. They frequently lick the surface of her body, particularly her head and protruding membranes on her gaster that are richly endowed with glands.

7. The queen's influence over her workers is very profound. Her presence guarantees strong colony cohesiveness. She maintains her dominance by actually suppressing the fertility of her daughters with potent chemicals, located in the glandular secretions. The workers so eagerly lick these chemicals from their mother's body and then pass on to the rest of the colony through grooming and regurgitative feeding.

8. On some cue from nature, the queen takes to her wings and mates, sometimes with many males, until she has a lifetime's worth of sperm in her abdomen. Then she establishes a new nest. After producing her first brood of daughters, she begins to release her powerful fertility-suppressing chemicals. The drone's role ends after supplying the sperm. He dies shortly after that, burned by his brief, energy-intensive life of sperm production and giving way to the queen, who will carry out the role of perpetuating the "race," assisted by her "retinue."

9. In order to cooperate so effectively, ants need a complex communication system that would at very least let them tell nestmates from strangers. This communication is carried out largely through chemistry. In fact, ants are little chemical factories, continuously producing an array of substances, called pheromones, that serve as their language. Through these pheromones the ants can convey messages ranging from the location of food to the presence of danger. They use pheromones as well to orchestrate social behaviors as diverse as tending the young, grooming the queen, marking their territory, and mating.

10. It is really amazing what these tiny insects can accomplish by mere instinct. They put us humans to shame. They do not need any blue plans, engineers, or architects to build their nests. They do not need any ballistic missiles to attack their enemies. There is no need of star wars either. Ant colonies survive in millions by nature's own power.

POSTREADING ACTIVITIES

1. Write down the new information you received from reading the above passage with reference to ants' :

   - Social behavior
   - Communication system
   - Propagation of the species

2. What new things have you learned about the queen ant's relationship with the rest of the members in the colony ? Compare this "matriarchal structure" of the "ant society" to the social structure of the community you belong to.
3. What role do the drones play in the colony ? How does this role differ from the male role in your society ?

Part 2: GRAMMAR

VERB TENSES: REVIEW

Problems for You to Solve

What tense is used in the underlined verbs in the following sentences ? What difference would it make in meaning if you used a simple past tense instead? Would you consider the simple past tense wrong in these contexts? Why?

S1.   They *have evolved* complex and subtle communication systems based on scents and body language. (Par. 2)

S2.   The construction of tentlike nests which the weaver ants literally weave from leaves and which *has given* them their name, is another example of the kind of cooperation and division of labor ants *have evolved*. (Par. 5)

PRESENT AND PAST PARTICIPLES AS ADJECTIVES

For Your Critical Thinking

Group the following into present and past participle phrases. How can you tell the present participles from the past participle? What position do these two occupy in each of the following groups of words?

1.   highly developed social behavior (Par. 2)
2.   self-contained unit (Par. 3)
3.   laying queen (Par. 3)
4.   specialized workers (Par. 4)
5.   living chains (Par. 5)
6.   protruding membranes (Par. 6)

Note

Making participles out of verbs and using them as adjectives is a handy device in writing. However, most second language students find it difficult to make the distinction between present and past participles. The following may help you distinguish the two kinds of participles.

1.   The present participle is usually derived from an active voice sentence.

Example :   In #3 above, "laying queen" is derived from the active voice sentence : "The queen lays (eggs)." Similarly, #6 above can be expanded into the sentence : "The membranes protrude."

2.   The past participle is usually derived from a passive voice sentence.

Example :   The phrase, "highly developed social behavior" (#1 above), is derived from the sentence : "Social behavior has been highly developed by the ants."

3. Both present and past participles are dependent on the stimulus-experience° relationship the verb affords. The experiencer is the one who is experiencing the action indicated by the verb. The stimulus or actor is the thing or person causing this action.

Example : In the sentence, "The professor bores the students a lot," The action is "bores." Those who experience this action (the experiencers) are the students and the one who gives the stimulus (the actor) is the professor. Applying the forms -*ing* and -*ed* to the verb *bores,* we get the present participle *boring* and the past participle *bored.* The present participle goes before the stimulus, namely, "the professor," and the past participle goes before the experiencer, namely, "the students." Thus we get "the boring professor" and "the bored students."

Application

For each sentence, follow these four steps :

1. Make present and past participles from the verbs.
2. Apply the questions (a) Who/what is the stimulus/actor ? and (b) Who/what is the experiencer of the action ?
3. Use both the present and past participles as adjectives, putting the present participle before the stimulus and the past participle before the experiencer.
4. Make sentences with each of the participial phrases.

Example of how to do this exercise :

1. Those children annoy their mother all the time.

Step 1. Verb : annoy
Present participle : annoying
Past participle : annoyed
Step 2a. Who are the stimuli of the action "annoy" ? The children.
Step 2b. Who experiences this action ? The mother.
Step 3. The annoying children (stimulus/actor)
The annoyed mother (experiencer)

---

*This idea is borrowed from Regina L. Smalley and Mary Ruetten Hank, *Refining Composition Skills : Rhetoric and Grammar for ESL Students,* Macmillan Publishing Co., New York, 1982, pp. 57–58.

Step 4.

    S1. The annoying children were taken out for a trip by their aunt. (present participle)

    S2. The annoyed mother could relax for a while. (past participle)

1. Those children annoy their mother all the time.
2. The machine answered all the questions.
3. The lady cleans the floor very well.
4. The news astonished my mother.
5. Exercise invigorates athletes.
6. My test results depressed my counselor.
7. Fred's girlfriend, Cathy, sometimes offends him by her rude behavior.
8. This lesson confuses the students.
9. The movie interested the audience.
10. The clown fascinated the guests.
11. The earthquake shattered the buildings into pieces.

ADVERBS

Form and Function

For Your Critical Thinking

1. What common form do you notice in all the underlined words below ?
2. What do you think are their functions in each of the sentences ? What difference would it make if these words were left out from the sentences ? Would it affect the structure of the sentence, making an ungrammatical sentence ? Or would it affect the meaning of the sentence ?

    S1. Ants belong to an <u>utterly</u> different species. (Par. 1)

    S2. The hallmark of ants is their <u>highly</u> developed social behavior. (Par. 2)

    S3. Soldier ants <u>automatically</u> risk their own lives to defend a territory needed to feed their colony's brood. (Par. 3)

    S4. The weaver ants <u>literally</u> weave tentlike nests from leaves. (Par. 5)

    S5. The queen carries the primary burden, which puts her <u>understandably</u> at the center of the colony's attentions. (Par. 6)

    S6. A crowd of workers <u>literally</u> covers the queen ant at all times. (Par. 6)

S7. They frequently lick the surface of her body, particularly her head and protruding membranes on her gaster that are richly endowed with glands. (Par. 6)

S8. The queen maintains her dominance by actually suppressing the fertility of her daughters with potent chemicals. (Par. 7)

S9. The workers eagerly lick the glandular secretions from their mother's body. (Par. 7)

S10. This communication is carried out largely through chemistry. (Par. 9)

S11. Ants are little chemical factories, continuously producing an array of substances, called pheromones. (Par. 9)

S12. It is really amazing what these tiny insects can accomplish by mere instinct. (Par. 10)

Note

The function of an adverb is to modify either an adjective or a verb.

For Your Critical Thinking

Which of the adverbs in the sentences above modify adjectives? Which modify verbs?

Note

Based on form and function, adverbs may be grouped into different categories. All the adverbs given above have the same form, that is, they end in -ly. Similarly, they are all derived from adjectives.

Exercise

Write the adjective forms of the adverbs:

adj.	adv.	adj.	adv.
_____	highly	_____	automatically
_____	literally	_____	understandably
_____	frequently	_____	particularly
_____	richly	_____	actually
_____	eagerly	_____	largely
_____	continuously	_____	really

All the adverbs in S1–S12 except *frequently* are **adverbs of manner,** which means they answer the question, "How?"

For example, in S2, *highly* modifies the adjective *developed* and answers the question, "How developed?" In S3, *automatically* modifies the verb *risk* and answers the question, "How do they risk their own lives?" However, *frequently,* in S7 answers the question, "How *often* do they lick the surface of her body?" This comes under a different category of adverbs called **adverbs of frequency** or **degree.** Some other adverbs belonging to this category are:

Group A		*Group B*	
occasionally	regularly	ever	never
usually	repeatedly	sometimes	seldom
generally		always	

Word Order of Adverbs of Manner

Usually, adverbs modifying adjectives or adverbs directly precede the word they modify. See S1, S2, S7 (*richly*), and S12.

Adverbs modifying a verb usually follow the verb and its objects. See S5 and S10 above. However, this position is often changed by writers for stylistic purposes, especially for emphasis. This is the case in S3, S4, S6, S8, S9, and S11 above.

For Your Critical Thinking

Change the position of the adverbs in S3, S4, S6, S8, S9, and S11 by putting them after the verbs and objects, and see why the writer preferred the pre-verb and not the post-verb position.

Word Order of Adverbs of Frequency

In affirmative sentences, adverbs of frequency generally precede the verb. See the use of *frequently* in S7 above. In affirmative sentences with auxiliaries, these adverbs usually follow the first auxiliary.

Ex. 1.   An ant colony would always have a division of labor.

When the first auxiliary is stressed, the frequency adverb precedes it.

Ex. 1.   An ant colony certainly would have a division of labor.

In questions, these usually follow the subjects.

Ex. 1.   Does the queen ant *always* suppress the fertility of her daughters?

In negative statements *always* usually follows the negative auxiliary.

Ex. 1.   I do not *always* understand animal behavior.

The adverbs *generally, often,* and *usually* can either precede or follow the negative auxiliary.

Ex. 1.   The older ants do not usually tend the queen.
Ex. 2.   The older ants usually do not tend the queen.

Adverbs Used as Sentence Adverbials

As sentence or clause adverbials, adverbs may be placed either at the beginning or end of the sentence or clause.

Ex. 1.   Anthropologists have made many research studies on animal behavior *recently.*
Ex. 2.   *Recently,* anthropologists have made many research studies on animal behavior.

Application

Do one of the following:

1.   Read an article from the *Encyclopedia Britannica* (or any other encyclopedia) on any animal, bird, or insect of your choice. Note down the key ideas. Write down a summary of what you read, elaborating your key ideas. (Do not copy sentences from the article. See Chapter 2, pp. 38–39 for a discussion of summarization.)
2.   Write a short story using your favorite animal, bird, or insect as characters.
       Find a partner. Have him or her go over your written piece and give you feedback on your use of adverbs.
       Go over your piece yourself, and make necessary changes. You may want to incorporate your partner's feedback. Add, delete, and/or make corrections. Rewrite the whole piece and hand it in to your instructor.

Part 3: SENTENCE COMBINING

CLAUSE MARKERS

Problems for You to Solve

How would you combine the sets of sentences in each of the following groups? How would you punctuate the combined sentences?

Write down your combined sentences. Check your answers against the writer's own sentences. If yours are different from the writer's, there are two possibilities: (1) Yours is an alternative way of combining the sentences. (2) Yours may be wrong. Discuss your answers with your group members and then with your instructor.

GROUP A

1a. Ant societies are exclusively female.
 b. They can have a million or more members.
 c. Each of these members is rigidly programmed to behave in the best interest of her sisters. (Par. 2)

2a. All its members have a common mother, the queen, and often, the same father.
 b. This father is one of the drones.
 c. The queen has mated this drone. (Par. 3)

3a. The ant colony also has a division of labor.
 b. This is often a caste system.
 c. This caste system assigns specific tasks to specialized workers. (Par. 4)

4a. The construction of a tentlike nest is another example of cooperation and division of labor.
 b. The ants have evolved this kind of cooperation and division of labor.
 c. The weaver ants literally weave these tentlike nests from leaves.
 d. This weaving of leaves to build tentlike nests has given the weaver ants their name. (Par. 5)

5a. The queen carries the primary burden.
 b. This puts her understandably at the center of the colony's attention. (Par. 6)

6a. The young worker ants lick the surface of the queen ant's body, particularly her head and protruding membranes on her gaster.
 b. These are richly endowed with glands. (Par. 6)

7a. Ants need a complex communication system in order to communicate so effectively.
 b. This communication system would at the very least let them tell nestmates from strangers. (Par. 9)

8a. Ants are little chemical factories.
 b. These factories are continuously producing an array of substances.
 c. This array of substances is called pheromones.
 d. These pheromones serve as their language. (Par. 9)

GROUP B

1a. Ants belong to an utterly different species.
 b. However, they, like the humans, have met many of the same problems human societies have had to face. (Par. 1)

2a. The female worker ants sacrifice their own fertility.
 b. The reason is that it is more efficient to help raise the eggs of a single, continually laying queen than to lay and rear their own eggs. (Par. 3)

3a. She produces her first brood of daughters.
 b. After that, she begins to release her powerful fertility-suppressing chemicals. (Par. 8)

GROUP C

1a. The middle-aged forage.
 b. In contrast, the oldsters serve as protectors. (Par. 4)

Note

The clause marker *while* has one of two meanings when it introduces an adverbial clause. The two meanings are : (1) *when*, and (2) contradiction. With the second meaning, it can be used as a substitute for *even though* or *although*.

GROUP D

1a. One ant grasps another's waist and so on.
 b. This activity goes on up to a certain time.
 c. At this time their chain of bodies reaches a leaf needed for a new nest. (Par. 5)

2a. The queen mates with many males.
 b. This mating goes on up to a certain time.
 c. At this time she has a lifetime worth of sperm in her abdomen. (Par. 8)

Note

Until is a time clause introducer meaning "up to" (a time).

GROUP E

1a. Chemical excretion makes the weaver queen very attractive to her worker offspring.
 b. As a result, a crowd of workers literally covers her at all times. (Par. 6)

2a. The ants need a complex communication system.
 b. The purpose is to communicate effectively. (Par. 9)

Note

So that is an adverbial clause marker, used to express purpose or result. In S1 of Group E above, it expresses result. The second set above in Group E could be combined with *so that* as follows:

S: The ants need a complex communication system *so that* they can communicate effectively.

However, in the text, the two sentences (2a and b above) are combined with *in order to,* a phrase marker, not a clause marker, to show purpose. This phrase marker may be reduced to *to,* in which case the sentence could be written:

S: The ants need a complex communication system to communicate effectively.

GROUP F

1a. Each colony is a self-contained unit.
  b. The members of each colony are working together for a common purpose.
  c. This common purpose is to ensure the reproduction and survival of its common genes. (Par. 3)

2a. The majors divide into age groups.
  b. The majors are charged with particular duties. (Par. 4)

3a. The oldsters serve as protectors.
  b. These oldsters are recognizable by worn mandibles and missing legs. (Par. 4)

4a. The ants act as guards and scouts.
  b. They have sharp eyesight and sense of smell. (Par. 4)

5a. The chain of bodies reaches a leaf.
  b. This leaf is needed for a new nest. (Par. 5)

6a. The living chain contracts.
  b. This living chain pulls or rolls the leaf into the desired position. (Par. 5)

7a. The queen maintains her dominance by actually suppressing the fertility of her daughters with potent chemicals.
  b. These potent chemicals are located in the glandular secretions. (Par. 7)

8a. The drone dies shortly after that.
  b. He is burned by his brief, energy-intensive life of sperm production.
  c. He gives way to the queen.
  d. The queen will carry out the role of perpetuating the race. (Par. 8)

9a. Ants are little chemical factories.
  b. They continuously produce pheromones. (Par. 9)

GROUP G

1a. Working together for a common purpose demands not just cooperation.
  b. It also demands altruism. (Par. 3)

GROUP H

1a. Young worker ants frequently lick the surface of the queen ant's body.
 b. They give particular attention to her head and protruding membranes on her gaster. (Par. 6)

For Your Critical Thinking

Did you find any common structural features in the sentences you made in each of the groups above (Groups A–H)? What are they? How are the sentences in each group different? Discuss the answers in your group and finally, have them checked by your instructor.

Part 4: SENTENCE RELATING

TRANSITION WORDS

Problems for You to Solve

What kind of relationship do you find in each of the following sets of sentences? What vocabulary word would you use to relate each pair? Why would you use that particular word in the context? Check your answers against the sentences in the text. Remember, what you find in the text is not the only answer. Discuss your answers in your group and then with your instructor.

1a. The female worker ants sacrifice their own fertility because it is more efficient to help raise the eggs of a single, continually laying queen than to lay and rear their own eggs.
 b. Soldier ants automatically risk their own lives to defend a territory needed to feed a colony's brood. (Par. 3)

2a. The colony also has a division of labor, often a caste system that assigns specific tasks to specialized workers.
 b. Among the weaver ants, the minors lick the scales to clean them, collect the discharge, and regurgitate it on demand. (Par. 4)

3a. The queen carries the burden, which puts her understandably at the center of the colony's attention.
 b. She fosters her daughters' devotion. (Par. 6)

4a. Communication is carried out largely through chemistry.
 b. Ants are little chemical factories, continuously producing an array
     of substances called pheromones. (Par. 9)

Part 5: VOCABULARY, WORD FORMS, AND IDIOMS

FILL-INS

Paragraph b in each of the following pairs is a paraphrase of a. Using synonyms and antonyms (which need not be exact), changing sentence structure, and changing word forms are some of the devices used in making the paraphrase.

Your task: Fill in the blanks with appropriate words or phrases. Each blank line indicates one word. The underlined words in the original may give you the clues. The asterisks in b tell you there are no clues provided in the original.

1a. As <u>premier</u> social insects, ants share a lot with <u>human beings. Even
     though</u> ants belong to an <u>utterly</u> different species, they, like the
     humans, have met, <u>throughout</u> their long evolution, many of the
     same problems human societies have had to <u>face.</u> These problems
     involve both war — <u>intense competition within and between
     species</u> — and peace — <u>coping with hunger and environmental
     stress.</u> We humans are but mere neophytes, <u>compared with</u> the
     ants, in <u>solving</u> these problems. (Par. 1)

 b. As social insects belonging to the (1) _____

     _____ , ants have a lot in common with (2) _____

     (3) _____ _____ _____ _____

     _____ that ants and humans belong to two

     (4) _____ different species, they are similar in one

     respect, namely, that they both have had to (5) _____

almost the same problems (6) _____ their long
(7)° _____ of evolution. (8) _____ for the
(9) _____ of the species involves going through stages of
war and peace. (10) _____ _____ with ants,
human beings are just novices in (11) _____ problems
(12)° _____ _____ survival.

2a. The hallmark of ants is their highly developed social behavior. Ant
societies, which are exclusively female, can have a million or more
members, each rigidly programmed to a division of labor and to
behave in the best interest of her sisters. To help in this cooperative
work of promoting the "society's" interest, they have evolved complex and subtle communication systems based on scents and body
language. Yet all their behavior is dominated by instinct, not by
such human traits as emotions or reasoning. (Par. 2)

 b. The most (13) _____ _____ of ants is their
highly (14) _____ social behavior. Each of the
(15) _____ of members in ant societies, made up of
(16) _____ females, (17) _____ in a
(18) _____ manner, all labor being (19) _____
to help her in (20) _____ the best interest of her sisters.
Working (21) _____ for the (22) _____ of the
"society's" interest in this way is (23)° _____
_____ by the complex and (24) _____
_____ communication system they have evolved, based
on scents and body language. (25) _____, it is instinct, not
any human (26) _____, such as emotions or reasoning,
that (27) _____ all their behavior.

3a. To the queen and drones fall the colony's paramount mission —
spreading the genes. The queen carries the primary burden, which

puts her understandably at the center of the ant colony's attentions.
Moreover, she fosters her daughters' devotion. (Par. 7)

b. Even though the colony's (28) _____ _____
mission — spreading the genes — is (29) _____
_____ by both the queen and drones, the
(30) _____ burden falls on the queen.
(31)° _____ , it is (32) _____ that she is
(33) _____ at the center of attention (34) _____
that she (35) _____ her daughters' devotion.

4a. The queen's influence over her workers is very profound. Her
presence guarantees strong colony cohesiveness. She maintains
her dominance by actually suppressing the fertility of her daughters with potent chemicals, located in the glandular secretions.
(Par. 7)

b. The queen is very (36) _____ _____ with
her workers, her very presence among them (37) _____
a strong bond of (38) _____ . She (39) _____
her (40) _____ position in the colony by actually
(41) _____ her daughters' fertility with the help of
strong, (42) _____ _____ chemicals,
(43)° _____ in the glandular secretions.

5a. In order to cooperate so effectively, ants need a complex communication system that would at the very least let them tell nestmates
from strangers. This communication is carried out largely through
chemistry. In fact, ants are little chemical factories, continuously
producing an array of substances, called pheromones, that serve as
their language. Through these pheromones the ants can convey
messages ranging from the location of food to the presence of danger. They use pheromones as well to orchestrate social behaviors

as <u>diverse</u> as <u>tending</u> the young, grooming the queen, marking their territory, and mating. (Par. 9)

b. To (44) _____ the purpose of such (45) _____ _____, ants (46) _____ a complex communication system that would (47) _____ _____ _____ level help them (48) _____ nestmates from strangers. This communication need is (49) _____ with (50) _____ by their body chemistry which involves the (51) _____ _____ of a (52) _____ of chemical substances called pheromones. (53) _____ as the language (54)° _____, these pheromones can convey a wide (55) _____ of messages, such as (56) _____ food and identifying (57) _____ situations. These pheromones are (58) _____ used to orchestrate social behaviors as (59) _____ as (60) _____ _____ the young, grooming the queen, marking territories, and mating.

Part 6: SUPPLEMENTARY READINGS

Supplementary Reading 1: CAFFEINE

1. The alarm clock rings, and you stumble from your bed to the kitchen. With sleepy eyes you measure out the fragrant brown granules, and soon you're savoring that first morning cup of coffee.

2. Within an hour the coffee will cause your adrenal glands to pour higher amounts of two stimulating chemicals into your blood stream, and your blood-

sugar levels will rise. Your blood pressure will increase by as much as ten percent as blood vessels constrict, but your pulse rate will slow slightly. After a strong cup of coffee, you, like most other people, perform physical and mental tasks at the peak of your ability.

3. The reason is caffeine. A single cup of drip or percolated coffee contains about 85 milligrams — roughly 1/300 of an ounce — of this alkaloid. Found in more than 160 plants, caffeine has been used by humans for thousands of years.

4. The ancient Aztecs drank ritual beverages brewed from the caffeine-laden cocoa bean, the source of our chocolate. In Africa, people used the kola nut, an ingredient in today's cola drinks. And most of the world drinks tea, a cup of which contains up to 50 milligrams of caffeine.

5. Each year Americans drink 2½ billion pounds of coffee, which accounts for 76 percent of our nearly 34 million-pound annual caffeine consumption. Eight out of ten adult Americans drink coffee, about 3.5 cups every day.

6. Many who abstain from coffee and tea also consume caffeine, often unwittingly. The drug is found in chocolate, colas and other soft drinks — some fortified with up to 54 milligrams of caffeine in each 12-ounce bottle. In addition, caffeine is present in diet pills, cold and allergy pills, headache remedies, and even as an unnamed "flavoring agent" in some puddings, frozen dairy desserts and baked goods.

7. Only recently have scientists begun to probe the hazards that all this caffeine might pose to our health. Here are some of the questions that have been raised and what scientific studies have found so far:

8. *Is caffeine addictive?* The most common problem for coffee drinkers is insomnia. Studies show that in many people caffeine disrupts their normal ability to fall asleep. As little as two cups of coffee can keep them awake. Perhaps, because insomnia bothers you one night, you decide to eliminate all caffeine from your diet the next day. If you're a heavy coffee drinker, by late afternoon you might feel depressed and moody and have a throbbing headache. If you stay off caffeine, these symptoms could last two or three days before disappearing.

9. Why? Because you were in withdrawal from a mild dependency on caffeine. Had you *gradually* reduced your daily intake, you might never have suffered.

10. Scientists have long known of caffeine's power to become habit-forming; 50 percent of regular coffee drinkers are hooked — pysically dependent to some degree. But only in 1981 did they begin to unlock the secret of that power. Researchers led by Dr. Solomon H. Snyder of the Johns Hopkins University School of Medicine in Baltimore discovered that caffeine is remarkably similar to one of the brain's "messenger" chemicals, adenosine. When adenosine molecules fit into the receptors or keyholes of brain cells, they inhibit or neutralize activity by offsetting the effects of other brain chemicals that excite activity. Caffeine fits into and blocks these receptors, preventing adenosine from doing its job. Caffeine therefore affects the mind and body indirectly, through its power to allow the brain's own arousing chemicals to go unbalanced by adenosine.

11. The brain cells react by quickly creating new receptor sites, enough to accommodate both the caffeine and the adenosine. When a person suddenly stops ingesting caffeine, adenosine occupies all the receptor sites vacated by caffeine. The brain then becomes overinhibited, understimulated. Blood pressure falls, and in most heavy coffee drinkers this sometimes produces severe headaches. Other symptoms could be depression, lethargy, irritability and moodiness, which will last until the brain adjusts by reducing the number of adenosine receptors.

12. This mild form of dependency with its potential withdrawal symptoms is considered by most medical authorities to be relatively harmless.

13. *Can caffeine hurt you?* Some people, perhaps as many as ten percent of coffee drinkers, experience such symptoms as nervousness, anxiety, and shortness of breath after ingesting 2½ cups of coffee (more than 200 milligrams of caffeine) in one day. For another ten percent, more than 10 cups of drip coffee (1000 milligrams) in a day can cause toxic symptoms — ringing in the ears, mild delirium, flashes of light, rapid irregular heartbeat, rapid breathing, muscle tension and trembling. However, a lethal dose is approximately 10 grams, and to get that from coffee you would have to drink more than 100 cups of it within a few minutes.

14.   *Does caffeine cause birth defects?* In September 1980, the U.S. Food and Drug Administration (FDA) issued a warning urging pregnant women to stop consuming products containing caffeine, but the agency stopped short of requiring a warning label for such products.

15.   Between 1978 and 1980 Dr. Thomas F. X. Collins, an FDA scientist, conducted experiments on pregnant rats. He reported that a caffeine dosage equivalent to what would be 12 to 24 cups of very strong coffee for a human could cause the rats to bear deformed litters. Even the equivalent of as little as two cups of very strong coffee could slightly retard bone development in rats.

16.   Some scientists who specialize in fetal deformity and genetic damage are skeptical about rat experiments. Such laboratory rats easily suffer deformities, and what causes deformity in one species often causes no harm in others. Also, their bodies metabolize caffeine differently from the ways humans do.

17.   Nevertheless, acting primarily on that study, the FDA Commissioner Jere E. Goyan proposed the suspension of caffeine from the FDA's "Generally Regarded as Safe" list. One week after Goyan's warning, three FDA inspectors paid a scheduled visit to Collins's laboratory. It was, they reported, poorly organized and unsanitary. An embarrassed FDA hastily appointed a panel of government scientists to review Collins's work.

18.   That panel, headed by Dr. Robert Dixon of the National Institute of Environmental Health Sciences, discounted Collins's study, noting that many of its results occurred because the extreme doses of caffeine probably poisoned the pregnant rats.

19.   On January 21, 1982, a team of Harvard scientists published their own study of 12,205 pregnant women and concluded that no link could be found between birth defects and the amount of coffee the women consumed. Additional studies in the United States and Finland reached the same conclusion.

20.   A mother-to-be might wish to err on the side of caution and limit her caffeine intake, since the alkaloid does pass through the placenta and enter the unborn infant's body. But the best research studies on humans dismiss any connection between caffeine consumption and birth defects.

21.   *Does caffeine affect the heart?* In 1972 and 1973 Dr. Hershel Jick and fellow researchers at the Boston University Medical Center published two studies on coffee and myocardial infarction, the most common type of heart attack. They concluded that people who drank one to five cups of coffee daily ran a 50-percent greater risk of heart attack than those who drank no coffee, and that those who drank six or more cups daily were at 110-percent greater risk. On the surface this made sense, for coffee can influence pulse rate and blood pressure.

22.   But other scientists criticized Jick and questioned his methods of selecting subjects for the study. They noted that Jick had found no link between myocardial infarction and the drinking of tea, which also contains caffeine. And they asked why he had overlooked the possibility that heavy coffee drinking and heart problems might *both* be results of certain personality traits.

23.   Other major studies contradicted Jick's findings. In the Framingham heart-disease epidemiology study, researchers began in 1949 to monitor more than 5100 citizens of the Massachusetts town. They found no link between coffee consumption and heart problems. A similar study on 2500 Georgia residents and another on 1700 men in Chicago also failed to connect heart disease and coffee drinking. Dr. Jick's studies have been interpreted by other scientists to show that coffee drinkers are more likely to *survive* a heart attack than are non-drinkers, because caffeine acts as a mild stimulant.

24.   For people with arrhythmia (irregularity of heartbeat), coffee drinking should be approved by a physician, because heavy doses of caffeine can alter heart rhythms. Those with high blood pressure should also consult their doctors because caffeine might raise that pressure. Several studies on laboratory animals have found evidence that caffeine can elevate the level of free fatty acids, lipids and cholesterol in the blood. But most of the major studies find little or no link between heart disease and coffee drinking.

25.   *Does caffeine cause cancer?* In 1981 *The New England Journal of Medicine* published a study by Dr. Brian MacMahon and colleagues at the Harvard School of Public Health. It concluded that drinking one to two cups of coffee daily doubled — and five cups a day tripled — a person's risk of getting cancer of the pancreas, the fourth largest cause of cancer deaths.

26.   Four eminent scientists, headed by Dr. Alvan R. Fienstein of the Yale University School of Medicine, discovered a bias in choosing subjects for the MacMahon study, which put his findings in doubt. A follow-up study by Dr. Harvey R. Goldstein of Scripps Clinic and Research Foundation in La Jolla, California, failed to detect any link between coffee and pancreatic cancer.

27.   While scientists continue to study the effects of regular coffee consumption on human health, they are also examining the potential dangers of drinking *decaffeinated* coffee. In 1982, one out of seven Americans had switched to decaffeinated coffee (20 years ago only one in 25 used the product).

28.   To remove caffeine from coffee beans, processors use solvents. Until 1975 the solvent in widespread use was trichlorethylene, replaced when the FDA threatened to ban it as a carcinogen. Since then companies have removed 97 percent of coffee's caffeine with methylene chloride. This solvent is applied in coffee beans, then rinsed away, but some researchers have been concerned that a potentially dangerous residue remains in the coffee. The National Coffee Association agrees that a trace residue lingers, but its scientists estimate that a consumer would have to drink 25 million cups of decaffeinated coffee a day to suffer ill effects from it.

29.   One of the world's pre-eminent caffeine researchers, geneticist Bengt A. Kihlman of the University of Uppsala in Sweden, presents what may be the final verdict on caffeine. When all the evidence is weighed, he has written, only pregnant women and those with some special health problems such as arrhythmia, seem even remotely at risk from heavy consumption of regular coffee. "For everybody else, since the risks are negligible or nonexistent, the risk–benefit evaluation is not difficult to make : caffeine can be acquitted."

Supplementary Reading 2: THE AWESOME POWER TO BE OURSELVES

1.   One afternoon, when I was a little girl, the teacher announced that there would be no school the next day because the old man who lived in the turreted mansion had died. I was puzzled. Many people died. Why close the school for this man?

2.   I asked Stuart, who was in the eighth grade and usually knew everything. "He owned the factory, didn't he?" Stuart said, amazed at my ignorance. "That's about as powerful as you can get around here."

3.   Isn't this how many of us think of power — the richest man in town, the man who can control others?

4.   But power has many guises. My father was a kind and gentle country minister in Nova Scotia. He had neither money nor fame. No one, I am sure, was ever afraid of him. When he was 64 years old, he received a letter from a church official in one of his old parishes. "We hear that you will soon be retiring," the man wrote. "Would you come and settle here? We feel that we'd be a better community and better neighbors for having a man whose life is so genuine living among us."

5.   Imagine changing a community just by being oneself. *That* is power.

6.   I think of a homely little man in Athens more than 2000 years ago who died because he asked dangerous questions. His audiences were very small ; yet there is no literate person in the world today who has not heard of Socrates. I think of St. Francis of Assisi, who gave up a pampered life to live in poverty while comforting the poor and the sick, and of Mohandas Gandhi, who freed his people from the most powerful empire of his time, without any force except what he called "truth force."

7.   What do these individuals have in common? They all spoke and acted as themselves, resolutely standing up for what they believed. They have had the inner purity of people true to their ideals. They have been "authentic."

8.   Many critics nowadays decry the "be yourself" philosophy as leading to selfishness. But *authenticity* doesn't do this. It proceeds from the center of a person's life, but is not self-centered. It sets a glowing example for others and moves them to action. This is its uncanny power, and it is available to all of us.

9.   The concept that we ought to know and be ourselves goes back to the first time a human wondered, "Who am I?" Socrates taught that to "know thyself" is the basis of all knowledge; Shakespeare wrote, "To thine own self be true... thou canst not then be false to any man." Like all the great ideas, the concept rises and falls with the tides of history.

10.   In the 1960s, after a period of conformity in America, young people began again to search for identity. They struggled against authority and insisted on obeying their own consciences. That crusade may be over, but the search for the self goes on. Always, we seem to be asking, "How can I make my life count for something?"

11.   Authenticity makes each person's life count by restoring *power* to the *individual.* To be oneself is a natural, human and universal power which brings with it a cornucopia of blessings. What are the attributes of an authentic person?

12.   Today, best-sellers are written on the powers of assertiveness and manipulation. But in our society the assertive manipulators often do not win. Many of our institutions are headed by authentic people, who rise because others are drawn to them, admire them, imitate their example. Here is an upright business leader who has risen to the top over others who are more clever. Why? His associates might say he is "fairer," or that he has a longer "vision," but it is more than that. The man possesses an inner strength; he radiates confidence. Instinctively honest, he never weakens his moral authority by a dishonest compromise. This honesty is one prime attribute of authentic people. Others include:

13.   *A sense of direction.* Authentic people recognize the direction in which their lives are meant to go. When Albert Schweitzer, the great missionary doctor, was a boy, a friend proposed that they go into the hills and kill birds. Albert was reluctant, but afraid of being laughed at, he went along. They arrived at a tree in which a flock of birds was singing; the boys put stones in their catapults. Then the church bells began to ring, mingling music with the birdsong. For Albert, it was a voice from heaven. He shooed the birds away and went home, disregarding what his friends thought about him. From that day on, reverence for life was more important to him than the fear of being laughed at. His priorities were clear.

14.   *Self-generated energy.* Fatigue is a common symptom of people who suppress what is truly themselves. They are not really tired but *tired of.* Dr. Josephine A. Jackson, in an early primer of psychotherapy, *Outwitting Our Nerves,* describes patients so fatigued that they could scarcely drag one foot after the other. Summing them up she said, "The sense of loss of muscular power was really a sense of loss of power on the part of the soul!"

15. We, too, are often tired, not from "the loss of muscular power" but from the effort not to be ourselves. We are actors trying to impress other people. That's hard work.

16. By contrast, the authentic person does not dissipate energy in contradictions. His self-honesty reduces internal conflicts, and he feels alive, exhilarated. His energy is turned on by doing what matters to him. He does not dissipate energy on conflicts or deceits.

17. *The power of example.* The authentic person also mobilizes the energies of others, by inspiring them. Just by being himself, he makes a statement about what is to be done.

18. During the French occupation of the Saar in the 1920s, when German feelings were running high against reported excesses by black colonial troops, Roland Hayes, the great black singer, faced a noisy and hostile audience in Berlin. For almost ten minutes, he stood quietly but resolutely by the piano, waiting for the hissing to cease. Then he signaled his accompanist and began to sing softly Schubert's "Du bist die Ruh" ("Thou Art Peace"). With the first notes of the song, a silence fell on the angry crowd. As Hayes continued to sing, his artistry transcended the hostility, and a profound communion between the singer and audience took place.

19. *The power of self-love.* A person who respects and values himself is much more likely to be able to do the same for others. When we are not sure who we are, we are uneasy. We try to find out what the other person would like us to say before we speak, would like us to do before we act. When we are insecure, our relationship to others is governed not by what they need but by our needs. Authentic people, on the other hand, are *there,* not only for themselves but for others. No energies are wasted in protecting a shaky ego.

20. *The power of the spirit.* No one can summon spiritual power just by wanting to. But it seems to come often to those most centered on the deep self where discovery begins. I think of Martin Luther King, Jr., marching between the clubs and baying dogs to Selma, Ala., and electrifying a huge audience in the Washington Mall. It was impossible to be with him for any length of time without realizing that the spirit was the spring from which he took his life's responses. Few of us can be great leaders, but any person who is true to himself enhances his access to this power of the spirit.

21. STRIVING for authenticity is not easy. This is a lifetime endeavor and nobody ever makes it all the way. It is a becoming rather than an ending, something we learn day by day. Here are some ways to begin.

22. *Pay attention to what is going on in your life, inwardly and outwardly.* Keep a journal to see how you change over time and to discover what muffled longings are being expressed. Few of us are so monolithic that we don't harbor conflicts within ourselves. Admit them. Listen to the dialogue within and record it in your journal. As May Sarton wrote in *World of Light,* "Everything free from falsehood is strength."

23. *Accept the idea that nothing is wrong with being different from other people.* The truth is, all of us are different, and we are meant to be. "Each one of us," wrote philosopher Paul Weiss, "is a unique being confronting the rest of the world in a unique fashion." Seek out your deepest convictions and stand by them, live by them.

24. *Spend time with yourself.* Solitude is at the heart of self-knowledge, because it is when we are alone that we learn to distinguish between the false and the true, the trivial and the important. "Solitude," said Nietzche, "makes us tougher toward ourselves and tenderer toward others."

25. As with the splitting of the atom, the opening of the self gives us access to a hidden power. Authenticity is a sensitizing and blessed power. It comes with feeling at home with oneself, and therefore, being at home in the universe. It is the greatest power in the world — the power to be ourselves.

Part 7: WRITING

ESSAY DEVELOPMENT AND PARAGRAPH STRUCTURE: REVIEW

This section will help you check on your background information on paragraph development. You may want to review Chapter 2, pp. 40–41 before you try to answer the questions.

For Your Critical Thinking

Discussing the following on the reading, "The Ant and Her World," in your groups will help you understand the process of thought development in each of the paragraphs in the reading passage above.

COHESION

1. What single characteristic trait about ants do you think the writer had in mind when he started to write this essay?
2. Locate the sentence which states this characteristic trait of ant life.
3. What key words does the writer use to explain this trait?
4. Locate the paragraph where the writer places these key words.

5.　According to the writer, by what two ways do the ants accomplish this trait?

6.　What is the point of comparison the writer wants to convey to the reader in Par. 3? What is this point compared to?

7.　What point does the writer want to make clear to the reader in the last two sentences of Par. 3?

8.　What is the single idea that runs through Par. 4-6?

9.　What device does the writer use to keep the reader focused on this single idea?

10.　What information does the writer convey to the reader in the second part of S1, Par. 4? ("... *that assigns specific tasks to specialized workers*")?

11.　What key idea does the writer want to develop in Par. 4?

12.　What device does the writer use in this paragraph to explain the key idea?

13.　Pick the words the writer has used in Par. 5 to relate this whole paragraph to the previous one (Par. 4).

14.　What information about weaver ants does the writer convey to the reader in Par. 5?

15.　How does the writer develop this idea in this paragraph?

16.　What is the specific information given to the reader in Par. 6-8?

17.　What device does the writer use to keep this single idea running through the three separate paragraphs?

18.　Does the writer deviate from the main idea in Par. 9?

19.　Is there any new information given the reader in the last paragraph?

20.　How does the writer appeal to the reader in this last paragraph?

COHERENCE

1.　Why does the writer begin the last sentence in Par. 2 with "yet"? Can you think of some synonyms for this word?

2.　Why did the writer begin the following sentence in Par. 3 with "this"?: "This demands not only cooperation but altruism."

3.　Do the last two sentences of Par. 3 express the same idea or different ideas? Underline the word the writer uses to relate these two sentences. Replace this word with synonyms.

4.　What role does "For example" in Par. 4 play in developing the idea expressed in the paragraph? (See Questions 11 and 12 above.)

5.　Pick the transition word that connects Par. 5 to Par. 4.

6.　What are the transition words the writer uses to relate the sentences explaining the different processes of nest construction? (Par. 5)

7.　Why does the writer use "Moreover" in Par. 6? What are some of the synonyms you would use for this transition word?

8. How are the following two sentences in Par. 9 related to the previous sentence, (that is, S1) ? Are the ideas expressed in the two sentences different or the same ?

   • "This communication is carried out largely through chemistry."
   • "In fact, ants are little chemical factories, continuously producing an array of substances, called pheromones, that serve as their language."

TOPIC SENTENCE AND PARAGRAPH DEVELOPMENT
BY GIVING EXAMPLES

1. How is the first sentence in Par. 3 related to the rest of the sentences in the same paragraph ?
2. Pick the one sentence in Par. 3 which is directly related to the last two sentences in the same paragraph.
3. Why does the writer begin sentence 5 (the next to the last) in Par. 3 with "For instance" ?
4. Pick the key statement in Par. 4 about the behavioral trait of ants.
5. How does the writer try to convince the reader of the authenticity of this statement ?
6. What is the key idea in Par. 5 ? Pick the sentence that gives this key idea.
7. How are the rest of the sentences in Par. 5 "tied" to this key sentence ?

Note

Each paragraph of an expository essay should talk about one and only one aspect of the thesis statement given in the opening paragraph (introduction). Many writers accomplish this unity of ideas (cohesion) by (1) beginning each paragraph with a statement of the key idea in one sentence, which is called the *topic sentence*, and (2) explaining or supporting this key idea with details.

The topic idea may be expressed in statement or question form. It may even be expressed in phrases. Also, it does not have to be the first sentence. However, for beginners it is always advisable to place the topic sentence at the beginning of the paragraph.

There are several ways of supporting the key idea. Giving examples or anecdotes is one way. Examples can be drawn from your own life, from people you know, or from history, literature, your reading, etc. Another very effective technique is to quote data from research studies. For people who have done research on the topic this is easy. However, those who haven't made a study of the topic can quote data from published studies.

For Your Critical Thinking

Compare the paragraph development in "The Ant and Her World" with that used in the two supplementary reading passages by finding the topic sentence of each paragraph and the techniques used in supporting the topic sentence.

THE EXPOSITORY ESSAY: PROCESS

The Thesis Statement

In Chapter 3 you learned how to brainstorm for ideas. (See pp. 72-73.) Free writing and questioning were suggested as two methods for getting ideas. It was also recommended that after getting ideas about the topic by brainstorming, you should choose the *one*, and *only one single idea* to be developed into an essay. This single idea, stated in a statement or question form is *the thesis statement* of your essay.

The thesis statement has two parts: (1) the topic (2) the comment. The "topic" part tells the reader about the broad theme of the essay. The "comment" part is your specific viewpoint on the topic, which you are going to talk about in the developmental paragraphs. The thesis statement helps both the writer and the readers. For the writer, it provides a definite framework to follow in the rest of the essay. For the readers, it provides a guide for a clear understanding of what to expect from the rest of the essay.

The thesis statement should be placed in the introductory paragraph. As mentioned in Chapter 3 (see pp. 69-70), the introductory paragraph begins with a broad description about the topic and gradually narrows down to the *thesis statement*. The thesis statement could be placed anywhere in the introductory paragraph, but it is advisable for beginners to place the thesis statement at the end of the introductory paragraph. The advantage of doing this is that it will help you be correctly focused when you write the developmental (body) paragraphs.

Organizing Ideas into an Outline

Once you have decided on the *single idea* you want to develop, the next stage in the process is to make an outline of how you would present this idea to the readers. Remember, the thesis statement is only your focus of explanation. The burden is on you to present this idea to the readers in the most informative way possible. The readers may or may not have the same viewpoint as you on the topic. In either case, remember that the readers are expecting to get some new information about the topic. Otherwise, they will consider the time spent in reading your essay wasted, and you will be rated as a poor writer.

This means you should have "informative ideas" about the topic. Where do you get these ideas from ? In cases of take-home writing assignments, you have enough time to go to the library and do some research. If your assignment is an in-class one, you can discuss the topic in your group. Or, you may already have gotten some ideas from your preliminary "brainstorming." If these ideas are too broad and not limiting enough to develop the thesis statement, do another brainstorming session focused *only* on the comment part of the thesis statement, *not* on the topic part. Take only the ideas most relevant and directly related to the comment and discard the rest.

After discarding all those ideas irrelevant to the thesis statement and the ones with which you are not comfortable, the next step in the process is to organize the rest systematically and logically into an outline. You do not have to worry about grammatical accuracy at this point. The only thing to consider seriously at this step is the logical or chronological ordering of your ideas.

Even though not all writers start with outlines, to avoid being a "sloppy" writer, it is advisable to make an outline of what you want to express in the essay. The outline does not have to be in any strictly grammatical form. However, it has to be organized. The outline plays the role of a blueprint before construction.

You may want to begin the outline with a statement of your thesis. Decide how many subpoints about the comment in the thesis statement you want to talk about. If you decide on three subpoints, for example, write them down and note down one example, anecdote, or item of research study or data for each of them. You can also note down the explanations you want to give to support each subpoint. You do not have to write complete sentences for the outline.

After writing the outline, check that all the subpoints are directly related to the comment part of the thesis statement and if the explanations, examples, etc., are relevant to the subpoints.

Problems for You to Solve

The following questions are based on "From Quill to Computer" (Chapter 3), "The Ant and Her World," "Caffeine," and "The Awesome Power to Be Ourselves" (Chapter 4). Answer them.

1. How many introductory paragraphs are there in each of the essays ?
2. In what number paragraph does the writer place the thesis statement in each of the above essays ?

3. In what part of the introductory paragraphs is the thesis statement of each of the four essays placed?
4. Write down the thesis statement of each of the four essays. What is the topic and what is the comment in each thesis statement?
5. Suppose the writers of the above essays made outlines before they began writing the complete essays. Write the outlines as the writers would have done.

WRITING ACTIVITIES

Reaction Journal

Write in your journal:

- What makes you happy about the three readings in this chapter
- If there is anything in the readings that makes you annoyed or angry, and why
- If any idea in the three reading passages confuses you, what they are, and why they are confusing
- What ideas you would change if you wrote these articles
- How helpful/not helpful the discussions in the chapter have been
- If you would like to see any section in the chapter taken out and why

Learning Log

Write in your learning log:

- What you already knew about ant behavior, coffee drinking, and how to be a powerful man or woman by being yourself
- What new ideas about these topics you learned from the readings
- If your reading of these articles changed your views about yourself and your behavior in any way; how and why
- If you have any new suggestions to make to your friends or relatives based on the information you received from the reading, and what they are
- How much of the information in Parts 2–6 you will be able to apply in your writing situations
- If any of the discussions have been unclear or confusing and what you would do to make them clear
- If you wrote the grammar and vocabulary sections what you would change or take out and why

Writing Assignment

Overview

Write a review of one of the articles in this textbook or any book, magazine, or newspaper on the content and the way of presentation.

> *Real-life Purpose of Assignment:* To get the review published in a student newspaper, if not in a popular magazine or newspaper
> *Academic Purpose:* Practice brainstorming, outlining, writing an expository essay
> *Real-life Audience:* Student and faculty readers on campus or the American public
> *Classroom Audience:* Your peers and instructor

Procedure

OUT-OF-CLASS ACTIVITY

1. Scan the pages of this textbook or of any book, magazine, or newspaper and find an article that interests you.
2. Read it over and over until you get all the key ideas.
3. Write down these ideas in a summary form (See Chapter 2, pp. 38–39 for a discussion on summarization.)
4. Reflect for about ten minutes on these key ideas and how they are presented.
5. Free-write for about thirty minutes (in chunks of ten minutes) on these key ideas and the devices used by the writer to present these ideas convincingly.
6. Read to yourself everything you wrote.
7. By adding and/or deleting, narrow down these ideas to only the directly relevant ones.
8. Make an outline of these directly relevant ideas (See Chapter 4, pp. 106–107 on outlining.)
9. Elaborate on this outline and write an essay reviewing the article on:

   - The ideas presented
   - How impressive or unimpressive these ideas are
   - How well or badly they are presented

IN-CLASS WORK IN PAIRS

Find a classmember who has not read the article you reviewed and get feedback from him or her.

OUT-OF CLASS WRITING

Based on the feedback you received, revise and rewrite the piece, to be handed in to your instructor.

Alternate Writing Assignments

1. You are the president of an ethnic student organization and are going to address its first board meeting. Since the organization is in its initial stage, 100% cooperation from all the members is absolutely necessary.

    Write down your speech. Emphasize the need of cooperation and division of labor, drawing examples from ant behavior.
2. The Bible says: "Learn from the ants and be wise." In what ways can we learn from ants' lives?
3. You are a feminist who believes that women are not the weaker sex and that nature has designed that women play a more important role in society than men, especially in the perpetuation of the race. Explain your position, giving examples from ant colonies.
4. You are an anti-feminist who opposes the above view. Explain your position, emphasizing the differences between human societies and ant colonies.
5. What is a caste system? How does it differ from the division of labor? Compare and contrast the two.

UNIT · 2

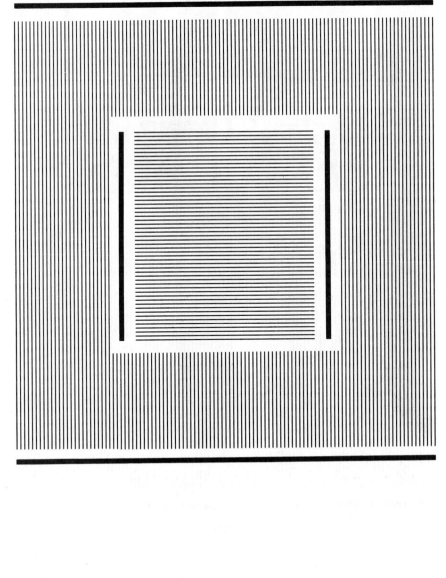

C H A P T E R · 5

Part 1: READING

PREREADING ACTIVITIES

Discuss the following questions in your group:

1. What implements are being used worldwide to eat solid food?
2. In what parts of the world are chopsticks used?
3. When were forks invented?
4. How did people manage to eat solid hot food before the invention of forks?
5. What is the best way to eat solid food?

Reading: *SOME REFLECTIONS ON THE TECHNOLOGY OF EATING*

1. All the world is divided into three parts — finger-feeders, fork-feeders and chopstick-feeders. Why people fall into these categories, however, is a mystery. "There is no comprehensive account of the ways of putting solid food into the mouth," according to Dr. Lynn White Jr., an emeritus history professor at University of California at Los Angeles and an expert on medieval technology.

2. Dr. White, who created a minor sensation in 1967 with his Science magazine article "Historic Roots of our Ecologic Crisis," stirred scholars in a recent speech at the American Philosophical Society meeting in Philadelphia. The society, which is rich in Nobel Prize winners and other illuminati, was founded by Benjamin Franklin in 1743 for the purpose of "promoting useful knowledge." Dr. White's contribution to the cause, at the society's request, was "Fingers, Chopsticks and Forks: Reflections on the Technology of Eating."

3. It is a topic rife with dispute over the utensils used to eat food. Those uneasy about the subtleties of an elaborately-set table can sympathize with Oscar Wilde's purported lament that "The world was my oyster, but I used the wrong fork." It is also a subject fraught with chauvinism: Devotees of one implement may often regard others as uncivilized or downright barbaric.

4. On Dr. White's tripartite globe, fork-feeders predominate in Europe and North America, chopstick-feeders in most of Eastern Asia and finger-feeders in much of Africa, the Middle East, Indonesia and the Indian subcontinent. That means fork-feeders are currently outnumbered 2 to 1. Academics agree fork-users have historically been in the minority ; humans have eaten with their fingers for most of the species' existence. As little as three centuries ago, most Western Europeans still used fingers, regarding the fork as foppish, decadent or worse. French historian Fernand Braudel tells of one medieval preacher in Germany who condemned the fork as "a dibolical luxury : God would not have given us fingers if he had wished to use such an instrument."

5. Forks and chopsticks won favor because they made it easier to handle hot food. Before their advent, people generally scooped up hot meals on flat bread. The major exception was China, where, Dr. White said, there is no evidence of flat bread being eaten. According to Dr. K. C. Chang, the chairman of Harvard University's anthropology department and editor of "Food in Chinese Culture" (Yale University Press, 1977), Chinese cooking was characterized by small portions, which did not require cutting by a knife and fork, eaten from bowls. "There was a need for morsels to be carried from a bowl to the mouth, and chopsticks came along to meet that need," he said.

6. Some of the oldest Chinese chopsticks date to 1200 B.C., Dr. Chang said. Apparently, the fork made its way to Western tables several hundred years later. It was not readily accepted. Forks were used for many years in Europe and the Near East, but only as kitchen implements, says historian Rhea Tannahill in "Food in History" (Stein and Day, 1971). She ascribes the widespread use of small forks as eating instruments to the Byzantines in the 10th century A.D. (The Byzantine Empire extended through Southeast Europe and Southwest Asia, including what is now Greece and parts of Turkey, Italy and Africa.) Dr. White noted that the first illustration of their use at meals was in a manuscript from the monastery of Montecassino in Italy, cradle of the Benedictine order, in 1022 A.D.

The Nobility Unforked

7. While the fork first entered society on the tables of the rich and well-born, many a crowned head, including Queen Elizabeth I of England and Louis XIV of France, ate with their fingers. Indeed, Mr. Braudel has said that Louis XIV ate chicken stew with his fingers and forbade the Duke of Burgundy and his brothers to use forks in his presence. History has it that when Napoleon III of France, a fork man, met the Shah of Persia, a finger-feeder, the potentates sharply disagreed about the proper method of bridging the gap between plate and lip. As late as 1897, Miss Tannahill writes, "sailors in the British Navy were forbidden the use of knives and forks, because they were regarded as being prejudicial to discipline and manliness."

8. Dr. White, himself a confirmed fork-feeder, as seen in his virtuoso performance with Pennsylvania scrapple and eggs, acknowledged that fork-, finger- and chopstick-feeders can be militant in defense of their eating implements. A famed Filipino restaurant in Los Angeles, for example, warns away customers who will not feed with fingers. Though they cannot document it, some scholars believe finger-feeding may be undergoing an enthusiastic revival, in part because of a worldwide resurgence in ethnic pride after the collapse of Western imperialism, in part because the regions and social classes with some of the highest birthrates shun forks.

9. The exceptions are the Westernized segments of society in third world countries. Dr. Eqbal Ahmad, a social scientist from Pakistan, said upper-income people in the subcontinent or in the Middle East may eat with their fingers most of the time, but often use forks on public occasions, particularly if Westerners or guests are present.

10. Norge Winfred Jerome, a nutritional anthropologist at the University of Kansas School of Medicine, said upper-income people in finger-eating areas can become more European than the Eurpoeans in their devotion to forks. She recalled taking Egyptian guests to a Kansas City grill and finding them unable to adopt the American custom of eating barbecued ribs with the fingers. For many such Westernized people, Dr. Jerome suggested, "The fork has become a status marker, because it establishes distance between the food and the eater that the fingers do not."

POSTREADING ACTIVITIES

1. What percentage of the world uses fingers for eating?
2. What advantages do forks and chopsticks have over fingers?
3. What advantages do fingers have over forks and chopsticks?
4. Would you consider eating with fingers civilized or uncivilized? Why?
5. How comprehensive is the writer's classification of the world, based on the technology of eating? Can you think of any group of people that uses any other kind of technology for eating solid food?

Part 2: GRAMMAR

VERB TENSES

Unreal Conditions in the Past

For Your Critical Thinking

Answer the questions following the sentence:

S1. God would not have given us fingers if he had wished to use such an instrument. (Par. 4)

1. What situation is the writer talking about?
2. Is this a real situation?
3. According to the writer, why did God create man with fingers?
4. How many verbs are used in the sentence? What are they?
5. In what time period (present/past/future) did the situation happen or not happen?

Note

When we want to talk about things, situations, or events in the past which are contrary to what actually happened in the real world, we use the *past unreal conditional verb patterns* as follows:

$$\underline{\text{If}} + \text{subj.} + \underline{\text{had}} + \text{past perfect} = \text{conditional clause}$$

$$\text{subj.} + \underline{\text{would}}/\underline{\text{could}}/\underline{\text{might}} \ (+ \underline{\text{not}}) + \underline{\text{have}} = \text{main clause}$$

The idea expressed by the sentence above may be put in a different way:

> Ex. 1   God created fingers because he wanted food to be eaten with them, not with any man-made tools.

The conditional verb pattern emphasizes the idea expressed as above.

Application

Express the following ideas using past unreal conditional verb patterns:

1. I failed the test. I was sick.
2. He was not nice to his wife. She divorced him.
3. The boy could not be saved. Paramedics were not available.
4. My father wanted me to be professional. He sent me to college.

Passive Voice: Reinforcement

For Your Critical Thinking

Underline the passive voice verbs in the following sentences. Why does the writer use the passive voice in these sentences?
(See Chapter 1, pp. 10–12 and Chapter 2, p. 28.)

S1. That means fork-feeders are currently outnumbered 2 to 1. (Par. 4)
S2. A medieval preacher is said to have condemned the fork as a "diabolical luxury."

S3. The major exception was China, where there is no evidence of flat bread being eaten. (Par. 5)

S4. Chinese cooking was characterized by small portions. (Par. 5)

S5. There was a need for morsels to be carried from the bowl to the mouth. (Par. 5)

S6. Forks were used for many years in Europe and the Near East, but only as kitchen implements. (Par. 6)

S7. Forks may not have been used as an eating utensil until the 10th century. (Par. 6)

S8. It has been reported that Louis XIV forbade the Duke of Burgundy and his brothers to use forks in his presence.

S9. It is said that sailors in the British Navy were forbidden the use of knives and forks because they were regarded as being prejudicial to discipline and manliness. (Par. 7)

S10. It is reported that a famed Filipino restaurant in Los Angeles warns away customers who will not feed with fingers.

COMPARISON OF ADJECTIVES: SUPERLATIVE DEGREE

For Your Critical Thinking

1. Why is *the* used in the following sentences?

    S1. Which of the three is *the* best way to eat food?
    S2. Historically, finger-feeders have *the* longest tradition.
    S3. Fingers are *the* cheapest.
    S4. Some of *the* oldest Chinese chopsticks date to 1200 B.C.

2. How many people, things, or groups are needed for the superlative degree to be used?

3. Compare the form of the superlative adjectives (one-syllabled) used here with the forms of comparative and positive degrees. (See Chapter 1, pp. 12-13; Chapter 2, p. 30; and Chapter 3, pp. 52–53.)

4. How does *best* in S1 above differ in form from the adjectives used in S2-S4?

Application

Divide one of the following into three groups and write a six-sentence paragraph, comparing each of the three to the others. Use the three degrees of comparison and appropriate vocabulary words. (See Chapter 3, p. 54 for some vocabulary words.)

- Your classmates
- Your neighbors
- The countries, cities, or towns you have visited

Part 3: SENTENCE COMBINING

CLAUSE MARKERS

Problems for You to Solve

In each group of sentences below, use the clause markers given to combine each set of sentences into one sentence.

GROUP A: WHY (USED AS SUBJECT)

1a. People fall into these categories.
 b. The reason is a mystery. (Par. 1)

GROUP B: WHO, WHICH, WHERE, WHILE, SINCE, BECAUSE

1a. Forks and chopsticks won favor.
 b. The reason was they made it easier to handle hot food (Par. 5)

2a. The major exception was China.
 b. Flat food was not eaten there. (Par. 5)

3a. Chinese cooking was characterized by small portions.
 b. These small portions did not require cutting by knives and forks. (Par. 5)

4a. Historically, finger-feeders have the longest tradition.
 b. The reason is chopsticks and forks are man-made inventions.

5a. The fork first entered society on the tables of the rich and well-born.
 b. However, it is said that many a crowned head, including Queen Elizabeth I of England and Louis XIV of France, ate with their fingers. (Par. 8)

6a. A famed restaurant in Los Angeles warns away customers.
 b. These customers will not eat with fingers. (Par. 8)

(See Chapter 1, pp. 14–15; Chapter 2, pp. 30–31; Chapter 3, pp. 57–58; and Chapter 4, pp. 87–91.)

PREPOSITIONAL PHRASES: *BECAUSE* VS. *BECAUSE OF*

Problems for You to Solve

Combine the following two sentences into a single sentence:

S1. Finger-feeding may be undergoing an enthusiastic revival.
S2. One of the reasons is a worldwide resurgence in ethnic pride after the collapse of western imperialism. (Par. 8)

Note

The prepositional phrase *because of* is always followed by a noun, noun phrase, or its equivalent, such as a gerund or participial phrase.

For Your Critical Thinking

How does *because of* differ in use from *because*?

Part 4: VOCABULARY, WORD FORMS, AND IDIOMS

FILL-INS

Paragraph b in each of the following pairs is a paraphrase of a. Using synonyms and antonyms (which need not be exact), changing sentence structure, and changing word forms are some of the devices used in making the paraphrase.

Your task: Fill in the blanks with appropriate words or phrases. Each blank line indicates one word. The underlined words in the original may give you the clues. The asterisks in b tell you there are no clues provided in the original.

1a. Based on the technology of eating solid food, we can classify the world into three groups — finger-feeders, chopstick-feeders, and fork-feeders. Why people fall into these categories is a mystery, and there is no comprehensive account of the ways of putting solid food into the·mouth. Which of the three is the best way to eat food is a controversial issue. It is also a subject fraught with chauvinism.

b. On the (1) _____ of the technology of eating solid food, the world may be (2) _____ into three different (3)° _____ : finger-feeders, chopstick-feeders, and fork-feeders. People (4) _____ fall into these separate (5) _____, (6)° _____ there does not (7) _____ any (8) _____ account of (9) _____ people (10) _____ solid food into their mouths. The (11) _____ on the best way to eat solid food is difficult to (12)° _____, because people are (13) _____ in their opinions on this (14) _____.

2a. Fork-feeders predominate in Europe and North America, chopstick-feeders in most of Eastern Asia, and finger-feeders in much of Africa, the Middle East, Indonesia, and the Indian subcontinent. That means fork-feeders are outnumbered 2 to 1, and they are the minority too. (Par. 4)

b. Europeans and North (15) _____ (16) _____ _____ use forks, while (17) _____ _____ South and South (18) _____ Asians, (19) _____, and Middle Easterners use their fingers to eat solid food, (20) _____ means that (21) non-_____ are the (22) _____.

3a. Historically, finger-feeders have the longest tradition, since chop-sticks and forks are man-made inventions. Some of the oldest Chi-nese chopsticks date to 1200 B.C. The fork made its way to Western tables several hundred years later. At first forks were used in Europe and the Near East as kitchen implements. Forks might not have been used as an eating utensil until the 10th century.

b. The finger-feeders have the longest tradition in (23) _____, (24) _____ chopsticks and forks were (25) _____ by man. The (26) _____ record of the use of chopsticks in (27) _____ is (28) _____ to 1200 B.C. Forks might not have been used as an eating utensil until the 10th century (29)° _____ _____ they had been used as kitchen (30) _____ (31) _____ .

4a. Forks and chopsticks won favor because they made it easier to han-dle hot food. Before their advent, people generally scooped up hot meals on flat bread. The major exception was China, where flat bread was not eaten. Chinese cooking was characterized by small portions, which did not require cutting by knives and forks. (Par. 5)

b. One (32) _____ chopsticks and forks had over fingers was that they made it easier to (33) _____ _____ hot food. Before they made their (34)° _____ on tables, in most countries (35) _____ China, flat bread was (36)° _____ to scoop up hot meals. Forks and knives were not (37) _____ to eat Chinese food (38) _____ the food got cut into small (39) _____ before it was (40) _____ .

5a. Fork-, finger- and chopstick-feeders can be militant in defense of their eating implements. For example, it is reported that a famed Filipino restaurant in Los Angeles, warns away customers who will not eat with fingers. (Par. 8)

b. All (41)° _____ _____ can be (42) _____ (43) _____ about the kind of eating (44) _____ each of them (45)° _____ . For (46)° _____ , it is reported that a (47) _____ Filipino restaurant in Los Angeles warns away (48) _____ .

Part 5: SUPPLEMENTARY READINGS

PREREADING ACTIVITIES

Discuss the following questions in your group:

1. What are herbs?
2. What are they used for?
3. Do you use herbs for any purpose?
4. Are herbs different from vegetables? How?
5. Are herbs being used more in developing countries than in industrial countries? Why?

Supplementary Reading 1: HERBS

1. Any plant used for its flavoring, aromatic, medicinal, or dyeing property may be called an herb. However, based on the wide use to which these herbs are put by a large number of people all over the world, they can be broadly classified as culinary and medicinal.

Excerpted and adapted from Lonnelle Aikman, "Herbs for All Seasons," *National Geographic* (March 1983): 386-408. Used with permission.

2. The culinary arts that distinguish one nation's cuisine from another's are based largely on the wise use of herbs. More than just embellishment, they heighten the senses of smell, sight, and taste, thus stimulating appetite and aiding digestion.

3. Although some plants — like peppers and onions — are eaten as garden vegetables, their virtues as flavor-enhancers qualify them as herbs. For example, onion provides good salad. Garlic chives are used uncooked, chopped in salads, dips, or vegetable dishes. Sweet basil improves almost any dish.

4. Thyme adds flavor to stews, soups and sauces. "To me, thyme is the queen of herbs," says the chef of the White House. He continues, "Thyme is good for all kinds of meat and stuffings."

5. Parsley (a good source of vitamins A, C, and E), rosemary, marjoram, garlic, oregano, peppermint, and spearmint are some other herbs often used as seasonings for meats and salads.

6. As interest in herbs spreads worldwide, scientists of both industrial and developing countries are looking back to folklore's raw-plant materials for clues to more effective and safer drugs of the future. In fact, nature's handouts provided virtually the only drugs available to any physician before 19th-century chemists began isolating and analyzing the healing properties of medicinal herbs. From these models came much of today's pharmaceutical industry.

7. As chemical science advanced in 20th-century laboratories, man-made synthetics and semisynthetics were gradually developed from plant blueprints. Then came mass-produced, purely chemical copies. Often simpler and more precise than mother nature's compounds, they now flood commercial markets. Even so, it is estimated that roughly 50 percent of the millions of prescriptions filled in the United States still contain some natural products.

8. The garden plant called purple foxglove, or digitalis, holds in its leaves the formula for drugs widely prescribed for heart failure and other cardiac ills. One of the most successful treatments yet developed against childhood leukemia and Hodgkin's disease was launched in the 1950's after a minute amount of the cancer-fighting principle was isolated from the leaves of the Madagascar periwinkle.

9. East Indian snakeroot was dried and powdered more than 2,000 years ago and fed to mentally ill people struck with "moon madness." In natural and synthetic form, its derivatives now supply physicians with a leading drug to reduce high blood pressure.

10. Common aspirin is totally synthetic today, but its natural ancestor was an active compound found in the drooping willow tree studied by the first-century A.D. pharmacologist-naturalist Pedanius Dioscorides. In his medical work, Dioscorides noted that juices from the bark and leaves of the white willow eased aches related to colds and fevers treated now by the small white tablet familiar around the world.

11. Modern herbs find increasing use as substitutes for salt and sugar, for synthetic sleeping pills and energizing drugs. Instead of table salt, some doctors prescribe — and herb fanciers prefer — dried and ground herbs to add interest to food. Combinations may include winter and summer savory, cumin, coriander, sesame, and mustard seeds — or whatever pleases taste.

12. For patients denied refined sugar, there are alternatives in many kinds of herb honey. Weight-watchers can make desserts with herbs such as sweet cicely or licorice. Herb-book recipes recommend grinding leaves, blooms, stems, or roots to sprinkle over nonsweet desserts or to cook into cakes, pies, and preserves to satisfy a sweet tooth.

13. From time beyond memory, herbal teas have been brewed as sedatives on one hand and to promote alertness on the other. Herbalists consider tea made from valerian root to be one of the best tranquilizers known.

14. As a coffee substitute to keep awake for an exam or to finish an office job, herb lovers suggest drinking a tea from ginseng, ginger, or borage, the "happiness plant" of the ancients.

15. In the hidden treasures that lie within herbs nature speaks to us not only of beauty and history but also of hope and progress.

POSTREADING ACTIVITIES

1. Did the writer include all kinds of herbs in her classification? How would you classify them?
2. What are some of the culinary herbs used in your culture? How are they being used?
3. How would you compare the medical use of synthetic herbs with that of natural herbs?
4. Give some examples of herbs used for medical purposes in your culture. How do they compare with synthetic ones? Which ones do you prefer? Give reasons.
5. In the concluding paragraph the writer talks about the "hope and progress" mankind can expect through the "hidden treasures that lie within these herbs." Write a paragraph elaborating this idea.

PREREADING ACTIVITIES

Discuss the following questions in your group.

1. How many courses are you taking this semester?
2. What kind of courses are they? How would you classify them?
3. How many instructors do you have this semester? How would you classify them? What basis would you use to classify them?
4. How would you compare each group of instructors?

Supplementary Reading 2: COLLEGE TEACHERS

1. Before I came to college, I was told not to expect my professors to care much about me or my work; indeed, I was told that I would be lucky if any of them even knew my name! But when I came to the university, I soon learned that these generalizations were too broad. Not all teachers are the same. In fact, I have found that most of the professors here at State fall into three categories: the positive teachers, the neutral teachers, and the negative teachers.

2. The positive teachers are by far the most agreeable teachers. A positive teacher is one who seems interested in his subject and his students. The first thing a positive teacher does is try to learn all of the students' names. This kind of teacher allows for questions and discussions in class and does not seem to mind if a student disagrees with him. A positive teacher shows his interest out of class as well. Not only is he available for conferences, but he encourages students to see him if they need help. The students tend to feel comfortable in the presence of this teacher. A good example of a positive teacher is my French teacher, Monsieur Poirrot. He always allows time during the class hour for some free discussion. Once, when some of the students in our class were having trouble with the pronunciation of the rolled "r" in French, he took several hours of his own time to work with us in very small groups in his office until we had mastered the sound. Unfortunately, teachers like Monsieur Poirrot are relatively small in number.

3. Unlike the positive teachers, the neutral teachers are not very agreeable. In general, the neutral teachers just do not seem interested in either the subject or the students. These teachers usually do not learn all of the students' names, though they may learn a few. Their classes tend to be more boring than the positive teachers' classes because they allow less time for discussion. However, like the positive teacher, the neutral teacher allows for questions and some discussion, but he just does not seem to care if the students are interested enough to want to discuss the subject or not. Although the neutral teacher is available for conferences, he does not encourage students to come see him for help; as a result, most students feel slightly uncomfortable in his presence, especially during a conference. Professor Hilton, my economics professor, is typical of the neutral teacher. She comes into class, opens her notebook, lectures, allows questions and some discussion, and then leaves class. When I had a problem understanding one of the concepts we had discussed in class one day, I went to her office for a conference. She was polite enough but did not make any special effort to see that I understood the concept during the conference. She more or less repeated what she had said in class. Very few students go to see her for a

---

Regina L. Smalley and Mary Reuten Hank, *Refining English Composition Skills*, 1st ed. (New York: Macmillan, 1982), 202–3. Used with permission.

conference because they think she is simply not interested. From what I have gathered in my conversations with other students, the neutral teachers make up the largest category.

4. Of the three types of teachers, the negative teachers are the least agreeable. These are the kind that every student dreads. Not only do they not learn the students' names, but they seem almost hostile both in class and out of class. In class, the negative teachers, like the neutral teachers, primarily lecture ; they may want the students to learn, but unlike the neutral and positive teachers, the negative teachers allow virtually no questions and no discussion. The negative teachers also seem inimical to the idea of having conferences and are almost never in their offices. Students avoid seeing them for conferences if at all possible. An excellent example of a negative teacher is Dr. Wollen, my physics professor. His classes are twice as boring as any class of a neutral teacher, and he is often intimidating in class. One day, for example, when one student asked him to repeat his explanation of the theory of relativity, he became quite angry and refused to repeat what he had just lectured on. The negative teacher is too often inflexible; in fact, he seems more like a machine than a human being. Fortunately, this group is in the minority.

5. The type of teacher students get can directly affect how much they learn. Obviously, students learn more from a positive teacher; unfortunately, as we have seen, this type makes up the minority. Since the mission of the university is to educate, adminstrators should try to get the neutral and negative teachers to improve their teaching methods and attitudes; otherwise, the administrators should consider dismissing at least the negative teachers and make every effort to hire those teachers who promise to be positive ones.

POSTREADING ACTIVITIES

1. How are college teachers classified in this essay?
2. What basis is used for this classification?
3. What is the thesis statement in the essay?
4. Write the topic sentence of each of the paragraphs.
5. What device does the writer use to support his or her topic statement in each paragraph?

Part 6: WRITING

THE EXPOSITORY ESSAY: CLASSIFICATION

Review

As you have seen in earlier chapters, an expository essay, as distinguished from a narrative, descriptive, or analytical essay, has the following characteristics:

1. The writer takes a stand (expresses a point of view), and states this stand in the form of a thesis (*thesis statement*), which consists of the topic and subtopics to be discussed.

2. Each *subtopic* in the thesis statement is developed in the succeeding paragraphs (*body paragraphs*).
3. Each body paragraph has a *topic* sentence, which has two parts: namely, the broad topic and the comment (the controlling idea).
4. The *comment/controlling idea* of the topic sentence is explained further by giving supporting details.
5. The supporting details involve examples, data, statistics, or even simple explanations.
6. Each paragraph has coherence and cohesion.
7. The rhetorical style used to explain the thesis statement may vary according to the writer's preference. Explanation, classification, comparison and contrast, and argumentation are some of the commonly used rhetorical styles in expository writing.

Classification: Organizational Pattern

1. Introduction   The main task here is to introduce the group you are classifying. The basis of your classification and its divisions form the thesis statement. Important points to remember are: (1) only one basis should be used; (2) the classification should be comprehensive (relating to all the members in the group).

2. Developmental Paragraphs   These paragraphs explain each of the categories into which the group is divided. Important characteristics which distinguish one group from the other(s) should be explained. As in any expository essays, this can be done by giving examples, quoting data from history, or providing statistics from research studies.

3. Concluding Paragraph   Here you may give your preference of one class over the other(s) and make suggestions.

For Your Critical Thinking

Answer the following questions:

1. What rhetorical style is used in the three essays given in this chapter?
2. Which of the three would you rate as the best expository essay? Why?
3. Write down the thesis statement in each of the three essays.
4. How would you classify the following essays?

   • "From Quill to Computer" (Chapter 3)
   • "The Ant and Her World" (Chapter 4)
   • "The Technology of Eating" (Chapter 5)

- "Herbs" (Chapter 5)
- "College Teachers" (Chapter 5)

5. What basis did you use in classifying these essays?
6. What characteristics distinguish each group?
7. Which of the essays do you prefer? Why?

THE EXPOSITORY ESSAY: PROCESS

Review

In Chapters 3 and 4 you learned the steps involved in writing an expository essay: They are:

1. Prewriting, which includes brainstorming for ideas (Chapter 3. pp. 72–73)
2. Deciding on the specific idea you want to develop (Chapter 3, pp. 72–73)
3. Formulating the thesis statement (Chapter 4, p. 100)
4. Outlining the development of the subtopics in the body paragraphs (Chapter 4, pp. 106–107)

The First Draft

The next step in the process is writing the first draft. Remember, your outline already contains:

1. The thesis statement (which includes the subtopics)
2. The subtopic for each body paragraph, together with at least one explanation, example, or item of data or statistics to develop each subtopic

When the outlining has been done, writing the first draft is easy, because the organization of your essay is already completed. Writing the first draft just involves:

1. Introducing the topic and the thesis statement (writing the introductory paragraph or paragraphs)
2. Developing the subtopics in the thesis statement (writing the body paragraphs) giving supporting details, examples, data, or statistics. The number of body paragraphs depends on the number of subtopics you want to develop (something you have already decided on when you wrote the outline)

3. Summing up the discussion, giving your comments and/or suggestions (writing the conclusion)

While writing the first draft, do not spend too much time on mechanics (punctuation, grammar) and spelling, because at this step in the writing process your mind should be set on developing your ideas. Remember, language is a vehicle for expressing ideas and not *vice versa*. After all, this is just your first draft, not the final draft.

WRITING ACTIVITIES

Reaction Journal

Write in your journal:

- What — if anything — surprised you in the readings in this chapter
- Which article impresses you the most, and why
- Which article you would hate to read again, and why
- Which article you would like to read over and over, and why
- Which article you consider most applicable to you (explain how)
- Which of the writers of the three essays you would rate as poor (give the basis for your rating)
- Which of the writers you would rate as excellent (give the basis for your rating)
- Which of the essays you could write yourself (explain)

Learning Log

Write in your learning log:

- A summary of the new things you learned from this chapter
- How the chapter helped/did not help you improve your reading and writing skills
- Which section(s) in the chapter helped you most to think critically
- How much of the learning can be applied to your life (explain with examples)

Writing Assignment

Overview

Classify the learning experience you have had so far. Write a letter to a friend in another university, sharing the different kinds of learning experiences you have had.

Real-life Purpose: To share your learning experience with a friend of yours

Academic Purpose: To practice writing a classification essay

Real-life Audience: Your friend in another university

Classroom Audience: Your peers and instructor

Procedure

OUT-OF CLASS ACTIVITY

1. Review the learning log entries you have made so far.
2. Find a basis for classifying your learning (for example : application to real life or academic life ; long-term or short-term applications ; old or new materials, etc.).
3. Find examples for each group.
4. Write the outline.
5. Develop the outline and write the letter.

IN-CLASS GROUP WORK

1. Read the letter aloud to your group.
2. Get feedback from your group members.
3. Revise/rewrite (in class or out of class).
4. Hand in your work to your instructor. (following your instructor's directions).

Alternate Writing Assignment

Overview

Classify your class members based on one of the following and write a letter to a friend or relative abroad, explaining each classified subgroup.

1. Eating habits
2. Sleeping habits
3. Study habits

Procedure

IN-CLASS GROUP WORK

Group Size: Five

1. Pick one of the three topics above.
2. Prepare ten to fifteen questions you would like to ask your class members on this topic.

3. Have each class member answer the questions in writing.
4. Study the responses.
5. Find a basis for classifying the responses (for example : vegetarians vs. non-vegetarians ; those who mostly eat out or at home, etc.).
6. Get additional information from members for examples or explanations.
7. Develop an outline.

INDIVIDUAL WORK (IN OR OUT OF CLASS)

Write the letter.

OUT-OF-CLASS ACTIVITY

1. Read the letter aloud to a member of another class and get feedback, especially on clarity of expression.
2. Read it out loud to yourself.
3. Revise as many times as is needed (until you are satisfied with your work).
4. Hand in your work to your instructor (following your instructor's directions).

CHAPTER · 6

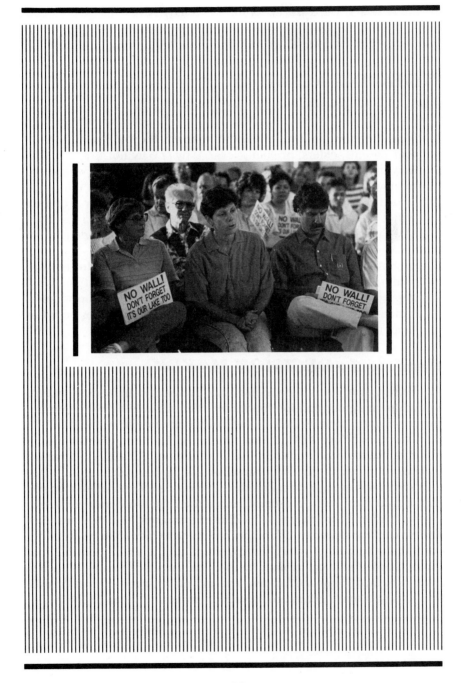

Part 1: READING

PREREADING ACTIVITIES

Discuss the following in multicultural groups:

1. In making serious decisions about yourself, do you usually consult your parents, elders, or counselors? Why?/Why not?
2. How did you make your decision on choosing the school where you are now enrolled? Are you happy with your choice? Why/Why not?
4. If you had a chance to do it all over, would you change your decision? Why?/Why not?
5. At what age do you think a child should be able to make independent decisions? Why do you think so?
6. Suppose you are the president of a student club. You want to get more funding for this organization from the school administration. What steps would you take before you send the application to the administration? How similar or different would those procedures be if this happened in a non-Western society?

Reading 1: DECISION MAKING

1. There are two kinds of decision-making prevalent in any society: individual decision and group decision. Significant differences exist between American and non-Western societies in both kinds of decision-making.

2. Americans believe that decision-making and the responsibilities that go with it rest with the individual. From a very early age, American children are encouraged to believe that they themselves are the best judges of what they want and what they should do. The children consult professionals or even parents to help them reach a decision. But those helpers are only considered sources of information; they are not expected to be engaged in the actual decision making. For example, high school seniors go to their college counselors, not with the purpose of having the counselors tell them which colleges they should choose, but to get information about the various opportunities open to them in the field of higher education. The students know for sure that the decision rests with them, not the counselors or parents.

This section is based on the ideas of Edward C. Stewart, "American Assumptions and Values," Part III of *American Cultural Patterns: A Cross-Cultural Perspective* (Yarmouth, Maine: Intercultural Press, Inc., 1972), 31-32.

3. In contrast, in many non-Western countries, parents make most critical decisions about children. For example, decisions, such as the field of study the children should follow in higher education and the kind of partners the children should have in marriage, are made by the parents, and in the absence of parents, by adults who are considered the "chiefs" in the "family tree." In such situations, the decision is made not by the person most affected by the decision, but by the occupant of a traditional role in the social group — for example, the parents. In a similar American situation, parents may make suggestions and the children may or may not follow their suggestions in deciding on their own course of action.

4. American individualization of decision-making is based on the American value system, which makes the individual responsible for both the motivation that precedes and the consequences that succeed the actual decision-making. The motivation that leads to the activity of decision-making should come from the individuals and not from any external sources. The responsibility for carrying out the decision and for dealing with whatever consequences may result, falls on the individuals. In contrast, in those societies where close-knit family and community relations exist, individuals are not expected to shoulder the absolute responsibility for decision-making, because in those societies responsibilities are shared.

5. In group decision-making too, the American situation differs from that in many non-Western countries. First of all, more kinds of decisions are likely to be made by the group in a non-Western society than in the United States ; many matters that require action by a family or community in the non-Western world are settled among Americans by a private decision. Furthermore, the manner in which the individual participates in the group may differ considerably. The American usually expects to be able to express his or her opinion and to exert a fair degree of influence in the final decision. To fulfill his or her expectations, an American can be quite concerned with procedures leading to the decision, such as "agenda" and "voting procedures." These procedures may be followed in non-Western societies, too. However, in many situations they are ritualistic and ceremonial and do not serve the purpose of ensuring fairness to all and facilitating action. Even when bypassing formal procedures, the American would give everybody a chance to speak and an equal voice in the decision, which does not occur in many non-Western societies.

6. Again, in group meetings, the American society expects active participation from as many members as possible. This concept is based on the assumption that, all those insofar as possible who will be affected by the decision are capable of making it. In many non-Western countries, group meetings held to discuss issues relating to decision-making function differently, for the purpose of those meetings may be to get public confirmation of a decision made in private by a smaller group who may or may not be represented in the larger group.

7. The American value of the majority rule is also absent in some non-Western societies. For example, the Japanese reject the majority voice in decision-making, because they believe that the decision-making is binding upon the majority and minority alike.

POSTREADING ACTIVITIES

Discuss the following questions in your multicultural groups:

1. What is the difference between individual and group decision making?
2. If and when you have children, what role would you play in your children's decision-making process? Would you prefer to have individualistic or shared responsibility in making decisions? Give your reasons.
3. How similar/different is the American society in its view of decision making compared with your parents' home society? Give examples.
4. What do you think about the Japanese belief that the decision-making is binding upon the majority and minority alike? How would you feel about the majority's rule on a particular issue if you were in a minority?
5. Why do you think Americans put so much emphasis on agenda, voting procedures, and so on in group decisions?
6. What does the author mean by: "These procedures may be followed in non-Western societies, too. However, in many situations they are ritualistic and ceremonial and do not serve the purpose of ensuring fairness to all and facilitating action"? (Par. 5)

PREREADING ACTIVITIES

1. How do you define feminism? Who is a feminist?
2. Do you think there are as many feminists in the Third World countries as there are in Western countries? Explain your answer.
3. What are some of the differences and similarities between Western and Third-World feminists?
4. How do social class differences affect the living conditions among Third World women?
5. Do these differences affect Western women too? How? Why?

Prereading Information

In 1975, the United Nations Women's Decade began with a Women's Conference held in Mexico City, to be followed by another conference in 1980 in Copenhagen, and the final conference in Nairobi in 1985.

The goal of the Women's Decade was to identify "women's issues" throughout the world and to make recommendations that would better the lives of women by the year 2000.

The writer of the article addresses some of the serious problems that both journalists and participants encountered when they met prior to the Copenhagen conference. These problems were not unique to that meeting; they were also present at previous and subsequent conferences.

Reading 2: FEMINISTS WORLDS APART

1. Last month, 27 journalists from around the world gathered under the United Nations' auspices to formulate recommendations to be submitted to the Mid-Decade U.N. World Conference of Women in Copenhagen in July. During the discussions leading to the final recommendations, one could discern once again the enormous gap that existed between the representatives of the developed countries and the Third World nations in their perceptions of what constituted the "women's problem." Western feminists at this meeting, like those at the 1975 Mexico City conference, saw the basic problem as being the denial of equality in the distribution of economic opportunity and responsibility to women. Often this perception led them to view men as the group responsible for their deprivation and oppression.

2. The third world champions of feminism, on the other hand, perceived the woman's fundamental problem as being the struggle to find for herself and her family the essential sustenance of daily life, like running water, medical services and stable shelters. As such, they expressed little or no criticism of men as a group, a fact that led one U.S. reporter covering the conference to remark: "There must be *some* feminists in the Third World."

3. These basic differences in perceptions are due in part to the inaccurate portrayals of women's roles as transmitted by the international media; even more important, they are due to the nature of the relations between social classes in the Western world and the Third World.

4. In the West, the vast majority of women — at least those with access to and representation in the media — share at some level the basis of a common national culture. They generally speak the same language, dress alike, and are affected by the same television and radio programs, films, newspapers and books.

5. When the majority of women feel part of the dominant culture, it is inevitable that they attribute the rights denied to them as being a question of

Salim Lone, "Feminists Worlds Apart," in Ellen W. Echeverria, *Speaking on Issues* (Orlando, Fla.: Holt, Rinehart and Winston, 1987), 141-42. Originally published in *The Washington Post*, June 1980. Reprinted by permission of the author. Mr. Lone is Editor-in-Chief of *Africa Recovery*.

access within the existing framework. This is not to say that class differences and antagonisms do not exist, but that women in the broad middle classes find genuine common cause around the issues of child care, jobs and wages and husbands ignorant of the value of domestic labor.

6. For most women of the Third World, the reality is incalculably different. The vast majority of them live in a state of acute deprivation. Their consuming pursuit is providing food for the family, finding and carrying firewood and water from distant places, selling surplus crops to buy clothing and to pay school fees and obtaining rudimentary medical care.

7. On the other hand, there is a class of Third World feminists who share almost the same views as their counterparts in the West. They have all the money, education and medical care they need. Consequently, their major worries are getting the right kind of jobs and deciding which school the children will attend, what to cook for dinner and which dress to wear to the office as they carve out roles for themselves in modern urban society.

8. Unlike their sisters, who are burdened under loads of water and firewood, their focus is not on economic oppression but on the unequal relations with the men in their class. They find that owing to this inequality, they have now been shut out of their traditional roles as full partners in the productive economy.

9. In all these economic and social concerns, this small elite group is heavily influenced by the Western image of women that is popularized in the foreign media.

10. As one can imagine, these privileged women are fast becoming foreigners in their own countries, sharing more with women of America and Europe than with the masses among whom they live. Ask them to go to work in the rural areas where they grew up, and they will candidly reply that they would rather work in London or Paris. Without question, many women of this class are feminists of the kind the reporter at the conference was wondering about.

11. However, feminists concerned about the Third World generally do not focus on the needs of the privileged. And the needs of the masses, their deprivations, their oppression, their disease, their illiteracy and their malnutrition are not confined to women alone ; the men who live with them are equally vulnerable. For this reason, feminism in the Third World does not isolate the problems of women from the problems of the rest of the society.

12. Nevertheless, this does not mean that Third World men do not have any responsibility for the economic and social misery the women are subject to. But on the whole, male oppression is not currently the primary focus of Third World feminists.

POSTREADING ACTIVITIES

1. Why do Western women look at men as the root cause of their problems, while Third World women do not have any such complaints ?
2. In what sense does the author use "feminists" in the sentence : "There must be *some* feminists in the Third World" ? (Par. 2)
3. What is the point that the author raises in Par. 3 ? Do you agree with this view ? Give your reasons.
4. What is the image of Western women the author talks about in Par. 4 ?

PREREADING ACTIVITIES

Discuss the following questions in your group :

1. Whom do you consider a friend ?
2. Would you group lovers and friends together as belonging to the same category ? Why ?/Why not ?
3. What are some characteristics common to both friendship and love ?
4. How does friendship differ from a love relationship ?
5. Can you have more than one lover in the same way as you can have more than one friend ? Give your reasons.

6. Why do you want to make friends?
7. What advantages/disadvantages does falling in love have over making friends and vice versa?

Reading 3: LOVE AND FRIENDSHIP

1. Love and friendship are the warp and woof of the social fabric. They not only bind society together but provide essential emotional sustenance, buffering us against stress and preserving physical and mental health. When those ties are severed, the loss can precipitate illness and even suicide in some people.

2. While we readily distinguish between friends and lovers in everyday life and value each differently, psychologists have not provided a systematic answer to how these two essential relationships differ.

3. My colleague Michael J. Todd and I developed a list of what we believe are characteristics central to friendship and romantic love. We then tested our model against the experiences and expectations of about 250 college students and community members, both single and married.

4. We found that love and friendship are alike in many ways, but that some crucial differences make love relationships both more rewarding and more volatile.

The Fabric of Friendship

5. The original profile of friendship we developed included these essential characteristics beyond the fact that two people participate in a reciprocal relationship as equals:

6. ENJOYMENT: They enjoy each other's company most of the time, although there may be temporary states of anger, disappointment or mutual annoyance. ("I find whatever we do more enjoyable when Jim and I do it together." "He has the ability to make me laugh.")

7. ACCEPTANCE: They accept one another as they are, without trying to change or make the other into a new or different person. ("She's not always on me to do things that I don't want to do." "He appreciates my style.")

8. TRUST: They share mutual trust in the sense that each assumes that the other will act in light of his or her friend's best interest. ("Even when he is bugging me, I know that it's for my own good." "I just know that I can count on her; whatever she says, she will do." "He would never intentionally hurt me — except in a fit of extreme anger.")

9. RESPECT: They respect each other in the sense of assuming that each exercises good judgement in making life choices. ("She doesn't give

---

Excerpted from Keith E. Davis, "Near and Dear: Friendship and Love Compared," *Psychology Today* (February 1985): 22-30.

advice unless asked, but then it is always good." "He will usually do what's right.")

10. MUTUAL ASSISTANCE : They are inclined to assist and support one another and specifically, they can count on each other in times of need, trouble or personal distress. ("I feel like doing things that she needs to have done.")

11. CONFIDING : They share experiences and feelings with each other. ("He tells me things that no one else knows about him.")

12. UNDERSTANDING : They have a sense of what is important to each and why the friend does what he or she does. In such cases, friends are not routinely puzzled or mystified by each other's behavior. ("I know what makes her tick." "I can usually figure out what's wrong when he's troubled or moody.")

13. SPONTANEITY : Each feels free to be himself or herself in the relationship rather than feeling required to play a role, wear a mask or inhibit revealing personal traits. ("I feel completely comfortable around him.")

The Tapestry of Love

14. We assumed that romantic relationships would share all the same characteristics as friendship but that they would have additional and unique ones. We identified two broad categories unique to love relationships.

The Passion Cluster

15.   This consists of three characteristics — fascination, exclusiveness and sexual desire :

16.   FASCINATION : Lovers tend to pay attention to the other person even when they should be involved in other activities. They are preoccupied with the other person and tend to think about, look at, want to talk to, or merely be with the other. ("I would go to bed thinking about what we would do together, dream about it and wake up ready to be with him again." "I have trouble concentrating ; she just seems to be in my head no matter what I'm doing.") A person worthy of this kind of attention is worthy of devotion. Thus, fascination provides one basis for idealizing the other, a phenomenon so often noted in romantic love.

17.   EXCLUSIVENESS : Lovers have a special relationship that precludes having the same relationship with a third party. ("What we have is different than I've ever had with anyone else." "We're committed to each other.") Thus, a romantic love relationship is given priority over other relationships in one's life.

18.   SEXUAL DESIRE : Lovers want physical intimacy with the partner, wanting to touch and be touched and to engage in sexual intercourse. They may not always act on the desire, even when both members of the couple share it, since it may be overridden by moral, religious or practical considerations (for example, fear of pregnancy or of getting caught).

The Caring Cluster

19.   This has two components : giving the utmost and being a champion/ advocate.

20.   GIVING THE UTMOST : Lovers care enough to give the utmost when the other is in need, sometimes to the point of extreme self-sacrifice. One of the best-known literary examples is in O'Henry's short story *The Gift of the Magi,* in which a man pawns his favorite pocket watch to buy his beloved a set of combs for her beautiful hair, while she sells her hair to buy him a gold chain for his watch. Each gives something priceless to make the other happy.

21.   BEING A CHAMPION/ADVOCATE : The depth of lovers' caring shows up also in an active championing of each other's interests and in a positive attempt to make sure that the partner succeeds. ("I realized that whatever my parents said that was critical of him just made me all the more determined to defend him."). ...

22.   If the findings of this research are valid, then the typical love relationships will differ from even very good friendships in having higher levels of fascination, exclusiveness and sexual desire (the passion cluster), a greater depth of caring about the other person (which would be manifest in a willingness to give the utmost when needed) and a greater potential for enjoyment and other positive emotions. Love relationships will also have, however, a greater potential for distress, ambivalence, conflict and mutual criticism.

23. One clear implication of these differences is that love relationships tend to have a greater impact on both the satisfaction and frustration of the person's basic human needs. It may be important, then, to acknowledge these differences in emotional significance as researchers study the mental and physical health implications of having — and of losing — lovers and close friends. ...

POSTREADING ACTIVITIES

1. Summarize the new information you received from reading the article.
2. Do you agree with the author's findings about the differences between love and friendship? Give reasons.
3. What additional statements would you make on the similarities and differences between friendship and love?

PREREADING ACTIVITIES

1. How do you define rhetoric?
2. Are logic and rhetoric related? How?
3. How would you relate the writing style of individual writers to their culture?
4. How do you find the writing style in English similar to and/or different from that in any other language you already know?

Reading 4: CULTURE, LOGIC, AND RHETORIC

1. Logic, which is the basis of rhetoric, comes from culture; it is not universal. Rhetoric, therefore, is not universal either, but varies from culture to culture. The rhetorical system of one language is neither better nor worse than the rhetorical system of another language, but it is different.

2. English logic and English rhetoric, which are based on Anglo-European cultural patterns, are linear — that is, a good English paragraph begins with a general statement of its content and then carefully develops that statement with a series of specific illustrations. A good English paragraph may also use just the reverse sequence: it may state a whole series of examples and then

From Alice O'Shima and Ann Hogue, *Writing Academic English* (Reading, Mass.: Addison-Wesley, 1981), 18-19. Copyright © 1981 by Addison-Wesley Publishing Company.

summarize those examples in a single statement at the end of the paragraph. In either case, however, the flow of ideas occurs in a straight line from the opening sentence to the last sentence. Furthermore, a well-structured English paragraph is never digressive. There is nothing that does not belong to the paragraph, and nothing that does not support the topic sentence.

3.   A type of construction found in Arabic and Persian writing is very different. Whereas English writers use a linear sequence, Arabic and Persian writers tend to construct a paragraph in a parallel sequence using many coordinators, such as *and* and *but*. In English, maturity of style is often judged by the degree of subordination rather than by the degree of coordination. Therefore, the Arabic and Persian styles of writing, with their emphasis on coordination, seem awkward and immature to an English reader.

4.   Some Asian writers, on the other hand, use an indirect approach. In this kind of writing, the topic is viewed from a variety of angles. The topic is never analyzed directly; it is referred to only indirectly. Again, such a development in an English paragraph is awkward and unnecessarily vague to an English reader.

5.   Spanish rhetoric differs from English rhetoric in still another way. While the rules of English rhetoric require that every sentence in a paragraph relates directly to the central idea, a Spanish-speaking writer loves to fill a paragraph with interesting digressions. Although a Spanish paragraph may begin and end on the same topic, the writer often digresses into areas that are not directly related to the topic. Spanish rhetoric, therefore, does not follow the English rule of paragraph unity.

6.   In summary, a student who has mastered the grammar of English may still write poor papers unless the rhetoric of English is also mastered. Also, the student may have difficulty reading an essay written by the rules of English rhetoric unless (s)he understands the "logical" differences from those of her/his own native tongue.

POSTREADING ACTIVITIES

1.   When you read the title, what did you expect the essay would be about? How similar to or different is the essay from what you thought it would be?
2.   What is the message the writer is trying to get to the audience?
3.   Who are the intended readers? How do you know this?
4.   Give an example of a digressive paragraph from any essay you have read.
5.   Give examples of subordination and coordination.
6.   Explain what the writer means by paragraph unity. What is another word for paragraph unity?

7. If you know another language, compare and contrast the rules of rhetoric in English with those of that language.
8. What new ideas have you learned from reading this essay?

PREREADING ACTIVITIES

Discuss the following questions in your group:

1. Are poets and politicians related in any way? How?
2. Can you think of any poets who had been politicians or vice versa? Who are they?
3. Who has more influence on the masses? Poets or politicians? Why?

Reading 5: POETRY AND POLITICS

1. Land of the unwashed, goodbye!
Land of the masters, land of knaves!
You, in neat blue uniforms!
You who live like cringing slaves!
In my exile I may find
Peace beneath Caucasian skies, —
Far from slanderers and tsars,
Far from ever-spying eyes.
    — Mikhail Lermontov

It seemed odd, on first hearing of it, that Nicholas Daniloff would quote lines of poetry to mark his release from Soviet imprisonment. Here was an incident that filled the news for a month, that brought the world's two titans into open confrontation, that in the end, perhaps, prodded them to agree on the pre-summit summit. Yet to cap off those momentous political events, Daniloff, the center of the storm, reached back into art for a poem by Mikhail Lermontov written almost 150 years ago for another world and circumstance. Grant that it was more diplomatic of Daniloff to quote Lermontov's exasperation with Mother Russia than to express his own. Still, it is curious that one would articulate feelings about so immediate and politically charged an event by using a form associated with indirection and repose.

2. Not that poets themselves have ever avoided politics as subject matter. Homer, Dante, Shakespeare, Milton, all found ways to hail or rage against kings and governments through their work. Yeats, unpolitical as anyone could look in his fluffy neckties, wrote stinging political lines. As did Robert Lowell.

Roger Rosenblatt, "Poetry and Politics," *Time,* 13 October 1986. Copyright © Time, Inc. Reprinted by permission.

As does Seamus Heaney. W. H. Auden's *September 1, 1939* is a beautiful muddle of a poem on Europe in the shadow of war. Bertolt Brecht's *To Posterity*, about Germany under the Nazis, is clear as a bell:

> Ah, what an age it is
> When to speak of trees is almost a crime
> For it is a kind of silence against injustice.

3. For their part, political leaders have courted poets, supported poets, quoted poets. Some have even been poets. Henry VIII, who liked to write verse when he wasn't making life brutish or short for his wives. Chairman Mao, who, when visited by the muse, commanded the largest audience for poetry in history. Poet Léopold Senghor, former President of Senegal. Poet José Sarney, current President of Brazil. If political leaders happen not to be poets, they can always seek one's company, so that he may write them into immortality or simply decorate a hard, unlyrical business. John Kennedy had genuine affection for the work of Robert Frost, but the poet's presence at Kennedy's Inaugural — the poem flapping in the wintry wind — also served to give a magic power to the occasion, like the blessing of the gods.

4. What clashes in the connection of poetry and politics is that on the surface, the two forms of expression seem antipodal not only in tone and structure but in the pictures of mind they convey. The poet is a vague and hazy animal, the politician hunched forward like a cat. What one would devour, the other would toy with in the air, angling the world in his paws so as to know not the world itself but the light-play on the world.

5. And yet, as the Daniloff incident suggests, these two sets of mind have a way of coming together in the strangest places, which would indicate that poetry and politics have basic things in common. One is the need to create a sense of urgency. Poets and politicians are alike in the frantic force of their opinions. When either speaks his mind, he is like the Ancient Mariner; he seizes the public by the collar as if to say: Accept my perspective and be converted.

6. Then, too, there are similar passions in poetry and politics. However dignified poetry or politics may appear, there is something sublimely irrational at their centers. Both appeal to the irrational as well, to the zealot in you stirring in the ice of your calm and stately nature. Zealots themselves, they seem to need to win something, to force a climax almost sexual.

7. At the same time, both also depend on the continuity of living, on the fact that no matter how heated the single moment, the realization of that moment is of necessity incomplete. The art of politics seems to dance between acting as if every issue were the end of the earth and simultaneously acknowledging that tomorrow will hold up a dozen fresh crucial issues. Poems imply this same incompleteness. Unlike prose, the place that a poem aims and arrives at is less important to the success of the poem than the ideas and images it uses to make the journey. By those ideas and images the poet holds the reader to the process, by which he suggests that the poem pauses more than finishes and that the end is somewhere in the middle.

8. Poems also create their own state of mind, and politics does that as well. Paul Valéry defined a poem as a "kind of machine for producing the poetic state of mind by means of words." The politician produces the political state of mind by means of words. Each does an act of hypnosis by persuading its audience that reality is the world that the poet or politician has constructed for them. In that, the two are equally imaginative. The world they create is an unreality. Yet that world must be grounded in reality, in facts — the real toads in imaginary gardens that Marianne Moore prescribed for poetry — or else the audience will not believe it.

9. Still, if poetry and politics are bedfellows in certain ways, the bed is rarely comfortable. Poetry has none of the active power that politics has. It can protest or commemorate a war but cannot cause one. Assessing the poet's responsibility in the world, Allen Tate derided the romantic notion that if poets "behaved differently ... the international political order itself would not have been in jeopardy and we should not perhaps be at international log-gerheads today." Poets do not have that sort of influence, and undoubtedly would abuse it if they did.

10. The power poetry does have, however, is staying power. It outlives politics mainly because the language of poets outlives the language of politicians — so effectively that Daniloff could recite Lermontov to the world last week, and the world could appear to have been waiting for those words. That eternity of language, reaching as far back as forward, is what politicians fear most about poetry, when they do fear it, and it can make a terrible enemy. Politics touches some people at particular times. Poetry calls to all people at all times. By its existence it demands generosity and expansiveness. "When power narrows the areas of man's concern," said Kennedy, "poetry reminds him of the richness and diversity of his existence. When power corrupts, poetry cleanses." Last week Lermontov, dead 145 years, mocked all the prisons and praised all the skies.

POSTREADING ACTIVITIES

1. Between poetry and politics, does the writer prefer one to the other? How do you know?
2. Why does the writer begin the essay with a quote from a poet?
3. What does the writer mean by his statement: "The poet is a vague and hazy animal, the politician, hunched forward like a cat"? (Par. 4)
4. Do you agree with the writer's statement that both poets and politicians force their opinions on others? (Par. 5) Give your reasons.
5. What do you think about the writer's statement: "Each does an act of hypnosis by persuading its audience that reality is the world that

the poets or politician has constructed for them." (Par. 8) Give your reasons.

6. Do you agree that "when power corrupts, poetry cleanses"? (Par. 10) Give examples to explain your reasons.

PREREADING ACTIVITIES

Discuss the following questions in your group:

1. Who are archaeologists? What do they do?
2. Can you think of any other profession which can be compared to archaeology? How do the two compare?

Reading 6: ARCHAEOLOGISTS ARE DETECTIVES WHO DIG IN THE DIRT

1. Archaeologists have often been compared with detectives, as they hunt for clues about the lifestyles of ancient peoples.

2. Like detectives, archaeologists go into the field to locate and preserve all kinds of information. They also use high-tech scientific tools to analyze the evidence they collect and then carefully interpret their data. In addition, like detectives, archaeologists today are not solely concerned with the traditional "what," "when," and "where" questions but try to answer the "how" and "why" ones, too. Moreover, like criminologists, archaeologists attempt to generalize from specific "why" answers to broader theories.

3. Like many comparisons, however, the similarities beween archaeologists and detectives cannot be pushed too far. One obvious difference is that archaeologists do not have informants or suspects they can question. The record that archaeologists study is mute. Thus, the archaeologists' problem is how to get the remains of the past — from broken bits of pottery to large monuments — to "talk."

4. Archaeologists accomplish such tricks by assigning meaning to patterns in the remains they uncover, frequently relying on the use of analogies. Things or patterns that have some similarities are presumed to have other similarities, as well. In the Maya lowlands of Yucatan, for example, where I have undertaken much of my field research, archaeologists find large numbers of rectangular and square arrangements of stone either situated on stone platforms or lying on the ground. Scholars believe these pieces of stone are the remains of wood and thatch houses.

Jeremy A. Sabloff, "Archaeologists Are Detectives Who Dig *In* the Dirt," *Newsday,* 4 March 1990. Reprinted by permission of the author.

5. Clearly, archaeologists don't actually *see* these houses, much of which has disappeared. But they do know, by studying the writings of clerics and soldiers from the time of the Spanish Conquest in the 16th Century and observations of modern Maya peoples in the Yucatan peninsula, that people in the area have lived in houses with walls made of thin tree trunks and branches and roofs of palm thatch — indeed, some still do.

6. Moreover, these houses often are situated on small raised platforms and the walls, which are sometimes plastered, sit on single rows of small boulders. The houses may have one or several rooms. When the wood and thatch rot away, the remains look almost exactly like those found by archaeologists at Pre-Columbian towns and cities. Thus, they feel justified in making analogies from partial remains — the patterns of stones — to the whole, houses with the patterns of stones plus the wood and thatch walls and roofs.

7. Ancient Maya civilization, which flourished for more than 2,000 years (from before the time of Christ to the Spanish Conquest) in the tropical lowlands of what is now Mexico, Belize, Guatemala, Honduras and El Salvador, has drawn considerable archaeological attention due to its marvelous accomplishments in architecture, art and science. Until recently, however, most research has focused on the remains of the Maya rulers: their temples, palaces, tombs and monuments. With important breakthroughs in the last few years in deciphering the Maya hieroglyphic writing system, much new light has been shed on the activities of the ancient Maya elite of the Classic Period (A.D. 300 to 800).

8. But what of the peasants who produced the food supporting the great Maya cities and provided the labor for the breathtaking buildings, or the craftspeople who manufactured the pottery or tools of everyday life? How did the cities develop, function and decline?

9. Archaeologists are increasingly turning their attention to such concerns, and in so doing have had to refine their detecting skills and use of analogies to new levels of sophistication.

10. Let me offer one small example of puzzle-solving from my own recent research at the site of Sayil in the Puuc region of the Mexican state of Yucatan, less than two hours drive south of the modern city of Merida. My colleagues and I have just completed five field seasons of research at the site, which flourished from 800 to 1000. Supported by National Science Foundation grants, we have mapped this large 1.7-square mile urban center that is now covered by dense forests, trying to understand how the land around Sayil and neighboring centers could have sustained a population considerably larger and denser than that living there today.

11. In studying how Sayil functioned, our attention has largely focused on the remains of the residences of the bulk of the population — those who were not of the ruling families.

12. We mapped these remains in the city and carefully examined the ground around and within a sample of the houses we identified, as well as areas between houses. In one case, we painstakingly examined the surface of a sample zone, slightly more than 300 feet on a side. Within this square were a number of structures including an extensive stone platform with the rows of stone that we identified by analogy as houses. Our team of workers cleared the vegetation in this zone and then subdivided the square into smaller squares to control our collections.

13. The team carefully collected all materials visible on the surface of the resultant 2,500 squares and chemically analyzed the soil in many of them too. The most frequent artifact was broken bits of pottery. By plotting the distribution of the potsherds, as well as their size and weight, we were able to locate the refuse dumps of the Maya who had lived in the houses from about 800 to 1000. We also found that areas of low pottery density coincided with a soil chemical signature that could be interpreted as resulting from prior fertilization and cultivation.

14. By analogy with peasant household lots studied elsewhere in lowland Mexico, our team of archaeological "detectives" was able to argue that the ancient Maya at Sayil apparently maintained extensive gardens around their houses and that the areas between house platforms probably were filled with fruit and vegetable plants. Using these areas, it was possible to supplement the maize (corn) fields surrounding the city and feed the dense population inhabiting Sayil for 200 years.

15. Modern archaeological work consists of such unromantic activities as rigorously sifting the soil for tiny bits of evidence of ancient materials, running precise tests of archaeological remains in the laboratory or studying the customs of modern peoples to use as analogies to the past. Just as most day-to-day detective work has little in common with the exploits of Hollywood private eyes, so the demanding research of today's scientific archaeologists bears no resemblance to Indiana Jones' searches for gold statues in jungle caves.

16. However, bit by mundane bit, modern archaeologists are building their understanding of how ancient peoples adapted to changing environments, and how and why some adaptations were successful and some failed.

POSTREADING ACTIVITIES

1. How do you justify the title of this article?
2. Summarize the writer's comparison and contrast of archaeologists and criminologists.
3. What new information have you received from reading this article?
4. Is the writer an archaeologist or a criminologist? How do you know it?

5. In your opinion, which of the two groups better serves society? Give your reasons.

PREREADING ACTIVITIES

Discuss the following questions in your group:

1. Where were you born?
2. How old were you when you came to the United States?
3. Compare your home town or city to the town or city where you are living now. Which one do you prefer? Why?

Reading 7: MY HOME CITY AND NEW YORK CITY

1. My home city, Ambato, and New York City share many characteristics. Nevertheless, both cities are different in three significant aspects: family life, education, and economic position. These are the keys to the development and integration of the city as well as the whole country.

2. The family life of my city is composed of grandparents, parents, and children. Children are raised by parents, who take care of them carefully. Parents give their kids much love, a sense of self-worth and responsibility for the future. Parents also teach children to show respect for old people. Children depend on parental guidance until they are mature enough to work out things by themselves.

3. Educationally, my home city has an average system. It has few schools; therefore, every child in a neighborhood knows every other child. School children have to do many assignments inside and outside the classrooms. Yet, school children are not allowed to use electronic machines, such as computers, calculators, etc. By not being permitted to use this type of equipment, children can add, multiply, subtract, etc. by hand. In addition, the government cannot supply the advanced mechanical devices because of their high cost. Also, professors teach moral values which are very important in the youngsters' lives.

4. In terms of the economy, my home city has a poor one. Its economic situation is worse than ever. An example is the high deficit.

5. In contrast to my home city, New York's family life is less dependent and more liberal. When a child reaches maturity, he will leave the house of his parents and find a place to live alone. Adolescents rarely follow orders given by

Melba Jordan, "My Home City and New York City," *The ESL Student Journal* (Fall 1985): 56.

their parents. Instead, they act the way they want to. The sense of respect for old people is almost gone. Youngsters go out mostly without getting their parents' permission. Its system of education is excellent because there is advanced technology. Electronic machines are being used in classrooms. These machines help the student make great improvements in a short time. Moreover, New York City is considered to be one of the richest and most powerful cities in the world.

6. Finally, these differences in relation to these three significant aspects are not unique with respect to my home city and New York; therefore, these aspects present to us a general view of how one city differs from another one. To conclude, I hope some day these two cities can join together to help people make up their minds for a better future.

POSTREADING ACTIVITIES

1. In Par. 3, does the writer imply that the unavailability of electronic machines is an advantage or disadvantage? Explain your answer.
2. What does the writer compare and contrast in Par. 2, 4, and 5? Which of the two systems do you think the writer prefers? How did you make this conclusion? Explain.
3. What message does the writer convey in the last paragraph?

PREREADING ACTIVITIES

Discuss the following in your group:

1. Where is Mexico? What country is the closest to Mexico?
2. What language do the Mexicans speak?
3. What are the political and geographical differences between Mexico and New Mexico?
4. Look up in an encyclopedia or almanac and find out the following about Mexico: (1) geographical location, (2) neighboring states (3) how similar to and different from New Mexico it is.

Reading 8: MEXICANS AND AMERICANS

1. The history of relations between the United States and Mexico has not been one of understanding and cooperation, though many persons on both sides of the border are working toward those ends. Even under the best of con-

From John C. Condon, ". . . So Near the United States," in J.M. Valdes, ed., *Culture Bound: Bridging the Cultural Gap in Language Teaching* (New York, Cambridge University Press, 1986), 85-92. Reprinted from *The Spring* 5, no. 1 (Spring 1980). Reprinted here with permission of Cambridge University Press.

ditions and with the best of intentions, Mexicans and North Americans working together sometimes feel confused, irritated, distrustful. The causes lie not
within either culture but rather can be best understood interculturally. Here
are four perspectives.

2. One perspective in which the two cultures differ is that of individualism.
In the North American value system there are three central and interrelated
assumptions about human beings. These are (1) people, apart from social
and educational influences, are basically the same ; (2) each person should be
judged on his or her own individual merits ; and (3) these "merits," including
a person's worth and character, are revealed through the person's actions.
Values of equality and independence, constitutional rights, laws and social
programs arise from these assumptions. Because a person's actions are
regarded as so important, it is the comparison of accomplishments — Mr. X
compared to Mr. X's father, or X five years ago compared to X today, or X
compared to Y and Z — that provides a chief means of judging or even knowing a person.

3. In Mexico it is the uniqueness of the individual which is valued, a quality
which is assumed to reside within each person and which is not necessarily
evident through actions or achievements. That inner quality which represents
the dignity of each person must be protected at all costs. Any action or
remark that may be interpreted as a slight to the person's dignity is to be
regarded as a grave provocation. Also, as every person is part of a larger family grouping, one cannot be regarded as a completely isolated individual. ...

4. Where a Mexican will talk about a person's inner qualities in terms of
the person's soul or spirit (*alma* or *espiritu*), North Americans are likely to
feel uncomfortable using such words to talk about people. They may regard
such talk as vague or sentimental, the words seeming to describe something
invisible and hence unknowable, or at the very least "too personal." The
unwillingness to talk in this way only confirms the view held by many Mexicans that North Americans are insensitive. "Americans are corpses," said one
Mexican.

5. Even questions about the family of a person one does not know well
may discomfit many North Americans, since asking about a person's parents
or brothers or sisters may also seem too personal. "I just don't know the person well enough to ask about his family," a North American might say, while
the Mexican may see things just the opposite : "If I don't ask about the person's family, how will I really know him ?"

6. The family forms a much less important part of an individual's frame of
reference in the United States than is usually the case in Mexico. Neighbors,
friends or associates, even some abstract "average American," may be the
basis for the comparison needed in evaluating oneself or others. "Keeping up
with the Joneses" may be important in New York or Chicago, but keeping up
with one's brother-in-law is more important in Mexico City. In the same way,
the Mexican depends upon relatives or close friends to help "arrange things"

if there is a problem or to provide a loan. While this is by no means rare in the United States, the dominant values in the culture favor institutions which are seen as both efficient and fair.

7. So it is that tensions may arise between Mexicans and North Americans over what seems to be a conflict between trusting particular individuals or trusting abstract principles. In a business enterprise, the North American manager is likely to view the organization and its processes as primary, with the role of specific people being more or less supportive of that system. People can be replaced if need be : nobody is indispensable. When one places emphasis on a person's spirit or views an organization as if it were a family, however, then it seems just as clear that nobody can be exactly replaced by any other person.

8. Both North Americans and Mexicans may speak of the need to "respect" another person, but here too the meanings of the word respect (or *respeto*) differ somewhat across the cultures. In a study of associations with this word conducted in the U.S. and Mexico, it was found that North Americans regarded "respect" as bound up with the values of equality, fair play and the democratic spirit. There were no emotional overtones. One respects others as one might respect the law. For Mexicans, however, "respect" was found to be an emotionally charged word involving pressures of power, possible threat, and often a love-hate relationship. The meaning of respect arises from powerful human relationships such as between father and son or *patrón* and *péon,* not a system of principles to which individuals voluntarily commit themselves.

9. Another area of difference between North Americans and Mexicans is that of "straight talk."... The Mexican is far more likely to flatter, tease or otherwise attempt to charm another than is the North American whose culture has taught him to distrust or poke fun at anyone who "really lays it on."... North Americans are often suspicious of one who seems effusive in praise ; they are also likely to make light of one who seems too enamored of titles. Mexicans, on the other hand, value one who has the wit and charm to impress another. Nor are titles or other indications of one's status, age or ability to be slighted. The owner of an auto repair shop may defer to a mechanic who is older and more experienced as *maestro* ; doctors, lawyers and other professional people will take their titles seriously. To make light of them is to challenge one's dignity. ...

10. North Americans and Mexicans also differ in their concept of truth. During the world congress held in Mexico for the International Women's Year, some first time visitors experienced the kind of problem that many North Americans have long complained about in Mexico. The visitors would be told one thing only to discover that what they were told seemed to bear no resemblance to the facts. A delegate who would ask where a meeting was being held might be given clear directions, but upon reaching the destination she would find no such meeting. "It was not that the Mexicans were unfriendly or unhelpful — just wrong !" North American managers working with Mexicans have sometimes voiced similar complaints : an employee says something is finished when in fact it has not even begun.

11. Rogelio Díaz-Guerrero, head of the psychology department at the National University of Mexico and a foremost interpreter of Mexican behavior patterns, offers this explanation. There are two kinds of "realities" which must be distinguished, objective and interpersonal. Some cultures tend to treat everything in terms of the objective sort of reality : this is characteristic of the United States. Other cultures tend to treat things in terms of interpersonal relations, and this is true of Mexico. ...

12. Viewed from the Mexican perspective, a visitor asks somebody for information which that person doesn't know. But wanting to make the visitor happy and to enjoy a few pleasant moments together, the Mexican who was asked does his best to say something so that for a short while the visitor is made happy. It is not that Mexicans have a monopoly on telling another person what that person wants to hear : perhaps in all cultures the truth is sometimes altered slightly to soften the impact of a harsh truth or to show deference to one's superior. It is the range of situations in which this occurs in Mexico and the relatively sharper contrast of "truth-telling" standards in U.S.–Mexican encounters that is so notable. ...

13. North Americans and Mexicans also differ in their perspective on time. Mexico may be best known as the land of *mañana*. Differences in the treatment of time may not be the most serious source of misunderstanding between people of the two cultures but it is surely the most often mentioned. Several issues are actually grouped under the general label of "time."...

14. North Americans express special irritation when Mexicans seem to give them less than their undivided attention. When a young woman bank teller, awaiting her superior's approval for a check to be cashed, files her nails and talks on the phone to her boyfriend, or when one's taxi driver stops en route to pick up a friend who seems to be going in the same direction, North Americans become very upset. North Americans interpret such behavior as showing a lack of respect and a lack of "professionalism," but the reason may lie more in the culturally different treatment of time.

15. Newly arrived residents seem to learn quickly to adjust their mental clocks to *la hora Mexican* when it comes to anticipating the arrival of Mexican guests at a party ; an invitation for 8:00 may produce guests by 9:00 or 10:00. What takes more adjusting is the notion that visitors may be going to another party first and yet another party afterwards. For many North Americans this diminishes the importance attached to their party, much as the teller's action diminishes the respect shown the customer. The counterpart of this, Mexicans' irritation with the North American time sense, is in their dismay over an invitation to a party which states in advance the time when the party will be over. This or subtler indications of the time to terminate a meeting before it has even gotten underway serve as further proof that Americans are slaves to the clock and don't really know how to enjoy themselves.

16. The identification of common problem areas in communication across cultures is always incomplete; there are always other interpretations and, since culture is a whole, the selection of "factors" or "themes" is never completely shown in its entire context. Nevertheless, a common effort to appreciate differences across cultures is essential, particularly in the relations between people of the United States and Mexico.

17. It is not an exaggeration to say that if North Americans cannot learn to communicate more effectively with Mexicans, [their] capacity to function in cultures elsewhere in the world will be doubted. Many of the well-springs of Mexican culture flow freely elsewhere, not only in other Latin American states but in such distant lands as the Philippines.

POSTREADING ACTIVITIES

1. What do you think the author means by "the uniqueness of the individual" and the "inner quality which represents the dignity of each person"? (Par. 3)

2. How do the three assumptions on which the American value system is based differ from (a) those of Mexicans (b) those of your home culture or another culture you know of?

3. Do you think the differences between American and Mexican value systems are the same as those between any industrialized and nonindustrialized countries? If so, how do you account for the differences between the Japanese and American value systems?

4. Explain how tensions can arise over what seems to be a conflict between trusting particular individuals and trusting abstract principles. (Par. 7)

5. When and how would "respect" become a system of principles to which individuals voluntarily commit themselves? (Par. 8)

6. Do you agree with the writer's statement: "Perhaps in all cultures the truth is sometimes altered slightly to soften the impact of a harsh truth or to show deference to one's superior"? (Par. 12) Give your reasons with examples.

7. Give some examples for the "truth-telling standards" in the United States. (Par. 12)

8. Do you agree with the statement: "Americans are slaves to the clock and don't really know how to enjoy themselves." (Par. 15) Give reasons.

9. Are you from a "*manana*" culture or a "clock" culture? Which one
    do you prefer? Why? Explain the advantages and disadvantages of
    these two different "time cultures."
10. The writer concludes: "Many of the well-springs of Mexican cul-
    ture flow freely elsewhere, not only in other Latin American states
    but in such distant lands as the Philippines." (Par. 17) What are
    some other cultures which share almost the same features as those
    of Mexicans?
11. Who are the intended readers for this article? How do you know?
12. What nationality do you think the writer belongs to? How did you
    come to that conclusion?

Part 2: WRITING

EXPOSITORY WRITING: COMPARISON AND CONTRAST

We all make comparisons and contrasts every day of our lives. For example, students compare and contrast schools and teachers. All of us compare and contrast supermarkets, department stores, friends, neighbors,
political, religious, and community leaders, and so on. Our decisions as to
which ones to choose are the result of these comparisons and contrasts.

Comparisons and contrasts do not always have to involve two people,
things, or events. Sometimes we compare and contrast the same persons
or objects to show how they have changed over the years, for example,
one's neighborhood as it existed ten years ago compared and contrasted
with what it is now; personality changes from childhood to teenage years,
or from teenage years to adulthood.

We also use comparisons and contrasts as devices to explain known
people or objects with reference to unknown ones. For example, teachers
explain new concepts by comparing and contrasting them with concepts
already being taught.

Academically, most of your courses, homework assignments, term
papers, and tests require the skill of comparing and contrasting. For
example, in your history class you may be asked to compare and contrast
the French Revolution and the Russian Revolution; your English professor may ask you to compare and contrast two novels, characters, poems,
and so on.

Since comparisons and contrasts are integral parts of our daily lives, it is of great importance to develop the academic skill of writing an expository essay using comparison and contrast as rhetorical devices.

> *Purpose:* Comparison and contrast are essentially two different approaches : comparison means pointing out similarities, and contrast means pointing out differences. When you compare people or objects, the assumption is they are different, so you are looking for similarities. On the other hand, when you contrast, the objects are supposed to be similar and you are looking for differences. Completely identical or different things do not provide meaningful comparison and contrast.
>
> In writing a comparison and contrast essay you can take one of five possible approaches.

Five Approaches

Approach 1

Choose two similar things and contrast them by explaining the differences.

EXAMPLE

Melbourne and Sydney, the two main cities with a combined population of more than six million, love to hate each other, and while both have become great cities of the world, they do indeed differ in spirit. Moralistic Melbourne cannot let go of principles, while on-the-make Sydney is content to count the numbers.

Hazel Hawke, wife of the prime minister, reflected on Melbourne and Sydney over coffee one morning in their Canberra residence. "The Opera House expresses Sydney — a wonderful, breathtaking place. Yet inside there's a lot lacking. As a place to produce opera, it's a headache. On the other hand, in Melbourne the arts complex is not stunning from the outside — it hides itself — but inside it works wonderfully."[1]

For Your Critical Thinking

1. Why do you think the writer emphasizes the differences between Melbourne and Sidney ?
2. Suppose the writer is Australian. Could he or she belong to Melbourne or Sidney ? Why ?

---

[1]Ross Terrill, "Australia at 200," *National Geographic* (February 1988) : 195-96. Used with permission.

Approach 2

Choose a dissimilar pair and explain how, in spite of the obvious differences, there are also some similarities. You may even want to mention both, but you actually have to emphasize one or the other.

EXAMPLE

Articles on Australia invariably ring the bell with United States readers — perhaps because no two nations so far apart geographically — are so close culturally. Like brothers growing up in different parts of the world, family traits show through. Both nations were founded by those rejected by Europe or who had rejected Europe. Prisoners, the persecuted, and the disinherited often led the way. The crowded poverty of the masses and the social and economic gridlock of class distinctions in Europe made both wilderness colonies seem utopian — there idealists could experiment with radical concepts of egalitarian, democratic government, and hard work and intelligence were rewarded. Word of fast fortunes and a free life also drew the adventurous and unscrupulous to both lands. Rough, tough, and often lawless immigrants swept over the sparsely populated frontiers and their indigenous populations like tidal waves. Those natives who survived found their cultures washed away. Most have yet to accommodate to the new ways. ... Still young as nations go, both exhibit similarities and differences as they mature. Social, economic, and racial problems of the kind thought left behind long ago surface like bad genes, but the response to them remains democratic. Both nations, for good reasons, remain favored havens for the restless and persecuted of this world. ...[2]

For Your Critical Thinking

1. After reading the above paragraph, do you look at Australia as having more similarities to or differences from the United States? Why?
2. What, according to the above paragraph, are the dissimilarities between the two nations?
3. If you wrote the paragraph would you emphasize the similarities or differences? Why?

Approach 3

You can show that both objects have a central idea or theme, probably in different ways.

---

[2]Wilbur E. Garrett, *National Geographic* (February 1988) : 157.

EXAMPLE

Familiar, informal, attractive, open, but different — a kind of not-American American, a not-English Englishman. The difference is underscored by the accent, for early on, classless Australia had unclipped the language and flattened out the vowels and kicked the ends of sentences up into questions, rather than shadow the downward drawl of a duke. ...[3]

For Your Critical Thinking

1. What are the two countries represented in this paragraph ?
2. What is the central point at which they converge ?
3. What are the differences ?

Approach 4

Show that one object is better, worse, more or less efficient, more or less of something, etc., than the other.

EXAMPLE

Probably, Australia will never become as American as it once was British. British influence was institutional, giving it a certain power to perpetuate itself. American influence is felt through the economy, popular culture, and technology, and is always in flux. "We are becoming Americanized only in the sense that we're becoming universalized," observed Tony Staley, a former cabinet minister. "It so happens that the U.S. is at the forefront of many things; the whole world is going in that direction."[4]

For Your Critical Thinking

1. How many countries are represented in the paragraph ? What are they ?
2. What nationality do you think the writer is ? Defend your judgment.

Approach 5

Use analogy (the most sophisticated, complicated, and difficult approach), that is, the use of a familiar idea to explain an unfamiliar one.

---

[3]Joseph Judge, "The Australians," *National Geographic* (February 1988) : 217.
[4]Terrill, "Australia at 200," 189.

EXAMPLE

"But this is an amazing country," said the Dutch-born director, who stressed the habitat. He summed up his art as an attempt "to make people more aware of their inner self. Like when we look at a tree. There's enormous strength under the earth to give that tree life. But we never see the roots, and we never think about them. You know, we admire the tree for traveling through the seasons, but where's the respect for the very roots that hold the tree deeply in the earth? It's exactly like that with people."[5]

For Your Critical Thinking

1. Look up "analogy" in the dictionary and define the word.
2. How many things does the writer talk about in this paragraph?
3. What is the point of the analogy?

ORGANIZATION

The Introduction

As in any introduction, begin with broad statements relating and narrowing down to the specific pairs you are comparing and contrasting.
    The thesis statement can be made in two ways:

1. State your point of view, for example, whether, in your opinion, similarities or differences count more.
2. Take a stand, for example, stating that one is better, more efficient, or of higher quality than the other. In this case, you have to defend your stand by arguing or debating.

Developmental Paragraphs

There are three ways of developing your thesis statement.

Paired Development

Here, one quality is discussed at one time for each of the two persons, things, or events you are comparing. This can be done in a single paragraph or in two different paragraphs. Many writers prefer this pattern, since it is easier to give details when one feature is dealt with at one time.

---

[5]Ibid., page 203.

Also, readers won't get lost, because the points of comparison and contrast run through the entire essay in a linear fashion.

For example, suppose you are comparing and contrasting two student residences (A and B). The outline of two of the developmental paragraphs could look as follows:

- Par. 1. Distance from university

    - Residence A: on university campus
    - Residence B: off campus

- Par. 2. Recreational facilities

    - Residence A: three student lounges with TV sets and video games; indoor games; in addition, can share all university facilities until 10 p.m.
    - Residence B: two student lounges with TV sets, but no video or other indoor games; no swimming pool

Block Development

Here, the points of comparison and contrast are discussed in two blocks: all the points relating to A go in one block and the same points relating to B, in another block. The number of paragraphs in each block depends on the number of points developed. If it is a short essay, each block may comprise one paragraph. If you follow this developmental pattern, the outline given above on the two student residences would be modified as follows:

- Par 1. Residence A

    - Location: on university campus
    - Recreational facilities: three student lounges with TV sets and video games in each; indoor games; in addition, can share all university facilities until 10 p.m.

- Par 2. Residence B

    - Location: off campus
    - Recreational facilities: very limited; two student lounges with TV sets, but no indoor games or swimming pool

Note that the points of comparison and contrast are exactly the same and in the same order as in paired development, but they are organized differently — not in pairs, but in blocks — all the points relating to each item forming one block. Each block may be divided into as many paragraphs as there are points, depending on the details given.

Most writers do not prefer this format because it is very difficult both to develop the points this way and to catch the reader's attention. In giving details about A in block B, readers should be reminded of each of the points of comparison and contrast made in the first block about A. This has to be done very carefully, with appropriate vocabulary and transition words.

Paired and Block Development Combined

In long essays, some writers use both block and paired development. However, for beginning and intermediate writers like yourself, it is better not to adopt this pattern.

For Your Critical Thinking

Discuss the following in your group and with your instructor.

1. One of the essays in the reading selections was written by a student. Which one is this? How did you find this out? How similar to/ different from the others, is this essay with reference to audience, purpose, and organization?
2. Classify the eight essays given in this chapter. (Review Chapter 4 for classification). How many groups would you classify them into? What would be your basis for classification?
3. Compare and contrast each group of essays you have classified.
4. Of the different groups of essays, which is easier and more comprehensible for you? Why? Would you adopt the purpose and organization of this group of essays when you want to write comparison and contrast essays? Why? Why not?
5. Do all the essays have conclusions? Which ones do not have conclusions? Add your own conclusions to these.
6. Find examples (from the reading selections) for the use of:

   • paired development
   • block development
   • paired and block development combined

7. Find examples of essays which:

    - Compare (stressing similarities)
    - Contrast (stressing dissimilarities)
    - Compare and contrast (giving equal importance to both)
    - Use analogy as a rhetorical style

8. Do any essays use research data to explain the points of comparison and contrast? Which are these essays? Compare and contrast them in their use of research data.
9. Do any essays quote experts to explain the points of comparison? Which are they? Comment on the use of the writers' use of quotations.
10. Which of the essays did you find most difficult to comprehend? Why did you find it most difficult? If you wrote this essay, what changes would you make? Why?

WRITING ACTIVITIES

Reaction Journal

Write in your journal:

- Which article(s) you most enjoyed
- Based on the information given, which article you found most useful and applicable to your daily life
- How factual you think the information given in each article is
- If you can guess where the writers got their information from (for example, from their experience, reading, or research)
- If you could write any of the essays yourself
- What deletions or additions you would make if you wrote any of the essays

Learning Log

Write in your learning log:

- What you learned from the chapter
- How and in what situations you would apply the learning
- What additional information you expected from the discussions and reading passages
- If you have anything to add either to the information in the essays or to the discussion on writing

Writing Assignment

Overview

Pick any pair from the list below. Compare and contrast the two groups of people in their service to the community.

1. Religious leaders/political leaders
2. Social workers/counselors
3. Medical doctors/lawyers
4. Real estate brokers/insurance agents

> *Real-life Purpose:* To learn more about the services rendered by the two groups of people you have chosen
>
> *Academic Purpose:* To practice writing comparison and contrast essays
>
> *Audience:* Your class members and instructor

Procedure

IN-CLASS GROUP ACTIVITY

Purpose: To make up a questionnaire for an interview
Group Size: 6

1. The group picks one pair from above (for example, medical doctors/lawyers).
2. The group divides itself into two subgroups for interviewing purpose. (For example: Three in the group will agree to interview medical doctors, and the other three will agree to interview lawyers).
3. Discuss the services offered by the two categories of people.
4. Discuss what you would like to learn about their services and what points of comparison you would like to make about their services.
5. Write down five to ten questions you would like to ask them at the interview.

OUT-OF-CLASS ACTIVITY

1. Each subgroup individually interviews the people of their choice, eliciting answers to questions. (See No. 5 above.)
2. Review the responses and summarize them.

IN-CLASS GROUP ACTIVITY

1. Discuss the responses in your group.
2. Make notes on points of comparison.
3. Make your outline of the essay.

OUT-OF-CLASS INDIVIDUAL WRITING ACTIVITY

1. Develop the outline into an essay.
2. Read it out loud to two people representing the two groups of people you are comparing and contrasting. Get their feedback.
3. Review/revise your draft as many times as is needed.
4. Hand in your work to your instructor.

Alternate Writing Assignment

Choose one of the following pairs. Write an essay comparing and contrasting them. You may use your life experience or your reading as the source for this assignment.

1. Music and poetry
2. Electronic and electric typewriters
3. Friendship and acquaintance
4. Actors and dancers

CHAPTER · 7

Part 1: READING

PREREADING ACTIVITIES

Form peer groups which have the following in two categories of people : (1) bicycle riders (or those who know people who ride bicycles) (2) non-bicycle riders. Discuss the following in your group.

1. What motivates people to ride bicycles ?
2. How do they learn to ride ? By themselves ? By going to a bicycle school ? By other means ?
3. What steps do they go through in the learning process ?
4. Name some parts of a bicycle. How do these parts help in riding ?
5. Do the members in Category 1 of your group use helmets when they ride ? Why or why not ?
6. Do they have their own bicycles ? How long have they been using them ? Where did they buy them ? How much did they cost ?
7. What lesson have they learnt from the buying process they went through ?
8. If they were to buy these bicycles now, would they change any of those buying processes they went through before ? Why or why not ?
9. Do you (nonriders) like to learn how to ride bicycles ? Why or why not ?
10. Have you known people using any kind of bicycle for any purpose other than riding ? What are those purposes ? How are those activities different from riding ?

Reading: STARTING TO CYCLE

1. Cycling is fast becoming the recreational pastime of choice for a growing number of Americans. One reason for its steadily growing popularity is that Americans are discovering both the pleasures and the physical benefits it offers. As with swimming and cross-country skiing, cycling dramatically improves cardiovascular fitness. Also, when done properly, the smooth, fluid movements of pedaling are non-injurious to joints, and they promote muscle flexibility and

Adapted from Skip Berry, "Starting to Cycle," *USAir Magazine* (November 1981) : 42–49.
Reprinted by permission of Pace Communications, Inc., Greensboro, North Carolina.

bone strength. It also provides participants with a vigorous aerobic workout without the joint trauma of running. And, cycling slows the aging process because it forces the heart and lungs to work.

2. However, as with any new physical endeavor, there is a caveat attached to cycling. While anyone who can balance a bike and pedal can take up cycling, no one is ready for long, strenuous rides right at the start. If your idea of exercise has been stepping out on the porch and stooping over to pick up the morning paper, don't expect cycling to be easy on your body. In fact, as with any exercise program, the first thing you should do is to check with your doctor before starting, especially if you are over 35.

3. If you haven't been on a bike since you got your driver's license, you will first need to condition your legs, your heart, and your gluteus. A novice only has to spend too much time in the saddle once to feel the effects of over-enthusiasm. There is not a cyclist around who hasn't had to sit gingerly on the edges of chairs for a few days following an extra-long ride.

4. However, before you have to worry about feeling saddle sore, you have to have a saddle to sit on. It is hard to take up cycling without a bike. In the interests of safety and comfort, don't dash off to a yard sale, slap down $25 for some rusty five-speed that has been gathering dust in someone's garage for the past fifteen years, and wobble off down the street. Times have changed, and so have bicycles. If you are serious about giving cycling a try, it is worth shopping for a new bike. Visit a couple of bike shops to find out exactly what is on the market.

5. The first thing you will discover is that the market is a tangle of choices — sport-touring bikes (also known as recreational bikes), all-terrain bikes (sometimes separated into city bikes and mountain bikes), racing and touring bikes. Make your choice based on what you want to do. Both racing and touring are specialized types of bikes ; the former comes in the form of track-racing bikes and road-racing bikes, while the latter is designed for long cycling tours. Neither variety is suited to beginners' needs. What you want to do initially is ride for fitness and fun — you can always try specialized riding once you have more experience. That means you have narrowed your options down to two basic types of bikes — sport touring and all-terrain.

6. Most bikes in these categories have 10 to 18 speeds, depending on the models. Sport-touring bikes usually have dropped (racing style) handlebars and narrow, grooved tires, while all-terrain bikes have rigid, upright handlebars and wide, knobby tires. The former kind is built for riding on paved streets and roads, the latter for riding off-road and on roads in off-road condition. Prices range from around $150 for a very basic 10-speed sport-touring bike to $900 and above for specially built all-terrain bicycles.

7. How much should you spend ? The gateway to good quality begins at about $300. As you move up to $600, there is a steady improvement in features, component quality, durability, and beauty. Though price is certainly a consideration, frame size is the most important factor when buying a bike. Getting the right frame size will determine how comfortable you feel riding — and that will determine how often and how long you ride. To find the right frame, the Bicycle Institute of America (BIA) guidelines suggest that you straddle the horizontal bar that runs from the handlebars to the seat, and put your feet flat on the floor. On a sport-touring bike, there should be a one- to two-inch clearance between you and the bar ; on an all-terrain bike, you will need a three- or four-inch clearance. A frame that is either too small or too large will make riding awkward, and turn what should be a pleasure into a chore.

8.　When it comes to accessories — racks, pumps, bags, lights, odometers, lights, heart monitors — there is only one essential : the helmet. While there is just as much disagreement among cyclists as among motorcyclists about the pros and cons of wearing helmets, the facts speak for themselves. According to the statistics collected by the BIA, every year nearly 70,000 bicyclists are involved in accidents that result in serious head injuries. Many of these injuries are debilitating ; some are fatal.

9.　It was once believed that helmets were heavy, hot, and awkward to wear. That is no longer true. Today's high-tech helmets weigh 7 to 14 ounces, are well-ventilated, and fit snugly and securely through the use of sizing pads and adjustable straps. Two strict testing standards created by the Snell Memorial Foundation and the American National Standards Institute insure the protective strength of helmets. Any helmet bearing a sticker from one of these organizations has been tested for durability and safety.

10.　Once you have a bike and a helmet, you are ready to begin cycling in earnest. Start off slowly ; it is better to ride five miles daily than fifteen miles once a week. Don't use gear settings that are so high they strain your knees. The BIA recommends shifting gears as necessary to maintain a cadence of seventy to ninety pedal rotations per minute. As you get used to riding, lengthen your distance and add short periods of hard riding, three to five minutes apart, to build strength and endurance. As you grow accustomed to cycling's demands, you will learn how to adjust your workouts according to your body's needs.

11.　Once you have gained some experience, you may want to follow the lead of the 160,000 American adults who ride in cycling competitions every year. Competitive events include track races, 10- to 200-kilometer road races, time trails, stage races that involve several types of events over several days (the Tour de France is the best-known stage race in the world), 200-mile-a-day ultra-marathon races, and off-road racing.

12.　To get started in competition, or just to learn proper training techniques and equipment maintenance skills, contact a local cycling club or organization. Cycling clubs not only offer helpful training tips, but they also usually sponsor a variety of group events ranging from informal rides to sanctioned competitions.

13.　But despite the excitement of racing, the reason most of us ride is the sheer pleasure of wheeling through neighborhoods and along country roads. A bike permits us to escape everyday stresses and strains for a while; it is not competition that interests us so much as contemplation.

14. For the uninitiated and those who put aside the pleasures of youth long ago, cycling is a form of moving meditation. There is something soothing about pedaling along a sparsely traveled road, miles from the daily duties that use up so much of our lives. On such a road, life is elemental — wide skies, bright sun, the pitiless wind. The rhythm of legs and lungs and heart is invigorating, the quick sprints are exhilarating, and the conquering of a steep hill is a triumph. Astride a bicycle with nowhere to be, it is impossible not to feel free.

POSTREADING ACTIVITIES

Discuss the following in your group :

1. Compare the steps you went through in learning how to ride a bicycle, drive a car, type, or use a computer keyboard to the steps described by the author in learning how to ride.

Part 2: GRAMMAR

MODAL VERBS: *SHOULD*

For Your Critical Thinking

Find the meaning expressed by *should* in the following sentences :

S1. In fact, as with any exercise program, the first thing you *should* do is to check with your doctor before starting, especially if you are over 35. (Par. 2)

S2. How much *should* you spend? (Par. 7)

S3. On a sport-touring bike, there *should* be a one- to-two-inch clearance between you and the bar. (Par. 7)

S4. A frame that is either too small or too large will make riding awkward, and turn what *should* be a pleasure into a chore. (Par. 7)

Part 3: SENTENCE COMBINING

IF-CLAUSES

Problems for You to Solve

1. Separate S1-S4 below into two sentences each, replacing *if* by another word or phrase.
2. What synonyms would you use for *if*?
3. What is the antonym for *if*?

> S1. *If* your idea of exercise has been stepping out on the porch and stooping over to pick up the morning paper, don't expect cycling to be easy on your body. (Par. 2)
>
> S2. The first thing you should do is to check with your doctor before starting, especially *if* you are over thirty-five. (Par. 2)
>
> S3. *If* you haven't been on a bike since you got your driver's license, you will first need to condition your legs, your heart, and your gluteus. (Par. 3)
>
> S4. *If* you are serious about giving cycling a try, it is worth shopping for a new bike. (Par. 4)

Note

The *if*-clauses in the above sentences introduce *real conditional sentences*, which express actions or state situations which the writer expects will happen or usually do happen, given the circumstances in the main clauses. In other words, the relation between the actions expressed by the verbs in the main and dependent clauses is real, which means the writer expects the action expressed by the main clause to be sure to happen or not to happen, provided the condition expressed by the *if*-clause is satisfied or not satisfied.

For Your Critical Thinking

Compare the situation expressed in the above sentences to that expressed in:

> S1. God would not have given us fingers if he had wished to use such an instrument. (Chapter 5, p. 114, Par. 4.)

Note

The relation between the actions expressed by the *if-* clause and the main clause in S1 above is unreal: in the real world the two actions expressed by the if-clause and the main clause did not happen and would not happen. In contrast, S1-S4 in the previous problems express real conditions and real situations.

The verb form formulas for the real conditional sentences (expressing present or future time) are:

subj. + *will*/modal verb/simple pres. + base v. = main clause
subj. + simple pres/pres. perf./cont. = *if*-clause

See pp. 115–116 for the past unreal conditional verb patterns.

WHILE- CLAUSES

Problems for You to Solve

1. Review the clause markers you have learned so far and find what clause markers can substitute for *while* in the following sentences. (In reviewing, pay special attention to Chapter 4, p. 88.)
2. Split each of the following sentences into two complete sentences, using appropriate vocabulary to relate each pair.

S1. *While* anyone who can balance a bike and pedal can take up cycling, no one is ready for long, strenuous rides right at the start. (Par. 2)

S2. The former comes in the form of track-racing bikes and road-racing bikes, *while* the latter is designed for long cycling tours. (Par. 5)

S3. Sport-touring bikes usually have dropped handlebars and narrow, grooved tires, *while* all-terrain bikes have rigid, upright handlebars and wide, knobby tires. (Par. 6)

S4. *While* there is as much disagreement among cyclists as among motorcyclists about the pros and cons of wearing helmets, the facts speak for themselves. (Par. 8)

For Your Critical Thinking

Compare the use of *while* in the above sentences with the ways it is used in the following sentences.

S5. At a brewery, Priestly used a primitive apparatus to pour water from one vessel to another while holding the contraption close to the fermenting vats. (Chapter 1 : "Soda," Par. 2 ; also see p. 13, no. 3a and b and p. 15.)

S6. The middle-aged forage, while the oldsters serve as protectors. (Chapter 4, "The Ant and Her World," Par. 4 ; also see Chapter 4, p. 88, Group C and Note.)

S7. While the fork first entered society on the tables of the rich and well-born, many a crowned head, including Queen Elizabeth 1 of England and Louis XIV of France ate with their fingers. (Chapter 5 : "The Technology of Eating," Par. 7 ; also see p. 118, No. 5a and b.)

NOUN CLAUSES

Problems for You to Solve

Find an appropriate pronoun to replace the underlined clause in each of the following sentences. Rewrite each sentence using this pronoun. Pay special attention to word order and grammar. These rewritten sentences may not convey the whole meaning of the original sentences, but they will look grammatically the same.

S1. Visit a couple of bike shops to find out exactly *what is on the market*. (Par. 4)

S2. Make your choice based on *what you want to do*. (Par. 5)

S3. *What you want to do initially* is ride for fitness and fun — you can always try specialized riding once you have more experience. (Par. 5)

S4. Getting the right frame size will determine *how comfortable you feel riding* — and that will determine *how often and how long you ride*. (Par. 7)

S5. A frame that is either too small or too large will make riding awkward, and turn *what should be a pleasure* into a chore. (Par. 7)

Note

Some noun clause markers are : *what, why, how* (often/long), *where, when, whether, if,* and *that,* which can also mark other kinds of clauses (adjectival, adverbial, conditional, etc.). What distinguishes noun clauses from other clauses is that the whole unit (including the clause marker) is used in place of a noun or pronoun and can be replaced by a noun or pronoun without affecting the grammar of the sentence.

Since a noun clause is used in place of a noun or pronoun, it can function as (a) the subject of the verb, (b) the object of the verb, (c) the object of a preposition, or (d) the subject/object complement.

Problems for You to Solve

Identify the function of each noun clause in S1–S5 of the previous problems: (a), (b), (c), or (d).

ONCE- CLAUSES

For Your Critical Thinking

Compare the meaning and use of *once* in the following sentences.

S1. It was *once* believed that helmets were heavy, hot, and awkward. (Par. 9)

S2. *Once* you have a bike and a helmet, you are ready to begin cycling in earnest. (Par. 10)

S3. *Once* you have gained some experience, you may want to follow the lead of the 160,000 American adults who ride in cycling competitions. (Par. 11)

Note

Once as a clause marker means "from the time that"/"when" and it introduces a time clause. *Once* as an adverb means "at one time"/"on one occasion."

Problems for You to Solve

Find which sentences above have clauses with *once* as a clause marker.

Part 4: SENTENCE AND PARAGRAPH RELATING

For Your Critical Thinking

Discuss the following in your group:

1. What are the topic and the controlling idea of Par. 1 in the reading passage above?

2. Do all the other sentences in the paragraph talk about the same topic? (paragraph unity/cohesion)
3. What structural devices does the writer use to relate each sentence in the paragraph to one another and to the topic sentence? (coherence)
4. Why does the writer begin Par. 2 and 4 with *however*?
5. What two sentences in Par. 2 are made to relate to each other by the use of *in fact*? Why does the writer use *in fact*?
6. Why does the author begin Par. 13 with *but*?

> *Note:* The transition word *in fact* is used to reaffirm the idea expressed in the sentence immediately preceding the one where it is used. (See Chapter 2, p. 39.)

Part 5: VOCABULARY, WORD FORMS, AND IDIOMS

FILL-INS

Paragraph **b** in each of the following pairs is a paraphrase of **a**. Using synonyms and antonyms (which need not be exact), changing sentence structure, and changing word forms are some of the devices used in making the paraphrase.

Your task: Fill in the blanks with appropriate words or phrases. Each blank line indicates one word. The underlined words in the original may give you the clues. The asterisks in **b** tell you there are no clues provided in the original.

1a. Cycling is fast becoming the recreational <u>pastime</u> of <u>choice</u> for a <u>growing</u> number of Americans. One reason for its steadily growing <u>popularity</u> is that Americans are <u>discovering</u> both the <u>pleasures</u> and the <u>physical benefits it offers.</u> As with swimming and cross-country skiing, cycling <u>dramatically</u> improves cardiovascular fitness. <u>Also,</u> when done <u>properly,</u> the smooth, fluid movements of pedaling are <u>non-injurious</u> to joints, and they promote muscle <u>flexibility</u> and bone strength. It also provides participants with a vigorous aerobic workout without the joint trauma of running. And, cycling slows the aging process because it forces the heart and lungs to work. (Par. 1)

b. An (1) _____ number of Americans have (2) _____ cycling as a (3) _____. One reason that cycling has become so (4) _____ is that Americans (5) _____ it a (6)° _____ tool for both (7) _____ and (8) _____. (9) _____ swimming and cross-country skiing, cycling improves cardiovascular fitness to a (10) _____ _____. (11) _____, pedaling, when done with (12) _____ smooth, fluid movements, makes the muscles more (13) _____ and bones (14) _____. (15) _____, the effects are similar to those of an (16) _____ aerobic workout. (17)° _____, there is no possibility of getting the joints (18) _____, which very often is a (19) _____ _____ you might have when running for exercise. Again, (20) _____ cycling (21) _____ the heart and lungs, the aging process is being (22) _____ _____.

2a. However, as with any new physical endeavour, there is a caveat attached to cycling. While anyone who can balance a bike and pedal can take up cycling, no one is ready for long, strenuous rides right at the start. If your idea of exercise has been stepping out on the porch and stooping over to pick up the morning paper, don't expect cycling to be easy on your body. In fact, as with any exercise program, the first thing you should do is to check with your doctor before starting, especially if your are over 35. (Par. 2)

b. (23) _____ all the benefits explained above, there
are initial (24) _____ (25) _____ in cycling,
(26) _____ in any new physical (27) _____ .
(28) _____ _____ anybody who can balance
a bike and pedal might (29) _____ _____ to
ride a bicycle, not (30) _____ can (31) _____
_____ with long rides. (32) _____
_____ your idea of exercise so far has been just to
(33) _____ out to the porch and (34) _____
_____ to pick up the morning paper, cycling is going to
be (35) _____ for your body. (36) _____

_____ _____ _____ _____ ,
those who are over thirty-five, are (37) _____
_____ to take (38) _____ care of their health by
(39) _____ their doctors (40) _____
_____ beginning any exercise program. This rule applies
to cycling, too.

3a. But despite the excitement of racing, the reason most of us ride is
the sheer pleasure of wheeling through neighborhoods and along
country roads. A bike permits us to escape everyday stresses and
strains for a while : it is not competition that interests us so much as
contemplation. (Par. 13)

b. (41) _____ _____ _____
_____ _____ that participating in a cycling
(42) _____ is very (43) _____ , what
(44) _____ most of us who go cycling is the
(45) _____ pleasure of wheeling through neighborhoods
and along country roads. A bike (46) _____ us the oppor-

tunity to (47) _____ _____ _____ the

(48) _____ and (49) _____ of daily life, at least

for a while. In (50) °_____ words, we are

(51) _____ (52) _____ in contemplation than in

competition.

Part 6: SUPPLEMENTARY READINGS

PREREADING ACTIVITIES

Discuss the following in your group:

1. Have you ever tried to sell a used car, bike, computer, etc.?
2. Did you get the price you asked for?
3. What have you learned from the selling procedures you went through?
4. If you did it over again, what changes would you make in your selling procedures?

Supplementary Reading 1: THE BEST WAY TO SELL YOUR CAR

Getting Top Dollar Can Be Easier than You Think

1. Each year, 15 to 20 million used cars change hands — a rate almost double that of new cars. The next time you buy a new car, you may choose to sell one as well. To obtain the greatest possible return on your investment, here's what you'll want to do.

2. Prepping. Most shoppers believe a used car that *looks* good probably *is* good. Your first step should be a good wash and wax. Clean the interior,

---

Ron Janus, "The Best Way to Sell Your Car." Reprinted with permission from the December 1988 *Reader's Digest.* Condensed from *Consumers Digest* (May / June 1988).

shampooing the carpeting and upholstery. Remove items that might rattle or look untidy. Tighten loose trim.

3. For a late-model or vintage auto, consider a professional "detail" job. This includes cotton-swabbing tiny nooks and crannies, touching up paint, and giving tires and plastic surfaces a polymer shine. The $50-to-$150 investment will likely spark more interest in your car. Look in the phone book under "automotive detailing" or ask a local garage, car wash or new-car dealer.

4. Be sure to have an oil change, fluid checks, grease job and tune-up. These reflect a well-cared-for automobile. Obviously, a flat tire or a broken starter must be repaired, but *major* work should be avoided — it isn't cost-effective. One caveat : safety hazards (bad brakes, for example) *should* be repaired. If they aren't, make sure you mention any such areas of concern to the purchaser.

5. By selling a car before it is three years old or has not been driven more than 40,000 miles, you often avoid replacing wear-and-tear items such as tires and brakes. When cars are six years old or reach 70,000 miles, repair costs begin to rise.

6. Pricing. To determine your automobile's value, first check one of the publications that track used-car prices. Ask your library or inquire at the loan department of a bank.

7. Each car is unique, so consider other factors. A car's value *increases* if it's loaded with extras (air conditioning, cassette stereo, sun roof, power windows), if paint and interior are in top condition, or if mechanical parts have been unusually well-maintained.

8. A car's actual value is set by local market conditions. Ask two or three new-car dealers what they would give for your car in an outright sale. Add as much as $1500 (on a late model) to determine your asking price — this represents the dealer's markup.

9. Another way to gauge the market is to review the classified ads in your newspaper. Throw out the highest and lowest prices — the remaining figures will give you a good idea.

10. Although some sellers put a fair price on their car and won't negotiate, it is usually wiser to leave room for haggling. For a reasonable cushion, add five percent to your asking price, or a couple of hundred dollars — whichever is more.

11. The Ad. When writing a newspaper ad, include the most essential information : make, model, year, body style (two-door, hatchback), transmission (automatic or manual), mileage, condition, price and phone number.

12. Some people tend to be coy — omitting mileage, for example, in the hope they can "sell" a prospect. ("It was all highway driving.") On balance, however, leaving out basic information discourages inquiries.

13. Include appealing descriptives such as "attractive two-tone blue" or "soft chocolate-brown leather upholstery." Phrases like "garage kept" and "one owner" can also be effective. But avoid expressions ("extra clean") and pricing ($5799) that suggest you are a dealer.

14. Rrrring! Post a note pad near the phone. Ask for the name and number of any interested party, in case your first buyer backs out.

15. Be honest. A flaw will have less impact if the buyer is informed ahead of time. No one expects a used car to be perfect, but most expect to be dealt with truthfully.

16. Don't be shy about your auto's good points, but don't appear anxious. If you've taken excellent care of your car, let the buyer know; maintenance records make a positive impression. If major repairs have been done, don't lie about them.

17. If the customer wants a test drive, ask to see a driver's license, and go along, or hold the keys to the buyer's car as security. In most cases when you permit someone else to drive your car, you and your insurance company are liable for accidents.

18. Occasionally, a potential buyer will want the car inspected by a mechanic. You may deny the request if you think you can sell the car without an inspection. If you decide to allow it, request a nominal deposit, refundable if the car doesn't check out. *Always* accompany the prospect on an inspection.

19. Sold! Once you have agreed on a price, insist on a nonrefundable deposit against the purchase price; $50 should be sufficient to hold the car for a few days. If the buyer needs more time (to secure financing, for example), require a larger deposit. Always give the buyer a receipt describing the car and giving the vehicle identification number, deposit, balance due and transaction date, signed by both parties.

20. Inform the buyer that the balance should be paid in cash or by certified check or money order. While a personal check may suffice for a small deposit, *never* accept one as final payment. Before money changes hands, write out a bill of sale stating that you are selling the car "as is, with no express or implied warranties." Make a copy for your files, signed by the buyer.

21. While states vary, title-transfer procedures usually require the seller to fill in the new owner's name, record the mileage and sign the back of the title. If the car was financed, you should find out the lender's procedure for paying off the loan and obtaining the title.

22. You'll want to check with your department of motor vehicles about license plates — some states allow their transfer, others do not. If required, also notify the department of motor vehicles that the car has been sold, freeing you from liability. And notify your insurance agent to receive a refund on the unused portion of your policy.

23. With the right preparation, selling your car can be a relatively pleasant experience: shine it up, price it right and watch the new owner happily drive it away.

POSTREADING ACTIVITIES

Discuss the following in your group:

1. What new information did you receive from your reading?
2. Do you think the information is useful? How?
3. Do you think the author left out any step involved in the process of selling a used car? Is there any step to be deleted? Give your reasons.

PREREADING ACTIVITIES

Discuss the following in your group:

1. Locate the following on the map:

    *   The Grand Canyon
    *   Lake Mead
    *   The Colorado River
    *   Boulder Dam

2. What is the Grand Canyon known for?
3. From reading the title below, what do you expect the writer to talk about?

Supplementary Reading 2: ADVENTURE ON THE COLORADO

1. One of the major tourist attractions of the United States is the Grand Canyon of the Colorado River. Every year thousands of visitors come to gaze into its awesome purple depths from vantage points along the road at the rim of the canyon or from the safety of a hotel window. Some of the more daring may venture down into it on mule back for a closer view. At the bottom is the Colorado River, considered by some to be the roughest in the world to navigate. To test the truth of this assertion and to see the most awesome aspects of the canyon, you should take a three-week trip down the river in a small boat that carries only an oarsman–guide and one or two other persons.

2. At first you do not realize how exciting it is to make the trip. You start where the river is calm some miles upstream from the canyon. Here the boat floats slowly along on clear water between limestone cliffs some 2,000 feet high. Farther down the river the view changes as the boat drifts between rock walls on which abstract sculpture has been produced by the force of the water against the rocks over a period of two billion years. Above these walls rise high promontories green with pine.

3.   As the boat glides on, you become conscious of a distant roar. The river narrows and suddenly you find yourself in turbulent water, its churning dark green crest edged in foam. Your boat drops dizzily. You are going through the first of the rapids. Before you have time to recover, you plunge through another series of rapids, then another. Caught in a whirlpool, the boat spins out of control, stands straight up on its stern, then shoots downward into a hole. You recall what the guide has told you — that the current of the river is so strong in some places that it can peel a man like a banana, stripping off his pants, belt, shirt, and shoes in a few minutes. Unbelievably, the boat rights itself.

4.   The river channel becomes even narrower. Now the boat is nearly crushed as it shoots down almost perpendicularly into seething water through a passageway between boulders. The noise makes your chest vibrate like a drum. You agree with those who say that few natural sounds on the planet are more intimidating than the thunder of water. Then it happens. The boat upsets, and you find yourself buffeted about in a churning maelstrom. At first it may be diffi-

cult for you to catch your breath, and you may wonder if it is possible to keep from being sucked under. Somehow your life jacket keeps you afloat, and the guide pulls you back into the boat, which is built to be unsinkable and which in a moment head on down the river.

5. As you go the rest of the 285 miles down the canyon, you will have many more adventures such as this. The river makes a 2,000-foot drop in the course of your journey, and you will negotiate 150 rapids. At night the guide will find a flat, sandy spot big enough for a campsite. He will build a fire and later, after a warm meal, you will crawl into your sleeping bag too exhausted to stay awake.

6. Eventually, the boat finds safer going. There are fewer boulders in the water, the rapids become less treacherous, and you finally float into Lake Mead, which is formed by Boulder Dam. The river will go on to the West Coast, but your boat trip is over. You have survived the dramatic run through the canyon, and the thrill will remain. Perhaps, like others, you will be so delighted with the trip that you will want to experience again the adventure of the water and the beauty of the canyon.

POSTREADING ACTIVITIES

Discuss the following in your group:

1. Did the writer talk about what you had expected from the title? How different is the content from what you expected?
2. After reading the essay do you feel you would like to go on the same adventurous trip? Why? Why not?
3. Have you had any similar adventurous trip? How different was it from that described in this essay?
4. How does the information given in this essay apply to you? Explain.

PREREADING ACTIVITIES

1. Do you think a "babbling" baby is verbally communicating? How? Why or why not?
2. How do you define "language?"
3. At what age do you think children start to express themselves in "language"?
4. How do you think pre-school children learn language?
5. What role does the mother play in children's language development?
6. What influence do a child's playmates have in his or her development of language?

Supplementary Reading 3: THE DEVELOPMENT OF LANGUAGE IN CHILDREN

1. Children acquire language in a fairly regular and systematic fashion. By the age of five, normal children complete the process of language acquisition and are able to verbally express themselves. To achieve this verbal mastery, children usually pass through four stages, namely, babbling, holophrastic, telegraphic, and recursive.

2. The babbling stage, also called the "prelinguistic" phase, may last from four to twelve months of an infant's growth. At this stage, infants experiment with all the different sounds the vocal cords are capable of producing, not just the ones in their parents' language. These sounds are functional in the sense that they are made in response to stimuli like hunger, irritation from diapers, fear, and the like. Mothers can contextually put meanings into these sounds. Contact with adult speakers during this period may shape their sounds, as they try to imitate the sounds they hear. By the end of this babbling period, most infants can repeat whatever language sounds are clearly spoken to them. Also, by this time, they will begin to select out and practice the sounds that belong to their language and drop those that do not.

3. The second stage, the holophrastic (meaning "whole phrase," or "whole concept") stage, may sometimes begin as early as eight months or as late as eighteen months. At this period the children begin to utter "one-word sentences" — single words that stand for a whole concept or sentence. Examples of such words are: "mama," meaning, "Mama is holding me now," "papa," meaning "Papa is coming" (pointing to him). Tone and pitch, rising and falling notes, together with loudness of voice, will express different concepts and emotions. For example, "mama," said in a soft tone might mean "Come here," but "mama" said in a loud voice might mean, "Mama, I am angry with you." Many children at this stage may also make generalizations. For example, any adult man may be called "papa." Anything round may be called "ball." This means they are learning to relate concepts (for example, roundness) to words. Also, when they hear any noise associated with the kitchen (for example, dishes being washed), they may say, "mama," "nanny," and so on. The second stage usually ends at the age of two.

4. At the third stage, namely the telegraphic stage, children make the progression from one-word sentences to telegraphic sentences — with pronouns, conjunctions, and articles left out (hence the name "telegraphic"). Examples are: "cookie gone," "mama come," "give baby," "see cookie." Also, at this

---

Adapted from Madelon Heatherington, *How Language Works* (Cambridge, Mass.: Winthrop, 1980), 16–20.

stage many children start experimenting with tense forms. Examples are: "mama going," "baby crying." They may make past tense verb forms, adding "-d's" to even irregular verbs, making sentences like "mama goed," "papa comed." The telegraphic stage may continue until the age of three.

5. The last stage, namely, the recursive, begins at around three years old and usually continues until the children enter school. At this stage they begin to understand meanings expressed by different grammatical structures. For example, a five-year-old child is able to understand the similarity involved in the sentences: "The dinner was cooked by papa today," and "Papa cooked the dinner today." Also, they learn to manipulate the language. For example, a girl might say, "Give that doll to me," when she wants to emphasize the recipient (her, not her brother), and "Give me the ball," when she wants to emphasize the object (the doll, not the ball.)

6. Everything children learn about language after the age of five is nothing but a modification of what they have learned up until that age and nothing new.

POSTREADING ACTIVITIES

1. Compare your background knowledge about the development of language in children to what you gained from reading this essay.
2. Do you think the information will help you in your future experience with children? How?

Part 7: EXPOSITORY WRITING

THE PROCESS ESSAY

A process is a continued set of actions or steps leading to a definitely planned result. A process essay describes these actions or steps. The writer of a process essay may have two purposes: (1) giving directions to the readers so that they can recreate the steps to reach the same end result as the writer describes, and (2) to inform the readers so that they get an idea of the different steps. The readers may or may not recreate these steps. Thus there are two types of process essay: (1) directional and (2) explanatory. Whatever the purpose may be, the pattern of organization is the same.

The first thing to make sure of is the audience. Even though awareness of the audience is very important in writing any kind of expository essay, the writer of a process essay has to be especially careful about the audience, because the decision what details to include or exclude depends on the kind of audience the essay will have. For example, suppose you are writing on "How to Make Pizza." If your audience does not have any idea of what pizza is, you will have to begin by explaining it. Similarly, suppose you are writing on "How to Bargain for a Used Car." If you are addressing novices who do not know anything about the car except that it is a vehicle for travel, you will have to include an explanation of the major parts of a car. However, it is reasonable to assume that the readers have some general idea about the topic. For example, most Westerners know what pizza is ; most adults are knowledgeable about the major parts of a car. But it cannot be assumed that everybody knows all the different steps involved in making pizza and in dealing with used car dealers.

A strictly chronological or spatial order should be followed throughout the development of the essay. Remember, you are writing about something that happened over time or will happen if the readers follow the directions you give. Therefore, steps should be ordered sequentially and in natural order. Otherwise, your readers will be confused.

The steps should also be all-inclusive — without leaving out any required step. This is especially important when you are writing a directional process essay, because if the process steps you explain are not complete, they won't produce the desired end result.

The Organization of a Process Essay

The Introduction

As in any introduction of an expository essay, narrow down your topic from the general to the specific — to something that is close to the reader in time and space, to some recent development related to the topic. For example, suppose you are writing about how the human brain works ; you can mention in the introduction how advanced technology like the microprocessor and micro chips has turned people's interest to study the working of their own brain.

End the introduction with the thesis statement, giving the major steps involved in the process of the activity, happening, or event. Try to put it in encouraging (discouraging, if that is your purpose) terms so that the readers feel invited to read your essay. Example : "Bargaining for a used car may consume a great deal of your time and energy. However, if you follow the steps given below, you will get the maximum satisfaction from your buy."

Developmental Paragraphs

The number of the developmental paragraphs depends on the number of steps involved in the process. At least one paragraph should be devoted to each major step. Each major step should be broken down into individual steps. Use appropriate transition words (for example, *first, second, next, finally,* etc.) to relate the steps to one another. Any new, technical, or unfamiliar terms, tools, or equipment should be explained clearly. Also, the readers should be warned against any difficulty they might have in understanding or recreating any step in the process. For example, suppose you are writing a process essay on "How to Bargain for a New Car." Readers should be alerted against salesmen who might try to talk buyers into cars in stock, which may have more options than they want. Options can make up 25 to 30 percent of the list price of many U.S. cars, so buyers should be sure they really want to pay for a radio with "seek and scan," a sun roof, or six-way power seats.

The Conclusion

The conclusion may be used to emphasize the end result of the process or to convince the reader of the final product they may expect to get, if they follow all the steps described.

Application

Bearing in mind the discussion above on how to write a process essay, critically examine the four readings in this chapter and discuss the following in your group :

1. How many paragraphs does the writer use in "Starting to Cycle" for introduction ?
2. What is the thesis statement ? Does it invite you to read on and gain information ? How and why ?
3. What purpose do the last sentence in Par. 2 and the second sentence in Par. 3 serve in describing the process ?
4. How many major steps are involved ? What are they ?
5. Is each step described clearly ? Will you be able to recreate the steps without being confused ? How or why ?
6. What is the end result to which the writer is drawing the readers' attention ?
7. Classify the four essays into directional and instructional. Explain the basis of your classification. (Review Chapter 5, pp. 127–128 on classification.)

8. How does the end result of the steps involved in "Starting to Cycle" compare with that of "Adventure on the Colorado ?" Do the writers aim at having the readers recreate the steps ? Explain.

Writing Assignment: (Reinforcement and Review)

1. Make up outlines of the four essays in this chapter. (Review pp. 106–109 for outlining.)
2. Classify the four readings in this chapter and write an essay comparing and contrasting each group in organization and structure. (Review Chapter 5, p. 128 for classification and Chapter 6, for comparison and contrast.)

ESSAY: PROCESS, REVISION

In Chapter 5, you were told how to write the first draft of your essay. Remember, you were told that when you write the first draft you should not worry about "how you write," but should pay attention to "what you write." The reason, as you have already learned, is that the primary purpose of your writing is communication of your ideas. However, these ideas should be presented clearly and systematically. Otherwise, you won't gain the readers' attention.

Not even professional and experienced writers make the first draft of their writing the final draft. They revise it over and over, until they make sure that everything goes where it belongs.

What do they actually do when they revise ? Revision involves :

- Reading your writing piece aloud to yourself (better, to somebody else), critically analyzing it, *adding* more statements, examples, data, or statistics (if any idea presented needs more explanation for clarity).
- *Deleting* unnecessary details which do not relate to the main topic and the subtopics in any of the developmental paragraphs.
- *Reorganizing* or *rearranging* paragraphs or sentences to see that everything goes in the right place. Always bear in mind, you are writing for an audience. In your case, your audience may be your professor, but he or she is an artificially created audience, since you are actually being trained to write for a larger audience. The ideas presented may be clear in your head, but when written down, they may not be clear to your readers. Therefore, the best way to see that your audience gets your message the way you want is to have a classmate or friend read your writing piece. If you are writing your essay out of class, you will have ample time to find somebody more experienced in writing than you are and get feedback from him or her. However,

when you are writing an in-class essay, you do not have this opportunity. Therefore, your best bet is to have a classmate of yours read it. Never hand in an essay to your professor unless at least one of your classmates has read it and you make sure that your ideas are clear to at least this reader.

The following guidelines may help your peer reader read your essay critically and give you helpful feedback. These guidelines will also help you to be a peer reader for somebody else.

Guidelines for Peer Feedback to Student Compositions

1. CONTENT/IDEAS

1. Can you find the main idea? Write it down in one sentence and discuss it with the writer. In case you can't find the main idea, or the writer disagrees with your summarization of the main idea, there is probably a communication problem. Either you are not reading it properly, or the writer is not communicating to you.
2. Have you learned anything new from this writing piece? Write down this new information and discuss it with the writer.
3. Does the vocabulary used aptly express the ideas presented?

2. ORGANIZATION AND DEVELOPMENT

1. Has the writer organized all his or her ideas systematically so that when you read the piece, they are clear to you? If the ideas are confusing to you, what do you think are the reasons?
2. Are all the ideas well developed or are there any places in the essay where you need more information? Point this out to the writer.
3. Does the writer move smoothly from one point to the other so that you do not have to go back and forth in your reading to check and double-check what the writer is talking about?
4. Are the ideas presented in an interesting way so that you would like to read the essay again for information or enjoyment (not for feedback!)?

3. PARAGRAPH DEVELOPMENT AND ESSAY STRUCTURE

A. Introduction
1. Does the essay have an introduction?
2. Does the introduction clearly introduce the topic so that you get a clear idea of what the writer is going to talk about in successive paragraphs? (This means the reader should be able to get a clear idea of what the whole essay is about without reading the other paragraphs.)

3. Is the introduction developed from the general to the specific?
4. Does the introduction end with a thesis statement? (The thesis statement may be placed in the beginning, middle, or end of the introductory paragraph. However, student writers are advised to put it at the end.)
5. Does this thesis statement give you a clear idea of the main points to be developed in the developmental paragraphs?

B. Developmental Paragraphs

1. Does each developmental paragraph begin with a topic sentence? (Professional and experienced writers may put the topic sentence in the middle of the paragraph. However, until students get more advanced in writing, they should prefer the initial position.)
2. Does the topic sentence contain at least one controlling idea?
3. Is this controlling idea developed with ample supporting details, examples, facts, statistics, or data?
4. Are all these supporting details clearly related to the controlling idea (paragraph unity/cohesion)? If you find any sentences not directly related to the topic sentence, write them down and discuss them with the writer.
5. Does the writer use appropriate transition words to relate one sentence to the other (coherence)?
6. Does each paragraph relate to the others and to the main topic presented in the introductory paragraph so that the whole essay reads as one whole piece?
7. Is there any paragraph that does not relate to the main idea? If there is, discuss it with the writer.
8. Is there any paragraph or sentence that is out of order (not following a logical, chronological, or spatial order) and which needs to be reorganized? If you find any, draw the writer's attention to it.

C. Conclusion

1. Does the writer end the essay with a conclusion?
2. Does the conclusion logically follow the ideas expressed in the essay and exclude new information or ideas?
3. Is the conclusion given in a convincing manner, which helps you get a summarized version of the essay to store in your brain for easy recall later on?

4. FINAL EVALUATION

1. Tell the writer what you have learned from reading his or her essay. If you haven't learned anything new or haven't learned something (you

knew already) in a different way, your reading time has been wasted and the writer has failed to communicate her/his ideas.
2. What grade would you give the writer for content, organization, and development?

When once you get back your essay from your peer reader you should read it over again together with the written feedback the peer reader has given and whatever notes you made during the discussion with him or her. Make marginal notes wherever changes are needed.

After rereading the essay critically, the next step is to rewrite it with necessary revisions. In revising, you will have to incorporate the peer reader's feedback and your own notes. Revision involves, DELETING unnecessary sentences or paragraphs, ADDING more sentences or paragraphs wherever more details are needed for better understanding by the reader and REORGANIZING sentences or paragraphs to enable the reader to read smoothly. Remember: DELETING, ADDING, REORGANIZING (DARe).

When once you rewrite by DARe, you will have your second draft. Depending on your availability of time, you can repeat the processes of peer reading and revision several times. As mentioned earlier, even experienced writers revise their writing several times. If peers are not available, read the revised version over yourself with the "Guidelines for Peer Reading" in mind, but make sure that there is at least one day between the time you rewrite the essay and the time you reread the revised draft. Make notes wherever you need DARe, and incorporate these changes in your revised draft.

Even the revised draft is not the final draft. Still more work is needed, which you will learn about in the next chapter.

WRITING ACTIVITIES

Reaction Journal

Write in your journal:

- Which of the articles in the chapter gives information most applicable to your life outside the college campus
- How this article compares to another one in the book, and which of the two you prefer
- If there is any information in any of the articles the relevance of which you question
- Which of the articles you did not want to finish reading, but did finish anyway, just because it has been assigned to you by your instructor

- Which of the articles does not relate to you because the information is so remote and unrelated to your life and experience

Learning Log

Write in your learning log:

- What you already knew about the topics discussed in the reading passages
- What you already knew about the grammar, sentence structure, and vocabulary discussions in the chapter
- All the new things you learned from the chapter
- Three academic and three real-life situations where you can apply this new learning
- Five to ten new words you learned, which you feel comfortable using in your writing
- What more you want to know about the topics discussed in the reading passages

Writing Assignment

Overview

Write an essay explaining a skill which you have mastered and which one of your classmates would like to learn.

Procedure

IN-CLASS GROUP ACTIVITY

Share with your group members some of the skills (technical or manual) you have (for example, using a word processor, assembling a computer or a radio, installing a new appliance, knitting a sweater, making a ceramic flower vase, etc.) and find which one they are interested in learning.

OUT-OF-CLASS WRITING

1. Reflect on how you perform this activity. Take as much time as you need to fill your brain with ideas. (Don't fall asleep!)
2. Free-write whatever comes to your mind about how you do this.
3. Read aloud to yourself the written piece.
4. Discard all unrelated information. (For example, if you wrote how you enjoy your skill, it does not belong in the essay you are going to write.)

5. Organize the steps in chronological sequence. (This is your outline.)
6. Read the outline aloud to yourself.
7. Read the free-written piece once again to find explanations or examples for each step in the performance of the activity.
8. Pick whatever is relevant to each step and add more if needed.
9. Read the piece aloud to check if you have enough explanations.
10. Add an introduction to the piece.
11. Write the developmental paragraphs, explaining each step.
12. End with a conclusion.
13. Using the formula DARe (delete, add, reorganize), make revisions on the organization of information.
14. Read the whole piece aloud to yourself once again and correct the errors on vocabulary, grammar, and sentence structure.
15. Rewrite the piece if needed.

IN-CLASS PEER FEEDBACK

Have your classmate to whom you are trying to teach the skill read the paper and check if all the steps are clearly explained and if he or she feels comfortable to try out the skill after reading the paper. If any step is unclear or confusing to him or her that means you need to revise that part. Discuss this problem area with your friend and make changes or corrections until everything is clearly expressed.

OUT-OF CLASS WRITING

Rewrite the entire piece, with all the changes or corrections incorporated. The final draft is the one you will hand in to your instructor.

Alternate Writing Assignment

Write an essay on one of the following:

- How to compete in a student election
- How to find an affordable apartment in the city/town where you live
- How to arrange for and enjoy a visit to a tourist attraction in your hometown
- The mummification process
- The development of the automobile or computer industry
- The development of space travel

(You may use your reading, research, or experience as sources for writing this essay.)

CHAPTER · 8

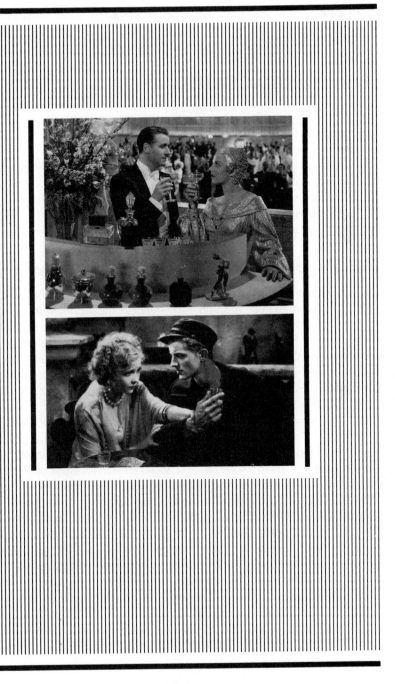

Part 1: READING

PREREADING ACTIVITIES

Discuss the following in your group:

1. How do you define alcoholism?
2. Do you drink? Why or why not?
3. What percentage of Americans do you think are heavy drinkers?
4. Do you consider drinking a social problem? Why or why not?
5. What are some of the negative effects of heavy drinking?
6. Why do you think people in general want to drink?
7. Can you think of any positive effects of drinking? What are they?

Reading: ALCOHOL AND AMERICAN LIFE

1. In defining the impact of alcohol on American life, it is tempting to begin with alcoholism and to go through the litany of its tragic consequences — birth defects, drunk driving, dereliction, deaths from cirrhosis, heartbreaking scenes in family court. Few of us, in fact, ever hit rock bottom in this fashion. Alcoholism is possibly the smallest societal problem arising from drinking. According to government statistics, adult Americans drank 2.73 gallons of pure alcohol per capita in 1982, but where drinking is concerned, "per capita" does not tell the whole story. For example, about one-third of the population never drinks alcohol, and another third has only one or two drinks a week. Moreover, 10% of the population consumes over half of all the wine, beer, and spirits sold.

2. "Drinking is ... heavily concentrated in a relatively small part of the population but contributes to a wide range of social and health problems for the society, and lowers materially the quality of life for communities across the country," writes Dr. Lawrence Wallack of the School of Public Health at the University of California, Berkeley, and the Prevention Research Center, also in Berkeley. The reduced quality of life he speaks of includes immeasurable emotional and psychological costs: the damage done to family life, for example, by a mother drinking secretly but chronically, by long-term marital quarrels over a husband's drinking habits, or by the devastating effects of a teenager's death in an alcohol-related car crash. But out-and-out alcoholism is not the only factor in much of the grief caused by drinking, and alcohol problems are not simply a matter of the drunk versus the rest of us.

Why Americans Drink

3. Alcohol has always been part of American life: "the good creature of God," colonial Americans called it. (They and their descendants also called it "demon rum.") Surprisingly, Americans today drink substantially less — about a third less — than their forebears. The day is long past when beer or whiskey was healthier to drink than well water, but modern drinkers of course share many motives with those of the past — the sociability of drinking, the brief but vivid sense of relaxation a drink can bring, the wish to be part of a special occasion. And quite apart from such psychological and personal needs, potent social and economic influences operate.

4. One reason Americans drink is that it is so easy. Alcoholic beverages are sold everywhere — on trains, boats, and airplanes, in liquor stores and bars on almost every streetcorner. Restaurants that serve an upscale clientele, particularly an expense-account crowd, must have a bar and a wine list in order to stay in business.

5. Another reason Americans drink is that alcoholic beverages are comparatively cheap. The relative cost of alcohol has declined substantially in the last 20 years. Since 1967 the cost of nonalcoholic beverages has increased four times over, and the cost of all consumer goods has almost tripled, but the cost of alcohol has not even doubled. This is because the excise tax on alcohol is not indexed to inflation, and Congress has not raised the tax since 1951. The price of alcoholic beverages is further reduced by the income tax law. Almost one-fifth of alcoholic drinks — over $10 billion worth annually — are sold for purposes of business entertainment, and thus are tax deductible.

6. And finally, another factor in the way Americans think about and use alchohol is the communications industry — advertising, television, and movies. In *Dallas, Dynasty,* and scores of other shows, rich, powerful, exciting people always drink and apparently pay few penalties. Movies, too, on television and in movie theaters, routinely depict drinking as part of the smart life-style: "Shaken, not stirred," says the invincible James Bond, ordering vodka martinis. Who does not yearn to exhibit such savoir faire?

7. In commercials as well as in print advertising, alcoholic beverages are inevitably depicted as part of affluence, good fellowship, and love. Real men may or may not eat quiche, but they do drink. For women, drinking is sold as a sign of sophistication and sexiness. "The civilized way to test the waters," proclaims one ad showing a bikini-clad beauty, brandy snifter in hand, dipping her toe into a swimming pool as her male companion watches. Given the media barrage glamorizing the use of alcohol, the surprise is not that some Americans drink too much, but that so many are moderate drinkers.

The High Cost of Drinking

8. The impact of alcohol on the nation's health and welfare is almost incalculable. According to the latest figures, alcohol causes or is associated with 200,000 deaths every year. These include deaths from alcohol-related diseases (such as cirrhosis of the liver, cancers of the mouth and larynx, chronic brain injury), traumatic events (including automobile crashes), and thousands of other injuries. Many of these deaths and injuries occur among the young. Alcohol-impaired driving is the leading cause of death and injury among those under 25 years of age (in 1984 an average of 9 teenagers were killed and more than 300 injured each day in alcohol-related car crashes). Alcohol contributes to falls in the home, house fires, and drownings. People who drink habitually are more likely to smoke and hence to doze off and start fires with unextinguished cigarettes. Half of the pedestrians killed on the streets are under the influence. Nor are the highways and the home the only places where trouble occurs. Lost work time due to drinking on the job and/or recovering from hangovers costs an estimated $7.9 billion annually.

9. The statistics compiled by various government agencies march inexorably onward, until the mind boggles and the huge sums of money lose their meaning. The Congressional Office of Technology Assessment currently estimates the total cost of alcohol use to the nation at $120 billion annually — medical costs, treatment, emergency service, and lost work time — money out of every taxpayer's pocket. But in this as in other mega-issues involving the health and happiness of millions of people, money is a feeble method for measuring the real price.

What Can Be Done

10. Nevertheless, amid all the bad news about alcohol, there is definitely some good, for the fact is Americans are drinking less alcohol — and lighter forms of it — these days. As a direct consequence of the nationwide campaign against drinking and driving, the number of accidents caused by intoxicated driving has decreased.

11. We may not be able to legislate an alcohol-free society. Nor is it necessary to aim for one : rather, our goal should be to alter our social habits enough to control the drinking that does the most damage to society and individuals. Since the problems are complex, solutions will also be complex.

POSTREADING ACTIVITIES

1. Why is alcohol called "demon rum" ?
2. Do you agree with the reasons the writer gives about the relationship between alcohol and American life ? Why or why not ?

3. How does drinking affect society?
4. Why do you think modern Americans drink much less than their ancestors?
5. Are the statistics given in Par. 5 currently applicable? (You may have to do some research to find the answer to this question.)
6. Do you agree with the author's statement: "Given the media barrage glamorizing the use of alcohol, the surprise is not that some Americans drink too much, but that so many are moderate drinkers." (Par. 7) Give reasons for your agreement/disagreement.
7. If you were the president of the United States, would you legislate an alcohol-free society? Why or why not?
8. Why do you think drunken driving is more prevalent among the young than among the old?
9. How does alcohol contribute to drownings and falls in the home?
10. Make some suggestions on how to solve some of the problems related to drinking.

Part 2: PUNCTUATION

QUOTATION MARKS

For Your Critical Thinking

1. What are the punctuation marks used in the following sentence? Why did the writer use these punctuation marks? If you wrote this sentence, would you use the same punctuation marks and in the same way as the writer does? Give your reasons.

S1. "Drinking ... is heavily concentrated in a relatively small part of the population but contributes to a wide range of social and health problems for the society, and lowers materially the quality of life for communities acrosss the country," writes Dr. Lawrence Wallack of the School of Public Health at the University of California, Berkeley, and the Prevention Research Center, also in Berkeley. (Par. 2)

2. Read the following sentences and compare and contrast them with reference to the use of punctuation marks.

    - The Professor said, "I won't accept late homework assignments."
    - "I won't accept late homework assignments from anybody," said the Professor in a very serious tone.
    - "Well," said some students, "we'll try our best."
    - "It's not a fair policy," said the students. "If we get sick, it's not our fault."
    - The professor continued, "I repeat. I won't accept late homework assignments from anybody, no mater what the reasons are."
    - "How ridiculous!" exclaimed the students.

Note

Quotation means repeating somebody's words exactly as they are. To indicate they are the exact words, the beginning and end of the quotation are marked by quotation marks ("...").

A comma goes before the beginning quotation marks if the quote is introduced by the reporting words like *he said.* The comma is placed before the end quotation marks, if the reporting words conclude the quotation. If the quotation is interrupted by the reporting words, commas should be placed before and after the reporting words.

If the reporting words interrupt sentences (not just words), put a comma before the reporting words and a semicolon or period after the reporting words.

No comma should be used if the quotation ends up with a question or exclamation mark.

ELLIPSIS PERIODS

Ellipsis periods are used to indicate the omission of words or sentences from a quotation. Put three periods (...) to indicate ellipsis in quotations. When an ellipsis comes at the end of a statement, put four periods (which include the end punctuation of the sentence).

Application

Bearing in mind the above discussion of punctuation marks, find examples of quotation marks and ellipsis periods in the reading, "Alcohol and American Life."

Part 3: VOCABULARY, WORD FORMS, AND IDIOMS

FILL-INS

Paragraph **b** in each of the following pairs is a paraphrase of **a**. Using synonyms and antonyms (which need not be exact), changing sentence structure, and changing word forms are some of the devices used in making the paraphrase.

Your task: Fill in the blanks with appropriate words or phrases. Each blank line indicates one word. The underlined words in the original may give you the clues. The asterisks in **b** tell you there are no clues provided in the original.

1a. The day is long past when beer or whiskey was healthier to drink than well water, but modern drinkers of course share many motives with those of the past — the sociability of drinking, the brief but vivid sense of relaxation a drink can bring, the wish to be part of a special occasion. And quite apart from such psychological and personal needs, potent social and economic influences operate. (Par. 3)

b. It was a long time (1) _____ when Americans (2)° _____ drinking beer or whiskey healthier than drinking well water. (3) _____, it is natural that many of the reasons that (4) _____ modern Americans to drink are almost the (5) _____ as those of their (6) _____. One such reason is that drinking on special occasions affords a (7)° _____ to (8) _____ and (9) _____. In addition to those psychological and personal needs, there are other (10) _____ social and economic factors (11) _____ in a very (12) _____ way.

2a. And <u>finally,</u> another <u>factor</u> in the way Americans <u>think about</u> and use alcohol is the communication industry — advertising, television, and movies. In *Dallas, Dynasty,* and <u>scores</u> of other shows, rich, powerful, exciting people always drink and <u>apparently</u> pay <u>few</u> penalties. Movies, too, on television and in the movie theaters, <u>routinely</u> <u>depict</u> drinking as part of the smart life-style. (Par. 6)

b. The (13) _____ (14) _____ that (15)° _____ Americans in their (16) _____ to and use of alcohol is the communication industry — advertising, television, and movies. (17)° _____ _____ , in *Dallas, Dynasty,* and (18) _____ other shows, rich, powerful, and exciting people always drink, and it (19) _____ they do not pay any penalties. Also, movies on television and in theaters (20) _____ (21) _____ drinking as part of the smart life-style.

3a. In commercials <u>as well as</u> in print advertising, alcoholic beverages are <u>invariably</u> <u>depicted</u> as part of <u>affluence,</u> good <u>fellowship,</u> and love. Real men may or may not eat quiche, <u>but</u> they do drink. For women, drinking is sold as a <u>sign</u> of <u>sophistication</u> and <u>sexiness.</u> (Par. 7)

b. In commercials (22) _____ print advertising, alcoholic beverages are (23) _____ (24) _____ as part of (25) _____ , good (26) _____ , and love. (27) _____ real men may or may not eat quiche, they all do drink. For women, drinking is sold as a (28) _____ of being (29) _____ and (30) _____ .

4a. The <u>impact</u> of alcohol on the nation's health and welfare is almost <u>incalculable</u>. According to the latest <u>figures</u>, alcohol <u>causes</u> or is <u>associated</u> with 200,000 deaths <u>every</u> year. These include deaths from alcohol-<u>related</u> diseases (such as cirrhosis of the liver, cancers of the mouth and larynx, chronic brain injury), <u>traumatic</u> events (including automobile <u>crashes</u>), and <u>thousands of</u> other injuries. <u>Many</u> of these deaths and injuries <u>occur</u> among the young. <u>Alcohol-impaired</u> driving is the <u>leading cause</u> of death and injury among those <u>under</u> 25 years <u>of age</u> (in 1984 an average of 9 teenagers were killed and more than 300 injured each day in alcohol-<u>related</u> car <u>crashes</u>). Alcohol <u>contributes</u> to falls in the home, house fires, and drownings. People who drink <u>habitually</u> are more <u>likely</u> to smoke and <u>hence</u> to <u>doze off</u> and <u>start</u> fires with <u>unextinguished</u> cigarettes. <u>Half</u> of the <u>pedestrians</u> killed on the streets are under the influence. <u>Nor are</u> the highways and the home the <u>only</u> places where trouble <u>occurs</u>. Lost work time due to drinking on the job and/or <u>recover</u>ing from hangovers costs an estimated $7.9 billion <u>annually</u>. (Par. 8)

b. The (31) _____ of alcohol on the nation's health and welfare is very difficult to (32) _____ . According to the most recent (33) _____ , about 200,000 deaths (34) _____ every year, (35) _____ among the young, (36)° _____ _____ _____ _____ problems (37) _____ _____ alcohol. These include diseases like cirrhosis of the liver, cancers of the mouth and larynx, chronic brain injury, as well as (38) _____ events such as automobile (39) _____ and (40) _____ other injuries. The (41) _____ (42) _____ for death among those who are

(43) _____ 25 years (44) _____ is

(45) _____ driving. Alcohol (46) _____ a major

role in such accidents as falls in the home, house fires, and drown-

ings. In all (47) _____, (48) _____ drinkers are

also smokers and for this (49) _____ it is

(50)° _____ that these "drinking smokers"

(51) _____ fires in the house when

they (52) _____ _____ unintentionally

without (53) _____ _____ their

cigarettes. (54) _____ _____

_____ of those who are killed while (55) _____

on the road are under alcoholic influence. Accidents are

(56) _____ limited (57) _____ to the high-

ways and homes. It is estimated that (58) _____

_____ the nation spends $7.9 billion to

(59) _____ _____ lost work time

(60) _____ _____ drinking on the job and/or

recovering from hangovers.

Part 4: SUPPLEMENTARY READINGS

PREREADING ACTIVITIES

1. What do you think is the average life span of Americans?
2. What is the average life span of people in the country in which you or your parents were born?

3. How old is the oldest of your relatives, friends, or acquaintances?
4. In your opinion when does old age begin? Explain the reasons for your opinion.
5. How long do you want to live? Give reasons for your choice.
6. At what age do you want to retire? Why? What do you want to do when you retire?
7. What are some of the advantages and disadvantages of a retired life?
8. What do you think is the secret of long life?

Supplementary Reading 1: LIVING A LONG LIFE

1. In the Caucasus region of the Soviet Union, nearly 50 out of every 100,000 people live to celebrate their 100th birthday, and many don't stop at 100! By comparison, in America only 3 people in 100,000 reach 100. But these Soviet old people aren't alone. The Pakistani Hunzas, who live high in the Himalaya mountains, and the Vilcabambans of the Andes Mountains in Ecuador seem to share the secret of long life too.

2. These peoples remain healthy in body and spirit despite the passage of time. While many older persons in industrial societies become weak and ill in their 60's and 70's, some Soviet Georgians, aged 110 and 140, work in the fields beside their great-great-grandchildren. Even the idea of aging is foreign to them. When asked, "At what age does youth end?" most of these old people had no answer. Several replied, "Well, perhaps at age 80." The very youngest estimate was age 60.

3. What accounts for this ability to survive to such old age, and to survive so well? First of all, hard physical work is a way of life for *all* of these long-lived peoples. They begin their long days of physical labor as children and never seem to stop. For example, Mr. Rustam Mamedov is 142 years of age. He remembers his life experiences: the Crimean War of 1854; the Turkish War of 1878; the Bolshevik Revolution in 1917. His wife is 116 years old. They have been married for 90 years. Mr. Mamedov has no intention of retiring from his life as a farmer. "Why? What else would I do?" he asks. Oh, he's slowed down a bit. Now he might quit for the day after 6 hours in the field instead of 10.

4. All these people get healthful rewards from the environment in which they work. They all come from mountainous regions. They live and work at elevations of 5,000 to 12,000 feet (1,660 to 4,000 meters) above sea level. The air has less oxygen and is pollution-free. This reduced-oxygen environment makes the heart and blood vessel system stronger.

Excerpted from Linda Markstein and Louise Hirasawa, *Expanding Reading Skills* (Rowley, Mass.: Newbury House, 1982), 29-30. Copyright © by Newbury House Publisher. Reprinted by permission of Harper & Row, Publishers, Inc.

5. Another factor that may contribute to the good health of these people is their isolation. To a great extent, they are separated from the pressures and worries of industrial society.

6. Inherited factors also play some role. Most of the longest-lived peoples had parents and grandparents who also reached very old ages. Good family genes may, therefore, be one factor in living longer.

7. Finally, although these three groups don't eat exactly the same foods, their diets are similar. The Hunzas, Vilcambans, and Soviets eat little animal meat. Their diets are full of fresh fruits, vegetables, nuts, grains, cheese, and milk. They never eat more food than their bodies need.

8. It is clear that isolation from urban pressures and pollution, clean mountain air, daily hard work, moderate diets, good genes, and a youthful approach to life all contribute to the health and remarkable long life of all these people.

POSTREADING ACTIVITIES

1. Why do you think that people in industrial countries have a shorter life than those in some agricultural regions?
2. What does a "youthful approach to life" mean?
3. Do you agree that a vegetarian diet is healthier than a nonvegetarian diet? Give your reasons.
4. After having read this essay, would you rather live on a farm than in a sophisticated town or city? Why or why not?
5. Why do people in industrial countries have more pressures than those in agrarian countries?

PREREADING ACTIVITIES

In mixed groups of men and women, discuss the following:

1. What is the minimum/maximum age for a man/woman to marry?
2. What is the ideal size of a family?
3. Do you think women are at a disadvantage in having a career-oriented life? How? Why?
4. Do you think a woman can be both a successful mother and a career woman? Give reasons for your answer.
5. Some people are of the opinion that pre-school children should get full attention from their mothers. These people do not endorse the idea of working mothers leaving their children with babysitters during the work day. What do you think about this? Give your reasons.

Supplementary Reading 2: THE CHANGING STATUS OF AMERICAN SOCIETY

1. By the middle of the 1970's it seemed clear that changes in behavior and attitudes among American women would continue to shape the social history of the country for the remainder of the 20th century. Although no single cause could be identified as decisive to the change, a constellation of social and economic forces had come together, each reinforcing the others, to create a total pattern that ensured an ongoing transformation of woman's place.

2. The birthrate continued to fall, each year setting a new record low. By 1975 the fertility rate of women 15 to 44 years old was only half of what it had been twenty years earlier.

3. This decline, in turn, coincided with a trend toward later marriages. By 1971, more than half of all women twenty years of age were single, in contrast to only one-third in 1960, and the number of unmarried women in the 20-to-24 age bracket had climbed from 28 percent in 1960 to 37 per cent a decade later.

4. Simultaneously, the greatest increase in the female labor force occurred among younger women of childbearing age. The proportion of women working in the 20-to-24-year-old age group increased from 50 per cent in 1964 to 61 per cent in 1973. Among college women in that age group the employment rate was 86 per cent. But the fastest rise of all took place among women with young children. From 1959 through 1974 the employment rate of mothers with children under three more than doubled, from 15 to 31 percent, and that for mothers of children three to five years old increased from 25 to 39 per cent.

5. Fourth, poll data as well as professional school applications suggested a new commitment on the part of women college graduates to carve out careers, and to view family life as only one part of their multiple interests. Between 1968 and 1980 the number of women college graduates was expected to increase by two-thirds (twice the rate of increase for men), providing a growing pool of potential career women.

6. Finally, the woman's movement continued to register a significant impact on the expressed values of young people, men as well as women, creating almost a cultural consensus that "equality" between the sexes was a good thing. A Roper poll which showed women supporting the movement toward equality also showed a majority of men endorsing change. Indeed, one survey of college students indicated that 86 per cent of men, as well as 92 per cent of women, believed fathers should spend as much time as mothers in bringing up their children.

From William H. Chafe, *Women and Equality : Changing Patterns in American Culture* (New York : Oxford University Press, 1977), 145-47. Copyright © by Oxford University Press. Reprinted by permission.

7. As each of these variables interacted with the others, they created a "multiplier effect," with shifting values and changing social and economic conditions building upon each other to produce new patterns of family and work life. By the mid-70's the shape of women's participation in the labor force had come close to matching that of men, and in some age groups, despite a lengthy recession, women's employment had already exceeded the Department of Labor's 1970 projections for the year 1990. Fewer children, a tendency toward later marriage, greater commitment to personal career fulfillment, and at least verbal acknowledgement of the value of equality, all appeared to have created a situation where radically different styles of male–female interaction were possible.

POSTREADING ACTIVITIES

1. Why did the writer give the title, "The Changing Status of American Society" to this essay? Does it mean that the structure of a society depends on the status of women? Defend your answer.
2. What are the advantages and disadvantages of getting married at a later age?
3. What are the advantages and disadvantages of being a working mother?

4. What does the writer mean by "at least verbal acknowledgement of the value of equality"? (Par. 7)
5. What are some of the "radically different styles of male–female interaction" the writer talks about? (Par. 7)
6. Find out from the Department of Labor what their projection is on the women's participation in the labor force for the year 2000.

PREREADING ACTIVITIES

1. How long do you watch TV everyday?
2. Do you think people should spend some time everyday watching TV? Why? Why not?
3. What advantages do you get by watching TV?
4. Why shouldn't children be allowed to watch TV for long hours?
5. What are some of the circumstances that lead children to spend long hours in front of the TV?

Supplementary Reading 3: TV VIEWING

1. "No parents in their right minds would invite a stranger into their home for three to four hours each day to teach their kids. Yet that is precisely what television, a powerful teaching medium, is doing." So says Dr. Victor C. Strasburger, director of adolescent medicine at Bridgeport (Conn.) Hospital and member of the task force on children and television of the American Academy of Pediatrics.

2. Ninety-six percent of American households have at least one television set, and more than half have two or more. In the last four decades, television has provided thousands of hours of entertainment and information at minimal expense for millions of viewers. In particular, public television and periodic specials on commercial television have had a considerable positive impact.

3. But in the view of Dr. Strasburger and others who have studied the issue, television is also having powerful effects on the health and minds of American children, effects that should prompt parents to think twice before they allow the intrusion of television to continue without some constructive input.

4. Children between the ages of 2 and 12 watch an average of 25 hours of television a week. By the time they graduate from high school, American children each will have spent 15,000 hours in front of a television set, compared with only 11,000 hours in the classroom.

5. In the course of their viewing, they will see perhaps 350,000 commercial messages, many for unhealthful food and other products that are not condu-

From Jane Brody, "Guidelines for Parents on Children's TV Viewing," *New York Times*, 21 January 1987. Copyright © by The New York Times Company. Reprinted by permission.

cive to health. The social messages are often no better : sex without affection or regard to the risk of pregnancy or disease ; frequent consumption of alcohol and drugs ; misrepresentations of women, minorities, and elderly and the handicapped ; unrealistically easy solutions to complex problems, and countless depictions to violence.

6. Recent studies have indicated that this barrage of televised messages can undermine children's health, resulting in obesity, lack of physical fitness, poor eating habits and behavioral problems. The passive nature of television viewing may also interfere with the development of imagination. And time spent in television viewing often detracts from reading and other active learning skills. This is especially so for children whose parents use television as an electronic babysitter or fail to limit what and how much their children watch.

Adverse Effects

7. Before the advent of television, children played outdoors with friends after school, and read and talked to their parents at mealtime. Today, many youngsters race home from school to catch their favorite television show, often a soap opera, sit-com, game show or cartoon. On Saturday mornings, instead of such activities as biking or playing baseball, televised cartoons are the leading entertainment.

8. A 1979-80 study of student achievement by the California State Department of Education found that the more television children watched, the poorer their school performance, even with differences in IQ, reading habits and homework time taken into account.

9. Television viewing has also been linked to increased between-meal snacking, the consumption of foods that are not nutritious and attempts to influence parental food purchases. A full 30 percent of commercials on programs for children are for foods, especially sugary breakfast cereals, candy, cakes, cookies and soft drinks.

10. A recent study by the New England Medical Center and the Harvard School of Public Health linked television viewing to the development of obesity in children 6 to 17 years old. Not only did fatter children tend to watch more television, but children who watched a lot of television were more likely to become obese as they reached adolescence.

11. Television viewing requires little more energy than sleeping, and it often supplants vigorous playtime. Children today are less fit than they were two decades ago. Children wedded to television may fail to develop athletic skills and learn to enjoy the type of physical activities necessary for long-lasting health.

12. The effect of repeated exposure to televised violence is still hotly debated, but more than 3,000 studies have linked it to increased aggression and violent behavior in children and adolescents. The exception was one long-term study that showed no lasting effect of television violence on aggressive behavior. At the least, the American Academy of Pediatrics said in a policy statement that such violence "promotes a proclivity to violence and a passive response to its practice."

13. In addition, children who watch a great deal of television (where violence occurs 10 times more often than in real life) regard the world as more violent than less frequent viewers, according to a study made at the University of Pennsylvania's Annenberg School of Communications.

14. Televised misrepresentations can give children a highly distorted view of life. For example, the elderly, who are seriously underrepresented, are often depicted as "silly, eccentric and sexually inactive," Dr. Strasburger noted in an article in *Contemporary Pediatrics*. "Sick, retarded, handicapped and fat people play small roles in the TV world ; men outnumber women by about three to one ; women's roles are minor compared to men's, with a comparative few working outside the home, and whites outnumber minorities disproportionately."

15. When minorities are shown, they are often depicted as stereotypes or the "bad guys." And while a majority of viewers are from blue-collar families, only a small percentage of the families on television shows are blue-collar, continues Dr. Strasburger.

16. Depictions of sex, and especially sex in casual relationships, have increased dramatically (the number of sexual references on television jumped nearly sevenfold between 1975 and 1979 alone, according to Dr. Strasburger).

17. Alcoholic beverages (often used as a problem solver, social lubricant and facilitator of scene changes on soap operas) are the most commonly consumed drinks on television, he says. And almost no one who gets into a car on television fastens a seat belt. About the only positive change in recent years has been the dramatic decline in cigarette smoking on television, to considerably less than what occurs in real life.

What Parents Can Do

18. Start by keeping a log of what and how much your children watch. View the programs yourself, and decide on their relative merits. Together, establish some reasonable rules, such as limits on viewing time or no television until homework assignments are done or none during meals. If a particularly desirable program would thus be missed, consider investing in a video-cassette recorder, and tape the show for later viewing. Each week, review the television listings with your children, and write down which programs each child can watch.

19. Dr. Patricia Greenfield suggests that parents help their children dissect commercials: "Point out that commercials are designed to sell by creating needs; question the methods used, and generally make commercials a subject for discussion, evaluation and questioning."

20. Dr. Greenfield, a professor of psychology at the University of California at Los Angeles, says that similar discussions should be held about programs. These talks can provide opportunities to discuss family values, distinguish between fantasy and reality and review the consequences of different courses of action.

POSTREADING ACTIVITIES

1. Make some suggestions for parents to control children's TV viewing.
2. Do you agree with the author's conclusions of the negative effects of TV watching? Give your reasons for agreement or disagreement.
3. Why do TV stations give so much importance to commercials?
4. What are some of the positive effects of commercials on children?
5. Suppose you want to start a TV station. What kinds of programs would you like to include? Give reasons for your choices.

PREREADING ACTIVITIES

1. How forced do you feel to compete in your present career as a student? Why do you have to compete?
2. Can you think of some professions or careers in which the pressure for competition is not felt as much as in some other fields? What are they? What are the reasons for this difference?
3. Why do you think politicians, institutions, or organizations compete with each other to be at the top?
4. Would you be satisfied with a mediocre kind of status or do you want to be at the top? Give reasons for your preference.
5. Do you think that industrialized societies are more competitive than agrarian societies? Why?

Supplementary Reading 4: THE COMPETITION COMPULSION

1. You've been thrust into the arena once again. The stakes are high, and you have no choice but to compete and win because losers don't count. You give it everything you have and more : The consequences of being second best are just too terrible to contemplate. But you put forth all your skill, and you've finally done it. The relief is immense ; the emotional high is wonderful. You're a winner. You've once again triumphed over your 8-year-old at checkers.

2. Let's face it. Competition is as American as apple pie and the Fourth of July. Winning is considered the major highway to the good life, free of economic worries and personal hardship. Despite looming obstacles and mountainous barriers, we persevere in the competitive world of our chosen life's work and push to the top.

From Bruce A. Baldwin, "The Competition Compulsion," *USAir Magazine,* (April 1990) : 28-25. Adapted from B. A. Baldwin, *It's All in Your Head : Lifestyle Management Strategies for Busy People !* (Wilmington, N.C. : Directions Dynamics, Inc., 1985). Reprinted by permission of Pace Communications, Inc., Greensboro, North Carolina. Dr. Baldwin is the director of Direction Dynamics.

3. It's certainly not bad to learn to compete even more effectively. In fact, competitive skills are a sound investment in your future. Millions of dollars each year are budgeted for learning these skills by individuals and corporations in order to get an edge on the competition. The object is to provide key personnel with the psychological and technical weaponry to get ahead. However, competition — like anything — can get out of hand. It can become all-consuming, reaching a point at which it is negative rather than positive. When you are unable to resolve any kind of conflict, become depressed over even the littlest of setbacks, worry excessively about rivals, or constantly seek praise from others, chances are you're in the throes of the Competition Compulsion.

4. Basically, the Competition Compulsion can be defined as a consistent and unquestioned need to aggressively compete and win in personally created win–lose contests with others, no matter what the situation and without regard for the appropriateness of the competitive interactions. As you can easily surmise, it's most difficult to really enjoy casual relationships, fun games, and an easy give-and-take with others when you are driven by the Competition Compulsion. Too many otherwise bright and savvy men and women never find out that, when you compete compulsively and must win to feel good about yourself, winning clearly becomes a losing proposition.

5. There is no single cause for compulsive competitiveness. Rather, a number of powerful psychological influences and reinforcements converge over a lifetime to create this personal and professional liability. Talented, achievement-oriented, and success-motivated individuals are especially vulnerable. It is ironic that while successful competition is of immense help in building a career, it backfires when carried too far because it interferes with enjoying the fruits of success once you get there. Here are four major determinant factors that together create the destructive and compulsive need to compete.

6. *The influence of innate dominance needs.* There is evidence of a biologically determined but socially manifested drive to become the dominant individual in a group. This deep need produces the motivation to compete to become the leader of the pack. Culturally, this survival-of-the-fittest competition is channeled into socially acceptable outlets for dominance combat. Beyond sports, the major arena for cultural competition is professional excellence, where the payoffs are economic rewards and power.

7. *The reinforcing effect of parental and peer modeling.* Parents are extremely important in shaping their children's perceptions of the world and their ways of interacting with it. Highly competitive parents often model a style of living and working characterized by constant comparisons, win-at-all-costs performance expectations, and evaluative remarks that are not lost on the children. Peer groups in academia and in the work world parallel these parental values to reinforce an intensely competitive mode of interacting that creates the Competition Compulsion.

8. *The constancy of external evaluation.* All individuals are evaluated on their performance throughout their entire life span. Judgments by parents, grades in school, and performance evaluations at work all provide you with positive or negative feedback as to how well you meet the expectations of others. Immersed since early childhood in an unremittingly evaluative environment that is highly performance-oriented, individuals develop an awareness of personal potential and high expectations for self that are internalized. The need to demonstrate competence by outdoing others is the result, and competition is the way to do it.

9. *The powerful performance–adequacy link.* An inadvertent but negative consequence of an evaluative performance environment is the development of a direct causal relationship between personal performance and self-esteem. In other words, the individual is only as personally adequate as his or her performance. If performance is up to par or beyond, then the individual feels personally adequate and acceptable. If performance is down, however, self-esteem drops correspondingly because it is perceived to be a direct negation of the self. Motivation is therefore fearfully directed to being a constant winner.

POSTREADING ACTIVITIES

1. What are some of the competitive skills? How many of these do you have? Do they help you to win your fights for success?
2. How does the author define Competition Compulsion? Do you agree with this definition? Why or why not?
3. Why does the author say that "when you compete compulsively and must win to feel good about yourself, winning clearly becomes a losing proposition"? (Par. 4)
4. Is it possible for us to avoid the destructive effects of Competition Compulsion the author talks about and still be successful? How? Why?
5. Do you think achievement-oriented people fail to enjoy life as much as those who are not achievement-oriented? Give your reasons.

Part 5: WRITING

THE EXPOSITORY ESSAY: CAUSE AND EFFECT

The rhetorical pattern used in the essays you have just read is different from the patterns used in the essays given in the previous chapters of this book. In Chapter 5 you learned how to analyze objects or persons by classifying them. In doing so, you were told that you were supposed to look for order and regularity among the members of the group classified. In analyzing things by comparing and contrasting them, you are again trying to find some order — by finding similarities and differences. In Chapter 7 you learned how to analyze the different steps involved in the process of producing something. The order of relationship here is sequential and if you follow this sequential order, you are sure to get the desired result.

However, in the essays in this chapter, the relationship is causal. Something or things caused something or things and this something resulted in something else. As in process analysis, here, too, we are saying that something produces something ; however, unlike process analysis, the different steps do not always have to be in the same order and the end result may not be the same in every case. In other words, the same cause does not have to produce the same effect, and the same effect need not have the same causes. For example, suppose a verbal fight between two neighbors resulted in a physical fight, which in turn resulted in the death of one of them. We know from our experience that all verbal fights do not end in death. We also know that all deaths are not the result of fights. It just happened unexpectedly, as it were.

Analyzing cause and effect is part of our daily life. You failed to reach the goal you wanted. You would like to know *why* you failed by analyzing the *cause(s)* that led to this failure (the *effect*) so that you learn from your failure. For example, you saw smoke coming out of your basement. You called the fire station. The firemen came and put out the fire. You would definitely want to find out *why* the fire occurred by analyzing the conditions or actions that *caused* it. You would do this because you want to avoid the conditions or actions that caused the fire (the *effect*) in the future. As another example, suppose your college board passed a resolution to cut the budgetary allotment for some student services. You would like to analyze the *effect* of this budget cut on the student organization(s) you belong to. Or suppose your department introduced a new curriculum. The curriculum committee would like to analyze the *effect(s)* of this new curriculum on student success.

Academically, cause and effect essays are required of you in all of your classes. Your history professor may ask you to analyze the causes of World Wars 1 and 2. Your chemistry professor may ask you to analyze the effects of Chernobyl on the body chemistry of the victims. Your social science professor may ask you to analyze the effect of tax raises on middle class families.

Cause/effect analysis is a required skill for successful careers, too. For example, to diagnose a disease, a medical doctor has to analyze the causes that result in the symptoms, which, of course, are the results of the disease. A detective has to analyze systematically the reasons that caused the murder before writing down the final report and making conclusions.

In short, cause/effect analysis is an important skill to learn. Writing a cause/effect essay means examining the topic carefully and thoroughly from a *logical* point of view.

Organization of Cause/Effect Analysis Essay

In a process analysis there is an order among the various steps which produce the end result, even though skipping one or two steps may produce the same result. In other words, each step in a process is related to the other. In a cause/effect analysis you may or may not find such an inter-relationship. Furthermore, the causes may be immediate or remote. It is possible that the more immediate the cause is, the more obvious it is. However, there may be several remote causes which lead to an immediate cause.

For example, suppose one of your close friends, who was the top student in the class, dropped out of school. In analyzing the reasons, you found the immediate cause was that the school sent a notice of dismissal because she had not paid her tuition for two consecutive semesters. However, the student's inability to pay the tuition was the result of her being laid off from the part-time job she had been holding for about two years. This was the result of her being constantly late to report to work, which in turn was the result of her boyfriend's involvement in some kind of drug business.

In the example above, you see that several causes led to your friend's dropping out. However, the immediate cause was financial. But there were other occupational and emotional reasons that precipitated the result. Another thing to notice is that the causes are related. However, look at the following example:

Effect: Your father is diabetic.

Causes:

1. His parents and grandparents were diabetic (hereditary).
2. He doesn't control his weight; he eats too much fatty food.
3. He has high blood pressure.

Here, the three reasons are not related to each other. Strictly speaking, these are not causes, but *factors*. Yet even though the three are unrelated, all three together must have contributed to his illness.

In organizing the causes — whether they are immediate (direct), remote (indirect), or related/unrelated, familiar/unfamiliar, interesting/uninteresting, important/unimportant, the writer makes his or her choice of order, depending on the kind of audience the essay is addressed to. Most professional writers prefer to go from immediate to remote, more familiar to less familiar, less interesting to more interesting, less important to more important, and more reasonable to less reasonable ones.

What specific organization you choose depends on both the nature of your topic and the audience for whom you write. Furthermore, the same two factors are involved in your decision whether you should emphasize the cause(s) or the effect(s) or both.

The *thesis statement* of a cause/effect analysis is much simpler than that of most other analytical patterns. Just state what the causes/effects were.

> Example : Social and domestic pressures, her own lack of knowledge about legal procedures, and her husband's constant threat to kill her made her sign the illegal document.

Having written the thesis statement, use the *developmental paragraphs* to explain each cause (in at least one paragraph) with sufficient evidence, examples, and/or data to support it. The *conclusion* may include your suggestions to help avoid the causes or on how to cope with the effect.

For Your Critical Thinking

Bearing in mind the preceding discussion on the cause and effect analysis essay, answer the following :

1. Which essays in the chapter emphasize both causes and effects ?
2. Which of them give more emphasis to causes than to effects ?
3. What kind of audience does each essay address ? How do you know this ?
4. Which essays have no conclusions ? Add conclusions to these essays.
5. What order of organization (example : from immediate to remote, from less important to more important, etc.) does each of the essays follow ? How did you identify this order ?
6. Find the thesis statement of each of the essays.
7. Classify the essays into different groups. Discuss the differences and similarities of each group. (See Chapter 5, pp. 127–128 for a discussion on classifciation.)
8. Which of the essays is the most comprehensible to you ? Why ?
9. Does "TV Viewing" develop all the points stated in the thesis statement ? If you wrote the thesis statement of this essay how would you state the points ?

10. Are the causes stated in each of the essays related to each other? How? Why?

THE EXPOSITORY ESSAY: PROCESS

Exercise in Revision

Review the discussion of the steps involved in revising (Chapter 7) and rewrite the essay, "TV Viewing." Remember the formula *DARe* (Deleting, Adding, Reorganizing). You may want to use the following questions as guidelines.

1. How many paragraphs does the introduction take? Would you delete and/or reorganize any of them?
2. Is the thesis statement rightly placed? Does it have to be rearranged?
3. Are all the points mentioned in the thesis statement developed in the developmental paragraphs? (This means if there is any point developed in the developmental paragraphs without being stated in the thesis, you have to *add* this point to the thesis.)
4. What do sentences 2, 3, 4 of Par. 6 and the sentences in Par. 8 talk about? Are they related? Do you need any *rearrangement* of these paragraphs? Is the main point discussed in these paragraphs stated in the thesis?
5. Is the main idea of Par. 7 and 11 the same or different? To what point stated in the thesis is this related?
6. Are the main ideas of Par. 12 and 13 mentioned in the thesis statement? What kind of revision is needed with these paragraphs? Deletion? Addition?
7. What does the author talk about in Par. 14-17? Are these points mentioned in the thesis statement?
8. Would you delete any sentence or paragraphs in the essay for the reason that they are unrelated to the thesis statement? Which ones? Why?
9. What kind of additions would you make to this essay?
10. Would you reorganize any paragraphs? Which? Why?

   Note: There isn't any "rule" which says that the points developed in the developmental paragraphs should be in the same order as they are in the thesis statement. However, for the purposes of clarity and easy comprehension by readers, you are strongly advised to discuss the points in the same order as they are mentioned in the thesis statement.

WRITING ACTIVITIES

Reaction Journal

Write in your journal:

- Which articles make you angry because the kind of world represented conflicts with your beliefs and way of life
- How you would like these to be changed
- Any new information you received which you would like to use in your life
- Any information the applicability of which you question, and why
- Any article(s) you would like to be taken out from this chapter, and why
- Which writer you would rate excellent or poor, and on what grounds
- Which learning materials make you feel happy or sad, and why

Learning Log

Write in your learning log:

- Things you learned which you would immediately put into practice
- Things you would never want to apply in your life
- Things you learned which you think are most helpful to you in developing your writing skills
- Things discussed in this chapter which are never going to be helpful to you either in your academic or in your real life
- What additional things you would like to see incorporated into this chapter

Writing Assignment

Overview

Visit one of the following:

- A crisis intervention clinic
- An outreach office, or any out-patient clinic for substance abusers
- An outreach house, or any in-patient treatment center for substance abusers

Interview one of the community or social workers on one specific problem area (for example, drinking, smoking, overeating, drug addiction, etc.). Write an article for the community newspaper of your choice, explaining the reasons for and/or the effects of the specific problem area you have chosen.

Real-life Purpose: To educate your community on the problem area you have chosen
Academic Purpose: To educate your class members on the problem area you have chosen
Real-life Audience: Your local community members
Academic Audience: Your class members

Procedure

IN-CLASS GROUP ACTIVITY

Group Size: 8

1. The group members meet and agree on the specific problem area they want to work on.
2. Members prepare the questionnaire for the interview (ten questions : five on causes and five on effects).
3. Members volunteer to visit centers in pairs (this means, each group will have four subgroups of two each : two will interview on causes and two, on effects).

OUT-OF CLASS PAIRED ACTIVITY

Paired groups visit the centers of their choice and interview the community or social workers available. Record the responses. Summarize the responses.

IN-CLASS GROUP ACTIVITY

1. Group members meet; go over the notes and summaries on the interviews.
2. The members come to an agreement on whether to give emphasis to causes or effects, or to both.
3. Members work together to write the article.
4. The group leader reads the article aloud to the members of another group who did not choose the specific area your group worked on. Get their feedback.
5. Applying the formula DARe, revise/rewrite your piece.

IN-CLASS PRESENTATION

Present your piece to the class and get feedback.

IN-CLASS GROUP WORK

Group members work together to make any more revisions needed.

OUT-OF-CLASS PUBLICATION ACTIVITY

The group leader sends the article out to a community newspaper of the group's choice. Remember, all your group members are the authors of this article.

Good luck on your publication!

Alternate Writing Assignment

Write an essay on one of the following topics. Review the process of writing given in the previous chapters and choose the kind of rhetorical pattern (classification, process analysis, cause and effect, or comparison and contrast) that best suits the expression of your ideas on these topics.

1. Air pollution
2. Poverty and illiteracy
3. Racism
4. Smoking

CHAPTER · 9

Part 1: READING

PREREADING ACTIVITIES

Discuss the following in your group:

1. Do you think women, by their very nature, are more caring and compassionate than men?
2. Do you think that the sick and the elderly should be under the care of women, and not of men? Why?
3. What are some of the women-dominated professions/careers? Why is it that these professions/careers do not attract men?
4. How does women's entry into the work force affect dependents like children, the elderly, and the sick?
5. Do you think that because of women's entry into the paid work force, the state is being forced to take responsibility for dependent children and aged and sick parents? Explain your position.
6. Recently in most developed nations and in some developing nations two-income families have become almost a part of the social structure. What does the society gain or lose from this new trend in family structure?

Reading 1: DEPENDENTS AND AMERICAN FAMILY STRUCTURE

1. In the past when women devoted their time and energy exclusively to home and family, dependents like children, the elderly, the sick, the disabled, the handicapped, and the retarded were taken care of mostly at home. Women assumed this responsibility as part of their domestic role. However, there have been changes in this pattern of caring for dependents. Although the vast majority of children still live at home and are cared for by parents, out-of-home paid or public care of children is increasing almost everywhere. Many elderly no longer live with their children, even when they are frail and in need of care.

2. Some people look at these changes as a threat to American family structure and attribute the cause to the changing role of women, most of whom do

---

From Mary Jo Bane, "Children and the Welfare State." Reprinted with permission from the Summer 1983 issue of the *American Educator,* the quarterly journal of the American Federation of Teachers.

not want to be considered one hundred percent housewives and mothers any more. Many people seem to think that compassion and responsibility, expressed through personal concern and care, which historically have been the virtues expected of women in their roles as wives, mothers, daughters, and friends, are lacking in modern women. As a result, the state is being forced to take the responsibility of caring for the dependents.

3. This is not actually the case. Most of the care of the old, the young, the sick, and the handicapped is still provided by women in their roles as wives, mothers, daughters, friends, and neighbors. It is true that there has been a dramatic growth in social welfare spending in recent years. However, not much of this growth can be attributed to the displacement of family care. It is mainly due to the provision of new and a higher quality of services by the social welfare sector in the fields of health, education, social services, and income security, and not to changes in family care.

4. Of course, the state is spending more and more money for social welfare. However, not all of this increase is due to the so-called "decline of the family system." For example, the vast bulk of health spending goes for hospitalization, physicians' services, drugs, and other goods and services that have never been, and indeed cannot be, provided by families. In the field of education, a good deal of the increase goes for higher education. There has also been significant increase in preschool education. However, most parents see nursery school as an educational and developmental institution and, thus, as supplementary to families. It could be argued that social services like day care, school breakfasts and lunches could have been provided by families, but not at the level of quality provided by professionals. As far as income security services like social security and pensions are concerned, they serve the purpose of relieving families of the financial burden of supporting the retired, disabled, unemployed, and otherwise poor. After all, a large proportion of these services are new. It might be argued that the quality of services the elderly are getting in nursing homes is inferior to the kind they used to get traditionally from home. This might be true in certain cases. However, it is also true that a lot of adult dependents have become more independent, and prefer to live away from family in privacy and autonomy.

5. So the new patterns of care for children, the elderly, and other dependents in the United States do not represent a decline of family structure. They only mean an improvement over what would have been provided in the absence of changes in families and the social welfare system. This is partly because families continue to provide the vast bulk of care for children and a substantial amount of the care of the elderly and chronically ill. Social welfare institutions and services supplement what families have always done and continue to do. Recent surveys on how children, the sick, and the elderly are cared for provide proofs to show that the entry of women into the paid work force has not had any drastic effect on the care of dependents. In 1975 only about 23 percent of children under two years and 25 percent of three- to five-year-old children were cared for by someone other than their parents for more than ten hours a week. Only 4 percent of children under two years and 11 percent of three-to-five-year-olds were in formal day care or nursery school more than ten hours a week. These numbers are no doubt higher than in 1960, but they are still not very high. In the late 1970's only about 5 percent of the elderly were in institutions. Of those needing help, most received it from family members.

6. Thus the movement of women into the work force does not seem to have been accompanied by a massive displacement of family care by the paid economy. Instead, women have taken on paid jobs in addition to their caretaking within the family. This has been partly assisted by other family members taking on additional responsibilities and by a decrease in the amount of housework that gets done by anyone. To some extent, this is because women are filling with paid work what was perhaps relatively unproductive time — while older children were in school, for example. (Only about 40 percent of the married mothers in the labor force are year-round full-time workers.) Or perhaps men and women are simply working harder and longer, sharing equal household responsibilities, including care for the dependents.

POSTREADING ACTIVITIES

Discuss the following in your group and write a paragraph on each:

1. Does income security relieve families of the financial burden of supporting the retired, disabled, unemployed, and otherwise poor? (Par. 4) How and why?
2. In Par. 4, the writer remarks: "A lot of adult dependents have become more independent and prefer to live away from family in privacy and autonomy." Do you agree with this statement? Or do you think these adult dependents are just adjusting themselves to the changing family structure?
3. Do you agree with the writer's views expressed in Par. 5? Give reasons for your agreement/disagreement.
4. Does the writer provide strong evidence to defend his or her argument re-emphasized in the conclusion? Give examples from the essay.
5. Update the statistical information given in Par. 5 by quoting the most recent data.

PREREADING ACTIVITY

Discuss the following in your group:

1. For what or whom are television commercials intended? Do you enjoy watching them? Why or why not? How do they relate to your life?

2. What role do women play in commercials? What image of women does the society get from commercials? Are they portrayed respectfully? Do you agree with these portrayals of women? Do you have any suggestions for change?

Reading 2: LESSONS IN SELF-HATRED

1. Television advertisers insult women. They do so by showing women primarily in three roles: hag, servant, and Playboy's Playmate.

2. The hag, though less prominent than she used to be, is still very much in evidence. Sometimes she is strictly a comic figure — intended, apparently, to bring forth chuckles from the men in the audience. The comic hag typically wears hair curlers and a baggy bathrobe as she shuffles from room to room, scratching and yawning, her voice a whine or a bellow. She bullies her befuddled husband, so that he escapes for some beer with the boys or, on the beach, ogles the curvaceous blonde who, of course, wears the scanty bathing suit the ad is trying to sell. But the comic hag appears less frequently than she used to, possibly because of protests from offended women, who control, as advertisers know, great buying power. The hag is now displayed as a warning: "Use our product or this is what you will become." One example is the commercial in which the woman yells uncontrollably at her teen-age daughter (who wallows in filth and pie plates in her bedroom) or cries "Honey, look out!" at her young son, who, speeding down the aisle on his fire-engine grocery cart, collides head-on with a stack of boxes. We learn that such uncalled-for tantrums could have been avoided had she only had the foresight to take Anacin.

3. But the woman who avoids becoming a hag is in danger of becoming a wife-mother servant. According to advertisers, this servant must be a cross between a miracle worker and Wonder Woman. She transforms her household every day, getting the grease out of her husband's fishing clothes, the smell out of the kitchen, and husband and kids out of the house in time for work and school in the morning. "And she even makes gravy," one proud husband exclaims. She is pretty, maternal, and extremely maudlin. But despite all the hugs and kisses, Mom has her problems. Because good old Mom is so kind and hard-working and long-suffering, her adoring family walks all over her. Seven-year-old Junior rides his tricycle across her freshly waxed floor or, outside, stomps through puddle after puddle, seconds after being asked to *please* stay dry. "Hey, Mom, will you wash out my tights?" says a teen-age daughter who is plenty old enough to do it herself. "Honey, I can't find my socks," says a help-

Excerpted from Robert Miles, *First Principles of the Essay* (New York: Harper & Row, 1975), 120–22. Copyright © 1971 by Robert Miles. Reprinted by permission of Harper Collins, Publishers.

less husband who was lucky to find the bureau drawer. Or, "Honey," he says, his voice straining with forced patience, "the bathroom bowl sure needs cleaning." Instead of a terse, "Well, clean it yourself. You use it as much as I do," his wife offers a worried "Think of all the germs!" and gets down on her knees to clean out the bowl. Mom perseveres and manages to maintain her efficiency by using such miracle products as Tide, Lysol, and Geritol. "I think I'll keep her," says the patronizing husband to his grateful servant.

4.   But she may well begin to fear that he will not always keep her, for each time she turns on her television set she sees the role towards which, apparently, she ought to aspire — the role of Playmate. This is the most prominent of the women's roles in television advertising. The ads are filled with smooth skin, shapely legs and, of course, large breasts. We are shown tall blondes in peek-a-boo bikinis and bosomy brunettes in low-cut evening gowns; or maybe these delicious morsels are simply lounging in towels or a bath. With almost any kind of product, a woman is offered as a decoration, invitation or prize. We see a car and a woman, a camera and a woman, a bottle of diet soda and a woman, a bra and a woman and a staring man. And whether the beauty is softening her skin with Calgon or coloring her hair with Miss Clairol or making herself smell sexy with Chanel, the message to women viewers is the same: "This is the kind of woman to be."

5. A woman who consciously or unconsciously believes in the advertisers' stereotypes will plunge more and more deeply into self-hatred. It is not enough that she strains to be a patient, efficient wife-mother servant. No, besides being eager to mop floors, she must be irresistible to men. She must have all the beauty of a well-paid model or prostitute. And if the ads are to be believed, woman in her natural state is anything but beautiful. Bombarded by all those commercials for deodorants and conditioners and cosmetics, a woman can only assume that without them her hair is too stringy, her skin too scratchy, her eyes too small, and her whole body too smelly. The ads are saying, "Women, without our help you look bad and smell bad, and you need our products to hide your natural inferiority." The advertisers have little concern for how many hang-ups they encourage or how many psyches they twist. Twisted psyches increase sales.

POSTREADING ACTIVITIES

1. Write two paragraphs each for and against the following statements by the writer.

   S1.   The nag is now used as a warning: "Use our product or this is what you will become." (Par. 1)

   S2.   But despite all the hugs and kisses, Mom has her problems. Because good old Mom is so kind and hard-working and long-suffering, her adoring family walks all over her." (Par. 3)

   S3.   "With almost any kind of product, a woman is offered as a decoration, invitation or prize." (Par. 4)

   S4.   A woman who consciously or unconsciously believes in the advertisers' stereotypes will plunge more and more deeply into self-hatred. (Par. 5)

   S5.   The advertisers have little concern for how many hang-ups they encourage or how many psyches they twist. Twisted psyches increase sales. (Par. 5)

   S6.   What kind of conclusion would you draw about the gender of the writer of this essay? How did you draw that conclusion?

   S7.   Could the writer be married or unmarried? On what clues from the essay did you base your judgment?

   S8.   Do you think the writer is a feminist? How and why did you reach or not reach that conclusion?

   S9.   Comment on the messages given by the writer to both men and women.

   S10. What kind of audience is the essay directed to? How do you know that?

S11. Does the writer imply the need for any kind of social change? Explain.

S12. Write a letter to the writer agreeing/disagreeing with him or her. Explain the reasons for your agreement/disagreement.

PREREADING ACTIVITIES

Discuss the following in your group.

1. What are some of the standardized tests given in American schools?
2. What do you think are the stated purposes of these tests? Do they serve these purposes? Explain.
3. What specific preparations do you, as students, have to make to take these tests? Do these preparations help you pass these tests? Do they help you in the long run (in your future life)? Explain your answers.
4. What are the advantages and disadvantages of multiple skills tests? Would you prefer a multiple skills test or a short answer test? Why?

Reading 3: STANDARDIZED TESTS

1. Over 100 million standardized tests are given annually in the U.S. public schools. Across the nation, teachers, parents, administrators, politicians, and the public increasingly are focusing attention on the harmful effects of this testing: damage to individual students, the curriculum, and accountability.

2. In many school systems, test scores routinely are used as the basis for high-stakes educational decisions such as whether a student will be placed in a "transitional" kindergarten or first grade, admitted into a "gifted and talented" program, placed in or removed from Chapter I or special education, promoted, tracked, or allowed to graduate from high school.

3. However, test scores are not necessarily reliable: that is, the score a child gets one day might be very different from the score he or she gets another day. Tests administered to young children are particularly unreliable. Because of limits to test reliability, no test should ever be the sole or primary basis for educational decision-making.

4. The consequences of making a wrong decision about a student can be disastrous. Children who need assistance may not get it, while children who do not need remediation may be placed into special programs from which there is often no exit.

From Monty Neill, "Standardized Tests," *New York Teacher* ([month or season]) [year]: [pp.]. Used with permission. Dr. Neill is the associate director of the National Center for Fair & Open Testing (FairTest).

5. Across the nation, African Americans are three times as likely as whites to be in programs for the "educably mentally retarded" or something similar. Hispanic students face similar problems. Although a federal judge banned the use of "IQ" tests for assigning African American children to special education programs in California, similar test use remains common elsewhere.

6. In many New York districts, test scores on "readiness" exams such as the Gesell are used to keep children out of kindergarten or first grade, or to place them in "transitional" programs. Independent studies have shown that half the students who take the Gesell are misplaced. Boys and children from low income or minority-group backgrounds are most likely to be deemed "unready."

7. Such early placement decisions tend to become self-fulfilling prophecies. Children labeled "not ready" or needing "special education" are often assigned to a track in which they are treated to a narrow, "dummied-down" program that guarantees they will never progress as quickly as their peers. Tracking, which effectively segregates students by class and race within schools, does not help advanced students and hurts lower-ranked students.

8. Achievement testing is an important factor in decisions to retain students in grade. Not only are the tests of questionable merit in such decisions, but retention itself is of dubious educational value. Current evidence indicates that as of the end of third grade, children who were retained in previous years do not perform better, despite being a year older, than students who scored the same but were not held back. Moreover, students who have been retained are substantially more likely to drop out of school.

9. For many students, particularly those who are not white and upper-income, the consequences of testing are disastrous : they are consigned to an inadequate education that reduces their life chances, damages their self-esteem, and precludes their exposure to a full education. But even for those not penalized by low test scores, testing narrows and warps the curriculum.

10. The misuse of tests also leads to an overemphasis on a limited range of academics at too young an age. Research indicates that such developmentally inappropriate programs do not help students make lasting academic gains and may turn them off from academics.

11. In many elementary and secondary schools, the emphasis on raising test scores has reduced education to test coaching for students and teachers alike. But multiple choice tests measure only a very limited range of knowledge and ability. They cannot measure personal qualities such as perseverance, ability to work with others, and creativity ; or the understanding, integration, use and creation of knowledge.

12. Reading tests, for example, test "reading skills," a set of isolated bits that have only a partial and indirect relationship to reading. Where the goal is high reading-test scores, students often do not read, discuss and write about real literature, even though many teachers would prefer to use such books.

Instead, students must read arid, irrelevant passages from basals, then do workbooks and answer multiple-choice questions.

13. Multiple-choice math tests are unable to measure whether a student understands quantitative reasoning and can apply it to new situations. They only measure whether a student can recognize a correct answer among four or five options. To raise test scores, teachers have little choice but to emphasize rote and drill instead of real uses for math and quantitative reasoning.

14. In science and social studies, the complexities of the subjects, the debates within them, and ultimately their real meanings, are lost in the push to memorize definitions and facts that can be recognized on a multiple-choice exam.

15. Increased testing has been justified as promoting accountability. But this notion of accountability is ultimately illusory, since the tests only measure a very limited range of skills and knowledge. Instead of making schools responsive to a partnership of students, parents, teachers and the community, tests make schools responsive to test companies, who are essentially unaccountable.

16. If teachers are to be held responsible for doing good work with students, they must be given the resources, support and freedom to do the job. Testing, however, disempowers teachers. At the same time, it shifts attention from reforms that are necessary to ensure good education for children to a punitive, threatening approach — get good scores, or else !

17. In conclusion, no test should ever be the sole or primary criterion for making educational decisions. Furthermore, tests should not drive curriculum and should not be used to judge the quality of teaching or programs.

POSTREADING ACTIVITIES

Discuss the following in your group and write one or two paragraphs on each.

1. According to the writer, what are the harmful effects of standardized tests ? Do you agree or disagree with the writer ? Why ? Why not ?
2. What kind of damage do standardized tests do to students ?
3. Do you agree with the writer's statement that across the nation African Americans and Hispanics are more likely to be in programs for the "educably mentally retarded" ? Give your reasons.
4. Give examples from the essay on the unreliability of standardized tests.
5. Is the author's statement, "For many students, particularly those who are not white and upper-income, the consequences of testing

are disastrous," (Par. 9) ethnically biased or based on reality? Give your reasons.

6. Comment on the writer's views on "test coaching." (Par. 11)
7. What does "a partnership of students, parents, teachers, and the community" mean? (Par. 15) How can this partnership be made effective? Suppose you were a district superintendent. Would you consider this suggestion? Why or why not?
8. Do you agree with the writer's statement that "tests make schools responsive to test companies, who are essentially unaccountable" (Par. 15)? Give your reasons.
9. The writer concludes: "No test should ever be the sole or primary criterion for making educational decisions." (Par. 17) Does this mean that tests could be a secondary criterion? What would be the primary criteria?
10. Which of the following categories do you think the writer belongs to:

    • An administrator
    • A teacher
    • A parent
    • A student
    • A board member of a test-making company

    Explain on what evidence from the essay you based the conclusion.

11. Who is the intended audience of this essay? How did you reach this conclusion?
12. Write a letter to the writer agreeing/disagreeing with the views expressed.

PREREADING ACTIVITIES

Discuss the following in your group:

1. What is science fiction? Give some examples.
2. What are some of the themes discussed in science fiction?
3. How different are the stories in science fiction from (1) romance, (2) mystery, (3) horror, or (4) wonder stories?
4. Do you like to read science fiction? Why or why not?
5. How real or imaginary are the themes dealt with in science fiction?
6. Would you like to read science fiction for enjoyment or information? Give your reasons.

Reading 4: SCIENCE FICTION AS MENTAL PUSH-UPS

1. "It is good to renew one's wonder," said the philosopher. "Space travel has again made children of us all." These words introduce Ray Bradbury's *The Martian Chronicles,* one of the world's most famous pieces of science fiction, and one of my own personal favorites from years ago.

2. Recently, I reread the *Chronicles* and discovered that it is as good a book today as it was when I first encountered it. Very few youthful enthusiasms can pass this test of time. When I was growing up, the *Martian Chronicles* were published one by one in shaggy-edged pulp magazines with names like *Thrilling Wonder Stories* or *Planet Stories*; they were sandwiched between the work of other obscure and unheard-of writers with names like Isaac Asimov, Robert A. Heinlein, and Arthur C. Clarke.

3. My friends and I read these stories under our desk tops in English class, when we should have been reading *Silas Marner.* The stories were chock-full of invasions from outer space, explorations of other worlds, and meetings with aliens; robots and starships and cities in space. Talk about a catalytic agent! Those stories taught us to *read*! They captured our interest and made us want to read more.

4. Furthermore, these books opened our eyes to the plausibility of the science behind the fiction. By 1950 Arthur C. Clarke had already detailed the mechanics of shooting rockets off the earth in *Interplanetary Flight,* and he even predicted that one day, the earth would be circled by an orbiting system of man-made satellites: a type of vast communications network. It made us wonder if such things could really happen, and how we could help to bring them about.

5. Our teachers and our parents took one look at the covers of these magazines and tore them into confetti. Our classmates looked askance at us and made tch-tching sounds with their tongues and then went back to preparing themselves studiously for minor clerkships in minor institutions, their little minds unclouded by such aberrant concepts as space travel. Orbiting spacecraft becoming communications networks? Men on the moon? Atomic power? Robots? Balderdash! No sensible person would even consider such crack-pottery!

6. How times have changed. The old pulp magazines have gone the way of the dinosaur, but science fiction is alive and thriving. Today, Ray Bradbury, Isaac Asimov, and Arthur C. Clarke aren't read beneath the desk but on top of it, included in thousands of high school and college curriculums across the country. Science fiction has invaded the mass media, producing a revolution in motion picture taste and providing some of the most commercially successful productions of all time : *E. T., Close Encounters of the Third Kind,* and *Star Wars,* to name a few. Television has featured *Star Trek* and *Buck Rogers* and *V,* while a British series, *Dr. Who,* recounting the adventures of a time-traveler from outer space, has become the longest-running series in British television history.

7. What happened ? History took over, just the way we thought it would. That "silly Buck Rogers stuff" proved not so silly after all, and the science fiction pulps began to look absolutely prescient. The space suits of the astronauts started to look like the ones on the old pulp covers, and the "flying belt" of Buck Rogers reappeared as the backpack used by present-day spacewalkers. Man has walked on the moon, landed spacecraft on Mars, and sent messages into outer space, inviting other civilizations to call. And while most of the world sits by with mouths gaping, the old science fiction fans will sit back and say, "we told you so."

8. Few recent developments have come as a surprise to the former members of the Buck Rogers solar scouts. We believed in things long before they happened. We had maps of the solar system, plans for model rocket ships, and badges for Flight Commanders and Chief Explorers (all of which are worth more than their weight in gold on today's memorabilia market). Therein, perhaps, lies one of the greatest strengths of science fiction. It gets rid of a lot of nay-saying in a hurry. You are not going to say that flying to the moon is silly claptrap if you have already accepted it as inevitable, even adventurous and desirable.

9. Why does science fiction act as a catalytic agent on men's imagination ? First, good science fiction has the unique power to evoke wonder and escort the readers to some marvelous part of the real or imagined universe which they cannot reach in real life. It arouses the readers' curiosity by having them see how they would react against such a background. What would you do if, for instance, you were confronted by an alien from outer space ? Space fiction has considered this situation from a thousand different vantage points, from H. G. Wells' *The War of the Worlds* to Steven Spielberg's *E. T.* One of the most engaging — and enduring — examples of this tale is Stanley G. Weinbaum's *A Martian Odyssey,* which describes mankind's first meeting with a Martian on Mars. Indeed, this is one of the central motifs running through all of Ray Bradbury's *The Martian Chronicles,* as well as William Sloane's novel *To Walk the Night,* which depicts the arrival of an alien intelligence on earth. As psychologist Elizabeth Thorne noted in *The New York Times,* "Our imagination has been totally captured by space travel ; we now use extraterrestrial figures as mythic figures. We're all on our way ; there may be an E.T. out there, or he may be coming to us."

10. The use of mythology and religious belief is another way science fiction evokes wonder. George Lucas' cinematic space fantasies, for example, are firmly rooted in mythology. Rebirth is another theme that science fiction deals with. This theme is explored explicitly at the conclusion of Walter M. Miller's *A Canticle for Leibowitz* and throughout all of John Wyndham's *Rebirth*. In "Towards an Aesthetic of Science Fiction," the writer Joanna Puss says science fiction "can deal with transcendental events. Hence, the tendency of science fiction towards wonder, awe and a religious or quasi-religious attitude towards the universe."

11. Although a fertile imagination is crucial to any writer, to the science fiction writer it is the mainstay, the top priority. Writers of science fiction are not bound by earthly contraints: they have a carte blanche that extends well beyond the realms of ordinary fantasy. In many ways, their fiction is an intellectual puzzle — a game for the mind. The author takes an imagined situation — a harsh environment or an unusual condition — and works out all the implications of that situation.

12. For example, what might happen if one of earth's radio telescopes began receiving signals from outer space? John Elliot and astronomer Fred Hoyle consider the possibilities in *A for Andromeda*. What would happen to the rest of us if mutation suddenly created a new being with radically increased intelligence? Poul Anderson's *Brain Wave*, Wilmar Shiras' *Children of the Atom,* and A. E. Van Vogt's *Slan* posit three possible outcomes, each told from an entirely different point of view.

13. In *The Watch Below,* James White considers the story of four people — two men and two women — who are trapped in a sunken tanker torpedoed by enemy submarines. Turned upside down, the ship descends to a depth of approximately 200 feet where the buoyancy of the air in its tanks stabilizes its position. It can't sink any farther but can't rise either; it just drifts helplessly along in the currents of the sea. In White's tale, several generations are born and raised in that closed environment. How? That is the story.

14. In the last analysis, however, it is the problem-posing and problem-solving aspects of science fiction that may be the most important reason for captivating the readers' mind. There are few problems we are likely to encounter in the future — in space or anywhere else — that have not already been treated in science fiction. Sci-fi writers have confronted problems of pollution, ecology, and overpopulation, and have even delved into sociology, archeology, and linguistics. They have pondered the problems of long-distance space travel at speeds close to the speed of light and created whole new worlds for humans to colonize. These thought-provoking considerations of future possibilities, simulations of "things that may come to pass," are a form of push-ups for the imagination: a necessary flexing of our mental muscles against the effects of future shock. As Isaac Asimov noted in *Asimov on Science Fiction,* "Our statesmen, our everyman must take on a science fictional way of thinking whether he likes it or not, or even whether he knows it or not. Only so can the deadly problems of today be solved."

POSTREADING ACTIVITIES

Discuss the following in your group and write one or two paragraphs on each.

1. How convinced are you by the writer's arguments? Explain.
2. What new information did you get from reading this essay? Did the reading change any of your views about science fiction? Will you read more science fiction than you used to? Why or why not?
3. Summarize the writer's arguments on how science fiction acts as a catalytic agent in promoting reading habits.
4. Give examples of some of the imaginative themes dealt with in science fiction which have been realized in real life.
5. What points do the two examples in Par. 12 and 13 explain? Do you get a clearer idea of the point from these examples? How? Why?
6. What is the writer's purpose in writing this essay? Who is the intended audience? How did you reach your conclusions?
7. What does the writer mean by the "problem-posing and problem-solving" aspects of science fiction (Par. 14)? Explain your answer from your life's experience.
8. Give some of the most recent examples of science fiction.
9. Would the writer be a man or a woman? How do you know this?
10. Write a letter to the writer explaining what you learned or did not learn from reading this essay.

PREREADING ACTIVITIES

Discuss the following in your group:

1. How would you explain "pro-life" and "pro-choice" with reference to abortion?
2. From your experience, what kind of people argue for "pro-life"? Why?
3. What are some of the arguments for and against pro-life?
4. Are you a "pro-lifer" or a "pro-choicer"? Explain why you made that choice.

Reading 5: ABORTION, RIGHT AND WRONG

1. I cannot bring myself to say I am in favor of abortion. I do not want anyone to have one. I want people to use contraceptives and for those contraceptives to be foolproof. I want people to be responsible for their actions ; mature in their decision. I want children to be loved, wanted, well cared for.

2. I cannot bring myself to say I am against choice. I want women who are young, poor, single, or all three to be able to direct the course of their lives. I want women who have had all the children they want or can afford or their bodies can withstand to be able to decide their future. I want women who are in bad marriages or destructive relationships to avoid being trapped by pregnancy.

3. I find myself in the awkward position of being both anti-abortion and pro-choice. Neither group seems to be completely right — or wrong. It is not that I think abortion is wrong for me but acceptable for someone else. The question is far more complex than that.

4. Part of my problem is that what I think and how I feel about this issue are two entirely different matters. I know that unwanted children are often neglected, even abandoned. I know that many of those seeking abortions are children themselves. I know that making abortion illegal will not stop all women from having them.

5. **Absolutes :** I also know from experience the crisis an unplanned pregnancy can cause. Yet I have felt the joy of giving birth, the delight that comes from feeling a baby's skin against my own. I know how hard it is to parent a child and how deeply satisfying it can be. My children sometimes provoke me and cause me endless frustration, but I can still look at them with tenderness and wonder at the miracle of it all. The lessons of my own experience produce conflicting emotions. Theory collides with reality.

6. It seems to me that both groups present themselves in absolutes. Each group of people think they have the right answer — the only answer. Yet I am uncomfortable in either camp. I have nothing in common with the pro-lifers. I am horrified by their scare tactics, their pictures of well-formed fetuses tossed in a metal pan, their cruel slogans. I cannot condone their flagrant misuse of Scripture and unforgiving spirit. There is a meanness about their position that causes them to pass judgement on the lives of women in a way I could never do.

7. The pro-life groups, with their fundamentalist religious attitudes, have a fear and an abhorrence of sex, especially premarital sex. In their view abortion

From Rachel Richardson Smith, "Abortion, Right and Wrong," *Newsweek,* 25 March 1985. Reprinted with permission.

only compounds the sexual sin. What I find incomprehensible is that even as they are opposed to abortion, they are also opposed to alternative solutions. They are squeamish about sex education in the schools. They do not want teens to have contraceptives without parental consent. They offer little aid or sympathy to unwed mothers. They are the vigilant guardians of a narrow morality.

8. I wonder how abortion got to be the greatest of all sins. What about poverty, ignorance, hunger, weaponry? The only thing the anti-abortion groups seem to have right is that abortion is indeed the taking of human life. I simply cannot escape this one glaring fact. Call it what you will — fertilized egg, embryo, fetus. What we have here is human life. If it were just a mass of tissue, there would be no debate. So I agree that abortion ends a life. But the antiabortionists are wrong to call it murder.

9. The sad truth is that homicide is not always against the law. Our society does not categorically recognize the sanctity of human life. There are a number of legal and apparently socially acceptable ways to take human life. Some examples of "justifiable" homicide includes the death penalty, war, and killing in self-defense. It seems to me that as a society we need to come to grips with our own ambiguity concerning the value of human life. If we are to value and protect unborn life so stringently, why do we not also value and protect life already born?

10. Mistakes: Why can't we see abortion for the human tragedy it is? No woman plans for her life to turn out that way. Even the most effective contraceptives are no guarantee against pregnancy. Loneliness, ignorance, immaturity can lead to decisions (or lack of decisions) that may result in untimely pregnancy. People make mistakes.

11. What many people seem to misunderstand is that no woman wants to have an abortion. Circumstances demand it; women do it. No woman reacts to abortion with joy. Relief, yes. But also ambivalence, grief, despair, guilt.

12. The pro-choice groups do not seem to acknowledge that abortion is not a perfect answer. What goes unsaid is that when a woman has an abortion she loses more than an unwanted pregnancy. Often she loses her self-respect. No woman can forget a pregnancy no matter how it ends.

13. Why can we not view abortion as one of those anguished decisions in which human beings struggle to do the best they can in trying circumstances? Why is abortion viewed so coldly and factually on the one hand and so judgmentally on the other? Why is it not akin to the same painful experience families must sometimes make to allow a loved one to die?

14. I wonder how we can begin to change the context in which we think about abortion. How can we begin to think about it redemptively? What is it in the trauma of loss of life — be it loved or unloved, born or unborn — from which we can learn? There is much I have yet to resolve. Even as I refuse to pass judgment on other women's lives, I weep for the children who might have been. I suspect I am not alone.

POSTREADING ACTIVITIES

Discuss the following in your group and write one or two paragraphs on each:

1. After reading the essay do you think you might change your views on abortion? Why or why not?
2. If you are pro-life, how would you account for unwanted children?
3. If you are pro-choice, how would you account for the children who might have been born and might have made significant contributions to the society?
4. In Par. 3 the author claims she is both anti-abortion and pro-choice. Does she prove this claim in her essay? Explain.
5. Does the writer contradict herself in her statement: "So I agree that abortion ends a life. But the anti-abortionists are wrong to call it murder." (Par. 8) Explain.
6. What is the point that the writer raises in Par. 9? Do you agree? Give reasons for your agreement/disagreement.
7. What impressions do you get about the writer's personality from the conclusion? Give reasons for your judgment.
8. How different do you think this essay would have been in the views expressed and in the examples given if it had been written by a man?
9. What new information did you receive from this essay?
10. Write a letter to the writer expressing your agreement/disagreement with her views.

PREREADING ACTIVITIES

Discuss the following in your groups.

1. How stressful is your student life? Compare an average American student's stress to the kind of stressful or relaxed life of a university student in any other country you know of. Do you think that American students have a more stressful life in comparison with the ones in developing countries? Give reasons.
2. If you think that your student life is more stressful than it should be, what are the reasons? What suggestions can you make to eliminate some of these reasons?

3. Do technological advances make modern man's life comfortable? How?

4. Do you think technology has partly to be blamed for modern man's stress? Give your reasons.

Reading 6: STRESS AND TECHNOLOGY

1. Stress- and pressure-filled days have become an almost normal part of contemporary life, due to the cumulative demands of careers, home maintenance, parenting responsibilities, and community involvements. Because of this, there is a general consensus that just doing all that daily needs to be done is an emotionally intense and complex process. In fact, a wit once commented, "Living these days is like a grammar lesson : the past is perfect ; the present is tense."

2. Resulting complaints are familiar : "Even when I'm away from the office, my mind keeps on speeding. I just can't stop it" ; Everything I try to do these days gets so complicated I can't stand it. I want to run away and live back in the woods" ; "There are so many little problems that interfere every day that I never get done what needs to be done. It's so frustrating, and I blow up constantly" ; "It's really strange. Even when I'm relaxing, I have trouble doing just one thing at a time."

3. These statements could easily be explained by the myriad of responsibilities of modern middle-class lifestyles, and to a substantial degree this perception would be accurate. However, a subtle and increasingly pervasive source of stress is the sophisticated technology that has become so much a part of our lives.

4. While new technology and information systems have been tremendous pluses in areas such as communications and health care, the catch is that they are also beginning to impact negatively on human functioning, especially emotional well-being. This influence is at once both elusive and powerful in its psychological effect, but it is not well understood by most men and women. With the passage of time, and as sophisticated technology becomes even more a part of life at work and at home, the potential for its negative impact increases.

5. The marvelous communication system made possible by technology, though beneficial in many ways, has caused a lot of strain on all career-bound people. No matter what our career paths are, we are constantly overloaded

From Bruce A. Baldwin, "Stress and Technology," *USAir Magazine,* (November 1989) : 30–42. Adapted from B. A. Baldwin, *It's All in Your Head : Lifestyle Management Strategies for Busy People !* (Wilmington, N.C. : Direction Dynamics, Inc., 1985). Reprinted by permission of Pace Communications, Inc., Greensboro, North Carolina. Dr. Baldwin is the director of Direction Dynamics.

with new and relevant information. The days are gone when virtually any professional could feel comfortably "up to date" on what is already known. A nagging guilt about not spending more time "keeping up" professionally, the pressure to constantly adapt skills and ways of doing things in light of new knowledge, and the consequent erosion of stability and predictability in life are some of the negative effects of this "ever changing" and "ever up-to-date" information system.

6. The Information Age brought in by advanced technology like electronic mail, electronic data processing, cellular telephones, miniature recorders, and portable computers, has made polyphasic activity possible, because we can get more done in a given time. However, when polyphasic activity becomes habitual, doing just one thing at a time makes us feel uncomfortable and we become no longer able to psychologically "let go" to enjoy just one activity. Instead, we are plagued by distractions that stem from the learned habit of constantly splitting our focus. As a result, genuine relaxation becomes difficult.

7. Modern technology intrudes into modern man's fun and relaxation. As the saying goes, "nothing is simple anymore," and this complexity has increasingly extended into leisure activities. Take for example, fishing, a pastime that many people enjoy. The "advances" are amazing : LED displays on fishing reels, sophisticated fish finders and sonar devices, charts that indicate the water turbidity to help select a lure of exactly the right color, fish "scents," and so on and on. The story is similar in virtually every other sport or leisure activity these days. However, the "gadgets" all require maintenance and can easily fail, leading to frustration and anger.

8. Technology makes it more difficult to separate ourselves from work. In times past, it was possible to leave a stressful workplace, go home, and relax. Since less work was mental and more was physical, it was relatively easy to remove oneself — physically and mentally — from it. The sophisticated communication technology available today was not yet developed. In contrast to the "good old days," it is no longer possible for busy men and women to go home or go on vacation and truly "get away from it all." It becomes difficult to relax when you are carrying a beeper that may go off any minute. The result is higher levels of stress in men and women because technology enables others to "find them anywhere."

9. It is ironic that much technology is designed to make work easier and faster ; presumably, this will make life easier for those who must operate the technology, but such is not the case. Witness the prophetic words of the great philosopher John Stuart Mill (1806-1873) : "It is questionable if all the mechanical inventions yet made have lightened the day's toil of any human being." How true this is despite the promise of "miraculous" new machinery ranging from a "new and more efficient" vacuum cleaner to the most sophisticated computer. The solution to living well lies not in new and better technology, but in the selective disuse of it so that life can be enjoyed in a more emotionally fulfilling way.

POSTREADING ACTIVITIES

Discuss the following in your group and write one or two paragraphs on each.

1. Comment on the writer's statement: "A subtle and increasingly pervasive source of stress is the sophisticated technology that has become so much a part of our lives." (Par. 3)
2. Do you think that the writer wants to go back to the "good old days" when everything was done manually and not mechanically as in the modern age? Give your reasons.
3. How do you define "Information Age?" How does the author relate this to stress?
4. What does the writer mean by the "'ever changing' and 'ever-up-to-date' information system"? (Par. 5) Does this negatively affect your student life?
5. In Par. 7 the writer states: "Nothing is simple any more." How does the writer explain this statement? Do you agree with the explanations and examples? Give your reasons.
6. What impressions do you get about the writer from the last sentence in the essay? Defend your answer.
7. What new information did you receive from reading this essay?
8. What kind of a profession do you think the writer belongs to? How did you make that judgment?
9. Suppose you were a technologist. How would you respond to this essay?
10. Write a letter to the writer agreeing/disagreeing with his or her views.

PREREADING ACTIVITIES

Discuss the following in your group:

1. Do you believe that women are the "weaker sex"? Give your reasons.
2. How different are men and women emotionally?
3. Do you think that the legal system in most societies treats women unjustly? Give examples and reasons.
4. What are some of the limitations that women are subject to in most societies?

5. In your family, who has the final voice in making serious decisions?
    Your father? Your mother? Your wife? Your husband?

Reading 7: WHO DECIDES FOR WOMEN?

1. A pregnant woman in Wyoming arrives at the police station to file assault charges against her husband. Instead, *she* is arrested, because she's intoxicated, and charged with abusing the fetus by drinking. A woman in Georgia is ordered by a court to have a caesarean section, after her doctors testify there is only a 1% chance the baby will survive a vaginal delivery and only a 50% chance the mother will survive it. (She fled and prayed and delivered a healthy baby — vaginally.) Anti-abortion forces demand that state "living will" legislation exclude pregnant women, so that if a woman has specified, even in writing, that she doesn't want to be kept alive by "extraordinary means," her wishes *must* be disregarded if she is pregnant. A couple agrees to have their six-year-old daughter donate bone marrow to their son, who has developed leukemia, after a court threatens to charge the parents with child abuse and take away their children.

2. On the other hand, an Arkansas man refuses to be a bone marrow donor for his brother, dying of leukemia — and no charges are filed.

3. Do we see a pattern here? Well, obviously. Women and children can be coerced into submitting to medical interventions or prevented from exercising their own judgment on a variety of grounds. Men cannot.

4. Courts, under various circumstances, make decisions for people deemed incompetent. The women and parents in these cases were not judged incompetent, at least not in the legal sense. The courts nonetheless saw them as *morally* incompetent, incapable of making a moral choice and so damaged as to need to have their decisions made for them by others.

5. But in the case of a man who refused to donate bone marrow to his dying cousin, morality was legally irrelevant. The judge in that case wrote, "The refusal of the defendant is morally indefensible." Yet, he went on, "to compel the defendant to submit to an intrusion of his body ... would defeat the sanctity of the individual and would impose a rule which would know no limits and one could not imagine where the line would be drawn."

6. When it comes to women and children, the line seems increasingly to be drawn on the wrong side. Clearly, society doesn't trust some women to make responsible moral or medcial judgments, either for themselves or their children. In fact, as Janet Gallagher, an attorney with the Project on Reproductive Laws for the 1990's, has pointed out, in many of these cases the women

---

From Andrea Boroff Eagan, "Who Decides for Women?" *American Health,* (September 1990): 42–43. Copyright © 1990 by *American Health Magazine.* Reprinted by permission.

involved are even seen as not susceptible to reason. "The very fact that [these cases] happen at all ... usually reflects a failure : of public policy, of the organization of medical care or social services, or of simple human communication. Since refusals [of treatment] are relatively uncommon, nonconsent to truly necessary interventions will be extremely rare."

Monstrous Medeas

7. In the worst example of forced intervention that has so far come to light, a pregnant woman dying of cancer was forced to have a cesarean section against her own wishes and those of her husband, parents, and doctors. The lawyers for the Washington, DC hospital summoned a judge, who hastened to the hospital and ordered the surgery, despite medical testimony that it would shorten her life.

8. An appeals panel, consulted by telephone, concurred. The baby died almost immediately ; the mother, within two days. (Recently, the judges' decision was sensibly overturned by the federal district court, which was apparently unable to understand why a woman's pregnancy was sufficient to obliterate all her rights as a human being. However, even this decision won't prevent some local judge from making the same fatal mistake in the future.)

9. What has happened to our traditional picture of Mom, the protector of the brood, who sacrifices her happiness, even starves herself so her children may eat ? When did we lose this view of mothers, and by extension, women, now portrayed as negligent, monstrous Medeas, who would willingly sacrifice their fetuses or children for "convenience," a better job, a religious belief most of us think bizarre, a hit of crack, or maybe a few more days of life ?

10. Writer Katha Pollitt, in an article in *The Nation,* opines that feminism has ruined the reputation of American women, that we are being punished for asking for autonomy, equality and a hand with the diapers. We only recently got to be full legal adults, with the right to vote, sign contracts and have custody of our children. Until well into this century, those rights were denied, and women were considered, legally, to be not much better than children. Now that way of thinking seems to have returned.

11. At the same time, we try to hold women, especially pregnant women and mothers, to a so-called "higher" legal standard than men. A drug-addicted woman in South Carolina who delivers an addicted baby is arrested for child abuse. Her partner, in whose company and with whose complicity she almost certainly used drugs, faces no similar charge. The man who could save his brother's life with an almost risk-free donation of bone marrow suffers, at most, the disapproval of his family and community. The woman who refuses to submit to major surgery on the *chance* of saving her fetus, and against her own religious principles, is ordered into the operation room.

Prenatal Child Abuse

12.   How far can this go? Ethicist John Robertson, a professor of law at the University of Texas and a member of the ethics committee of the American Fertility Society, is a man who apparently doesn't trust women very much. He has suggested that for a woman who has had sex and missed a period, even before a pregnancy is confirmed, "It does not seem unreasonable to require her either to have a pregnancy test or to refrain from activities that would be hazardous to the fetus if she were pregnant."

13.   This could, by some definitions, require her abstention from sexual intercourse, a glass of wine, horseback riding, and most prescription drugs — all of which are perfectly legal for the non-pregnant.

14.   "Woe to the woman," Gallagher comments, "who does not keep accurate track of her menstrual cycle and tidy records of sexual activity to disprove liability 18 or 21 years later," when her child could sue for "prenatal abuse."

15.   A baby damaged by drug abuse, the one who could have been saved by a cesarean section or some other procedure that *wasn't* done, the child who dies because her religious parents refuse any conventional medical treatment — these are indeed tragedies. So are the damaged children of women who conscientiously followed their doctors' orders and took DES, thalidomide or powerful diuretics to hold down weight gain during pregnancy (and the damaged children of women who lack prenatal care, enough to eat or a place to live).

16.   Neither doctors nor judges can predict the outcome of every action, though they sometimes act like they can. But women, as much as men, must be guaranteed their right to bodily integrity, the right not to be pressured into submitting to medical procedures they themselves don't want.

17.   If we deny this right to anyone — even to the lowliest drug addict — we set ourselves on a course where any woman may some day find herself incarcerated to keep her out of harm's way; or bound to a table, gagged and paralyzed by anesthesia, having done to her what someone else has decided she needs.

POSTREADING ACTIVITIES

Discuss the following in your group and write one or two paragraphs on the following:

1.   Substantiate the author's statement: "Women and children can be coerced into submitting to medical interventions or prevented from exercising their own judgment on a variety of grounds. Men cannot." (Par. 3)

2. Do you agree with the writer's allegation that the courts see women "as morally incompetent, incapable of making a moral choice, and so damaged as to need to have their decisions made for them by others"? (Par. 4) Give your reasons.
3. Why do you think most societies treat women as inferior to men?
4. Do you think that in fighting for equal rights women are neglecting their traditional roles? Give your reasons.
5. Why do you think American women were denied the right to vote until recently?
6. Discuss the double standard the writer mentions in Par. 11.
7. From your experiences, give some examples of women being subjected to unnecessary and unwanted medical procedures.
8. Who is the intended audience for this essay? Men? Women? Judges? Medical doctors?
9. What do you think about the writer's tone in this essay? If you wrote the essay, how different would the tone be?
10. Write a letter to the author of the essay, expressing your agreement/disagreement with the points of argument.

PREREADING ACTIVITIES

Discuss the following in your group.

1. How do you define aggression?
2. Differentiate between competition and aggression.
3. Do you need to be competitive and aggressive to survive in American society? Explain by giving examples from your experience.
4. Is it possible to be competitive without being aggressive? Explain with examples.
5. How do you explain Darwin's concept of the survival of the fittest?

Reading 8: IS AGGRESSION NECESSARY?

1. Some scholars have suggested that certain kinds of aggression are useful and, perhaps, even essential. Konrad Lorenz[1], for example, has argued that aggression is "an essential part of the life-preserving organization of

From Elliot Aronson, "Is Aggression Necessary?" in Vivian Rosenberg, *Reading, Writing, Thinking* (New York: McGraw-Hill, 1989), 159–60. Excerpted from E. Aronson, *The Social Animal* (New York: Random House, 1989). Used with permission.

[1]Konrad Lorens, *On Aggression,* tr. Marjorie Wilson (New York: Harcourt, Brace & World, 1966).

instincts." Basing his argument on his observation of nonhumans, he sees aggressiveness as being of prime evolutionary importance, allowing the young animals to have the strongest and wisest mother and fathers and enabling the group to be led by the best possible leaders. From their study of Old World monkeys, the anthropologist Sherwood Washburn and the psychiatrist David Hamburg[2] concur. They find that aggression within the same group of monkeys plays an important role in feeding, reproduction, and in determining dominance patterns. The strongest and most aggressive male in a colony will assume a dominant position through an initial display of aggressiveness. This serves to reduce subsequent serious fighting within the colony (the other males know who's boss). Furthermore, because the dominant male dominates reproduction, the colony increases its chances of survival as the strong male passes on his vigor to subsequent generations.

2.   With these data in mind, many observers urge caution in attempting to control aggression in man, suggesting that, as in lower animals, aggression is necessary for survival. This reasoning is based, in part, on the assumption that the same mechanism that drives one man to kill his neighbor drives another to "conquer" outer space, "sink his teeth" into a difficult mathematical equation, "attack" a logical problem, or "master" the universe.

3.   But this is probably not true. Overt aggression is no longer necessary for human survival. Moreover, to equate creative activity and high achievement with hostility and aggression is to confuse the issue. It is possible to achieve mastery of a problem or a skill without hurting another person or even without attempting to conquer. It is possible to reduce violence without reducing man's curiosity or his desire to solve problems. This is a difficult distinction for us to grasp, because the western mind — and perhaps the American mind in particular — has been trained to equate success with victory, to equate doing well with beating someone. M. F. Ashley Montagu[3] feels that an oversimplification and misinterpretation of Darwin's theory has provided the average man with the mistaken idea that conflict is necessarily the law of life. Ashley Montagu states that it was convenient, during the industrial revolution, for the top dogs, who were exploiting the workers, to justify their exploitation by talking about life being a struggle for survival, and about it's being natural for the fittest (and only the fittest) to survive. The danger, here, is that this kind of reasoning becomes a self-fulfilling prophecy and can cause us to ignore or play down the survival value of non-aggressive and noncompetitive behavior for man and other animals. For

---

[2]Sherwood Washburn and David Hamburg, "The Implications of Primate Research," in *Primate Behavior : Field Studies of Monkeys and Apes,* ed. I. De Vore (New York : Holt, Rinehart & Winston, 1965), 607–622.

[3]M. F. Ashley Montagu, *On Being Human* (New York : Hawthorne Books, 1950).

example, Peter Kropotkin[4] concluded in 1902 that cooperative behavior and mutual aid have great survival value for many forms of life. There is ample evidence to support this conclusion. The cooperative behavior of certain social insects, such as termites, ants, and bees, is well known. Perhaps not so well known is a form of behavior in the chimpanzee that can only be described as "altruistic." It goes something like this : Two chimpanzees are in adjoining cages. One chimp has food and the other doesn't. The foodless chimpanzee begins to beg. Reluctantly, the "wealthy" chimp hands over some of his food. In a sense, the very reluctance with which he does so makes the gift all the more significant. It indicates that he likes the food and would dearly enjoy keeping it for himself. Accordingly, it suggests that the urge to share may have deep roots, indeed.[5] But Kropotkin's work has not been given much attention — indeed, it has been largely ignored — perhaps because it did not fit in with the temper of the times or with the needs of those who were profiting from the industrial revolution.

4. Let us look at our own society. As a culture, we Americans seem to thrive on competition ; we reward winners and turn away from losers. For two centuries, our educational system has been based upon competitiveness and the laws of survival. With very few exceptions, we do not teach our kids to love learning — we teach them to strive for high grades. When sportswriter Grantland Rice said that what's important is not whether you win or lose, but how you play the game, he was not describing the dominant theme in American life ; he was *prescribing* a cure for our over-concern with winning. ... Vince Lombardi, a very successful professional football coach, may have summed it up with the simple statement, "Winning isn't everything, it's the *only* thing." What is frightening about the acceptance of this philosophy is that it implies that the goal of victory justifies whatever means we use to win, even if it's only a football game — which, after all, was first conceived as a recreational activity.

5. It is certainly true that, in the early history of man's evolution, a great deal of aggressive behavior was adaptive. But as we look about and see a world full of strife, of international and interracial hatred and distrust, of senseless slaughter and political assassination, we feel justified in questioning the survival value of this behavior. The biologist Loren Eisley paid tribute to our ancient ancestors, but warned against imitating them, when he wrote : "The need is now for a gentler, a more tolerant people than those who won for us against the ice, the tiger, and the bear."[6]

---

[4]Peter Kropotkin, *Mutual Aid* (New York : Doubleday, 1902).

[5]Henry Nissen, "Social Behavior in Primates," in *Comparative Psychology,* 3rd ed., ed. C. P. Stone (New York : Prentice Hall, 1951), 423–457.

[6]Loren Eisley, *The Immense Journey* (New York : Random House, 1946), 140.

POSTREADING ACTIVITIES

Discuss the following in your group and write one or two paragraphs on each.

1. Why does the writer quote Lorenz's argument that aggression is "an essential part of the life-preserving organization of instincts?" (Par. 1)
2. Have you found aggression necessary for your survival in American society? Can nonaggressive people be successful professionals in this society? Explain with examples.
3. How do you define overt and covert aggression? Which of the two kinds do you notice in American society? Give examples.
4. Comment on the statement: "Cooperative behavior and mutual aid have great survival value for many forms of life." (Par. 3) Substantiate this statement, giving examples from your own social or family structure.
5. What is the difference between teaching to love learning and teaching to strive for high grades? What is wrong in teaching the kids to strive for high grades? (Par. 4)
6. What does the author mean by the statement that "in the early history of man's evolution, a great deal of aggressive behavior was adaptive"? (Par. 5) Give examples.
7. Comment on the concluding quote: "The need is now for a gentler, a more tolerant people than those who won for us against the ice, the tiger, and the bear." Would you prefer to be aggressive or tolerant? Why?
8. Do you think the writer is a tolerant person? How did you make that judgment?
9. Who do you think is the intended audience of this essay? The American public? The elite? The international public? Give reasons for your answer.
10. Write a letter to the writer agreeing/disagreeing with the argument.

PREREADING ACTIVITIES

Discuss the following in your group:

1. If you went to public school in the United States, what do you think are the advantages and disadvantages of the American public school system?

2. If you went to school in another country and also in the United States, compare and contrast the school systems in the two countries. Which system do you prefer? Why?
3. What do you expect from a college education? Are you happy or unhappy with the kind of education you are getting now? How?
4. Would you send your children to private or public schools? Why?
5. If you were the Education Secretary, what reforms — if any — would you make on the present educational system in the United States? Why would you or would you not make changes?

Reading 9: WE SHOULD CHERISH OUR CHILDREN'S FREEDOM TO THINK

1. Americans who remember "the good old days" are not alone in complaining about the educational system in this country. Immigrants, too, complain, and with more up-to-date comparisons. Lately, I have heard a Polish refugee express dismay that his daughter's high school has not taught her the difference between Belgrade and Prague. A German friend was furious when he learned that the mathematics test given to his son on his first day as a freshman included multiplication and division. A Lebanese boasts that the average high school graduate in his homeland can speak fluently in Arabic, French, and English. Japanese businessmen in Los Angeles send their children to private schools staffed by teachers imported from Japan to learn mathematics at Japanese levels, generally considered at least a year more advanced than the level here.

2. But I wonder: If American education is so tragically inferior, why is it that this is still the country of innovation?

3. I think I found the answer on an excursion to the Laguna Beach Museum of Art, where the work of schoolchildren was on exhibit. Equipped only with colorful yarns, foil paper, felt pens and crayons, they had transformed simple paper lunch bags into, among other things, a waterfall with flying fish, Broom Hilda the witch, and a house with a woman in a skimpy bikini hiding behind a swinging door. Their public school had provided these children with opportunities and direction to fulfill their creativity, something that people tend to dismiss or take for granted.

4. When I was 12 in Indonesia, where education followed the Dutch system, I had to memorize the names of all the world's major cities, from Kabul to Karachi. At the same age, my son, who was brought up a Californian, thought that Buenos Aires was Spanish for good food — a plate of tacos and

From Kie Ho, "We Should Cherish Our Children's Freedom to Think," in Sharon Scull, *Critical Reading and Writing for Advanced ESL Students* (Englewood Cliffs, N.J.: Prentice-Hall, Inc., 1987), 267–69. Reprinted with permission of the author.

burritos, perhaps. However, unlike his counterparts in Asia and Europe, my son had studied *creative* geography. When he was only 6, he drew a map of the route that he traveled to get to school, including the streets and their names, the buildings and traffic signs and the houses that he passed.

5. Disgruntled American parents forget that in this country their children are able to experiment freely with ideas ; without this, they will not really be able to think or to believe in themselves.

6. In my high school years, we were models of dedication and obedience ; we sat to listen, to answer only when asked, and to give the only correct answer. Even when studying word forms, there were no alternatives. In similes, pretty lips were *always* as red as sliced pomegranate, and beautiful eyebrows were *always* like a parade of black clouds. Like children in many other countries of the world, I simply did not have a chance to choose, to make decisions. My son, on the contrary, told me that he got a good laugh — and an A — from his teacher for concocting, "the man was as nervous as Richard Pryor at a Ku Klux Klan convention."

7. There is no doubt that American education does not meet high standards in such basic skills as mathematics and language. And we realize that our youngsters are ignorant of Latin, put Mussolini in the same category as Dostoevski, cannot recite the Periodic Table by heart. Would we, however, prefer to stuff the developing little heads of our children with hundreds of geometric problems, the names of rivers in Brazil and 50 lines from "The Canterbury Tales" ? Do we really want to retard their impulses, frustrate their opportunities for self-expression ?

8. When I was 18, I had to memorize Hamlet's "To be or not to be" soliloquy flawlessly. In his English class, my son was assigned to write a love letter to Juliet, either in Shakespearean jargon or in modern lingo. (He picked the latter ; his Romeo would take Juliet to an arcade for a game of Donkey Kong.)

9. Where else but in America can a history student take the role of Lyndon Johnson in an open debate against another student playing Ho Chi Minh ? It is unthinkable that a youngster in Japan would dare to do the same regarding the role of Hirohito in World War II.

10. Critics of American education cannot grasp one thing, something that they don't truly understand because they are never deprived of it : freedom. This most important measurement has been omitted in the studies of the quality of education in this century, the only one, I think, that extends even to children the license to freely speak, write and be creative. Our public education certainly is not perfect, but it is a great deal better than any other.

POSTREADING ACTIVITIES

Discuss the following in your group and write one or two paragraphs on each.

1. In general, how different do you think the American education system is from that of some non-Western countries?
2. Summarize the author's argument in preferring the American system of education as it exists now.
3. Do you think that in its emphasis on creativity and imagination, the American education system does not promote critical thinking habits?
4. Do you think rote memorization helps in any kind of learning? Explain with examples.
5. Comment on the writer's statement that American children "are able to experiment freely with ideas: without this they will not really be able to think or to believe in themselves." (Par. 5)
6. What, according to the writer, is wrong in "being models of dedication and obedience"? (Par. 6) What do you think about this? Give your reasons.
7. Is it true that "American education does not meet high standards in such basic skills as mathematics and language"? (Par. 7) What, according to the writer, counteracts this deficiency in the American education system?
8. What, in your opinion, are the advantages of being given "the license to freely speak, write, and be creative"? (Par. 10)
9. Compare and contrast the advantages and disadvantages of having the "license to be free" with those of being forced to be "models of dedication and obedience," as described in Par. 6? Which of the two do you prefer? Why?
10. Who is the intended audience of this essay? How did you arrive at your conclusion?
11. Write a letter to the writer agreeing/disagreeing with the arguments.

Part 2: WRITING

EXPOSITORY WRITING: ARGUMENTATION

Chapters 1-8 were meant to help you develop skills in writing expository essays by describing, classifying, analyzing causes and effects, comparing and contrasting, and so on. Learning how to write an argumentative essay involves the most sophisticated skill of all, because it requires more than stating the thesis and developing it.

Purpose of the Argumentative Essay

To begin with, you have to know what an argument is. An argument is the result of the disagreement between two parties on a controversial issue. Each party tries to convince the other that her/his opinion is right. Since arguments are based on opinions, the issue is always debatable.

Statements of facts are not debatable. For example: The earth is round. Even though at one period in history this statement was debatable, this is now an accepted fact. Also, matters of faith (for example, the Christian belief in the Trinity, or the Hindu belief in reincarnation) cannot be debated. People may disagree on matters of faith. However, it is very difficult to convince the other party, because the issue is not one of opinion but of faith. So, also, preferences cannot be debated. For example, one person might prefer Chinese food to Cuban food or vice versa because to him or her one kind of food tastes better than the other. This cannot be debated because the issue is based on two people's taste buds. However, you can argue that one kind of food is more popular in certain parts of the country, because you can quote data to support your statement.

To summarize: For an argumentative thesis to be possible, it should be:

- Debatable
- Based on a controversial issue
- Based on opinion

but should not be based on facts, preference, or religious faith.

An argument is different from persuasion, propaganda, and fight. When you try to persuade others, you are trying to make them reject their opinions or beliefs, and accept yours. An argument, on the other hand, is meant to convince the opponents in such a way that they will be able to overcome doubts about your side of the issue. In the process, the opponents may or may not accept your point of view. However, they will certainly be convinced or at least be aware that your side of the argument has some logic. They may still hold on to their points of view and may come up with more counterarguments, and the debate may still go on indefinitely.

Propaganda is a sophisticated form of persuasion used by political parties, corporations, and so on, to promote their ideas and win over the competing opponents by defeating them. Propagandists may quote statistics and data, but these are often distorted to serve their purpose. Rather than appealing to the audience's reason, they appeal to their emotions. They use such devices as sweeping and hasty generalizations, name calling, and the like, none of which can ever be used in an argument. In an argument, there is no question of defeating the opponents and winning over. It is just a matter of convincing the opponent how reasonable your side of the issue is.

An argument is not a quarrel over an issue either ; it just presents reasons for or against something. In both quarrels and arguments people disagree. However, during a quarrel, may people get angry, call each other names, threaten each other, and may even become irrational and emotional. However, an argument is a reasonable presentation of ideas, providing proofs and evidence. Winning or losing is not the issue. Hence, in an argument there is no place for unpleasant or nasty references, attacks on the opponent's character or beliefs, scoffing, or sarcastic remarks.

Organization

The *introduction* of an argumentative essay (1) identifies the issue, (2) briefly explains both sides of the argument, and (3) states the thesis, which tells the reader what your stand is.

The *thesis* of an argumentative essay is different from that in other kinds of expository essays. First, you have to take a strong stand, proposing a course of action. This is often (not always) expressed by the modal verb *should*.

> Ex. Knowledge about sex *should* be imparted formally by school professionals and not informally by parents.

The *developmental paragraphs* develop the argument logically (as opposed to chronologically and descriptively) by giving verifying examples and evidence. Remember, you are trying to convince your opponents that your point of view is right and theirs is wrong. Therefore, audience awareness is very important in this part of your essay. Always remind yourself that the argument is directed against the opponents and not to those who favor your side of the issue. Therefore, knowing your opponents' views against yours is very important.

For example, in developing the thesis above, your reasons may be : (1) many parents do not have the kind of scientific knowledge about the topic that professionals have to answer teenagers' questions, (2) the parent-children relationship is so close that it makes it difficult for parents to look at the issue impartially. Your opponents may agree on these points, in which case there is no argument. Their contention may be that sex education in school gives the youngsters "the license" to experiment with sex, which may promote promiscuity. If you do not refute this counterargument, your opponents will not see any validity in your argument.

Refutation of possible counterarguments by the opponents may be done in two ways : (1) by incorporating the refutation in the developmental paragraphs, (2) by devoting a separate paragraph, preferably the last developmental paragraph, to a refutation. For beginning writers, the second method is easier.

Remember, you are not quarrelling. Arguing is a sophisticated way of debating. Therefore, do not make derogatory or sarcastic statements. For example, statements like : "Those who think that school is the right place for sex education are either stupid or ignorant" do not belong in an argument. Think of the strongest argument by your opponents against yours. Prove that yours is more reasonable and valid.

Inductive Versus Deductive Reasoning

Inductive reasoning argues from the specific to the general. That is, you examine specific details and make a generalization based on the evidence gotten from the examination of these details. You have been applying this kind of reasoning all through this book. For example, when you answer the question : "What message does the writer try to convey ?" you are analyzing the details given in the reading passage and coming to a conclusion. Again, when you classify items and compare and contrast them, you are applying inductive reasoning.

In deductive reasoning, you start with a generalization and arrive at a conclusion about a specific item, based on the generalization. When you start with a thesis statement, you do not have any choice except to apply deductive reasoning, because in stating the thesis, you have already made a judgment on the issue. Therefore, the burden is on you to prove this generalized thesis statement by explaining it convincingly. Explain your reasons for making this generalization by giving supporting details. Facts drawn from research studies, historical facts, scientific data, statistics, etc., are the best supporting details. The more convincing these supporting details are, the more convincing your argument would be.

The *conclusion* may summarize the points developed in the developmental paragraphs or restate the thesis statement in a different way. You may end up the essay with some kind of prediction about the issue, making a value judgment, giving a warning, making suggestions, etc.

For Your Critical Thinking

1. Analyze the readings in this chapter to find out if all of them refute the opponents' points of view ? Add refutations to those which do not include one.
2. What method of refutation do the other essays follow, incorporating the refutation into the writer's defense or giving it as a separate paragraph ?

3. Do you find in the reading selections given in this chapter any persuasive essays not fitting the format of an argumentative essay? What changes are needed to make these essays argumentative?
4. Are there any essays which are "colored" by the writer's anger on the issues? How would you "soften" the writer's tone?
5. Find the thesis statement in each essay. Are these thesis statements explained well in the body paragraphs?
6. Find the essays which are based on research studies and scientific data. Compare and contrast them with the other essays which do not use these data.
7. Do all the essays give examples? Do the examples help clarify the points argued?
8. Compare and contrast the introductions of the essays. Would you modify any of the introductions? Which ones? Why?
9. Do any of the essays sound unsophisticated? Explain your answer.
10. Do all the essays give conclusions? Add conclusions if needed.
11. Which of the essays do you find easily comprehensible? Why?

WRITING ACTIVITIES

Reaction Journal

Write in your journal:

- If any reading material given in the chapter offends you in any way, and how
- If the readings helped or did not help you to think more critically about the controversial issues presented, and how
- If any of the readings made you change some of your previously held views about some issues; how and why
- If any readings make you exclaim, "Outrageous!" or "How biased!" which ones did so, and why
- Which of the readings you enjoyed most, and why
- Which of the readings you would or would not recommend to your friends, and why
- How the chapter helped or failed to help you to improve your writing skills
- How it helped or did not help you to be to a critical thinker

Learning Log

Write in your learning log:

- What new things you learned from the chapter

- How and where you can apply this new learning
- Some new vocabulary words you learned from this chapter which you are confident to use in your writing
- How different or similar the discussion on the argumentative essay was compared to what you already knew

Writing Assignment

Overview

Write a letter to the writer of one of the articles, whose ideas you disagree with.

> *Real-life Purpose:* To express in writing your agreement/disagreement with the ideas expressed in the article
>
> *Academic Purpose:* To practice writing an argumentative essay
>
> *Real-life Audience:* The author of the article whose ideas you agree/disagree with
>
> *Academic Audience:* Your class members and instructor

Procedure

IN-CLASS GROUP WORK

Group Size: Four to six

1. Members come to an agreement about which article to review.
2. Make sure that the group members you have chosen are divided in their opinion about the writer's ideas. In case the members are unanimous in their opinion, change the membership of your group.
3. Form two subgroups of those who agree and disagree.
4. Argue for and against. Make notes on the major points mentioned. The purpose is to get ideas for both defending and refuting.
5. Pool the group's ideas and make an outline.

OUT-OF-CLASS INDIVIDUAL WRITING

1. Elaborate on the outline, giving reasons and quoting data or statistics.
2. Write the essay defending your stand and refuting the opponent's.
3. Read the essay aloud to yourself, and revise and rewrite, using the formula DARe.

IN-CLASS ACTIVITY

Exchange your paper with at least one of your peers and get feedback. Revise and rewrite, if needed. Hand in the final draft.

Alternate Writing Assignment

Take a stand on one of the following. Write an essay defending your position and refuting your opponent's.

1. Should attendance at class meeetings be a mandatory requirement for passing the course?
2. Should public transportation be free to all residents?
3. Should women be drafted?
4. Should men and women share equal responsibility for household chores?

You may use your reading on the topic and also your life experience as the sources for this assignment.

UNIT · 3

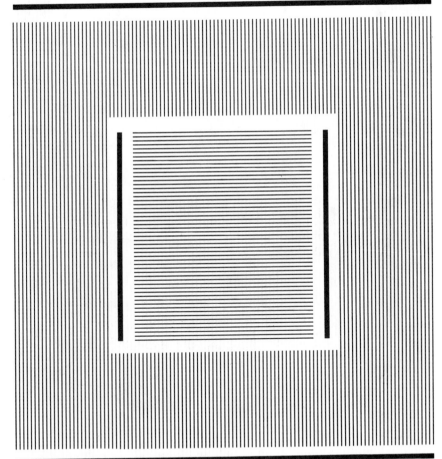

CHAPTER · 10

Part 1: WORD ORDER AND THE ENGLISH SENTENCE

THE EDITING PROCESS

Editing is the last step in the writing process. Revision relates to content and organization, whereas editing relates to language and usage. In other words, you revise to check *what* you wrote, and you edit to check *how* you expressed *what you wrote.*

Basically, editing involves reviewing your essay to see if you have followed the rules of syntax, grammar, and idiomatic usage. These rules exist in all languages, and most native writers follow these rules intuitively. However, second language learners have to remind themselves of these rules. Some of these rules and the most common errors that writers of English make are discussed below.

WORD ORDER

English has strict rules of word order, and violating these rules can lead to miscommunication. For example, the sentences below all use the same words, but when the words are arranged in different orders, the meaning changes.

S1.   The dog bit the boy.
S2.   The boy bit the dog.

S3.   The dog really bit the boy very little.
S4.   The very little dog really bit the boy.
S5.   The very little boy really bit the dog.

English has fixed positions for each grammatical construction. The three basic positions are:

1.   Subject
2.   Verb phrase
3.   Object

THE SUBJECT

The first position in a basic English sentence is that of the *subject* — the topic of the sentence. The usual constructions that go in the subject position are:

- Noun or pronoun
- Noun phrase or clause
- Infinitive, gerund, or participle phrase

A test you can use to check whether you are using the correct construction in this position is to replace the whole position by a pronoun. For example, in Sentences 1–5 above, *it* or *he* can be substituted for the subjects as below:

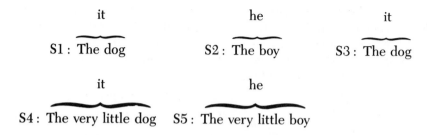

The Dummy Subject: *There, It*

Another construction that can fill the subject position is the dummy subject. There are two dummy subjects in English, *there* and *it*.

There

This dummy subject is usually used with *be* verbs.

Ex. 1. There are three computer laboratories in our school.

The actual subject of the sentence is *three computer labs*. However, in English there is no such structure as: "Three computer laboratories are in our school."

It

There are two kinds of *it* structures:

1. Impersonal *it*

   Ex. 1.   It is hot today.
   Ex. 2.   It is half past ten.

   In some languages, like Spanish, *it* can be left out and the sentence is still grammatical. English does not allow this. Omitting *it* in such structures is ungrammatical.

2. Anticipatory *it*

   Ex. 1.   It is very dangerous to go out now.
   Ex. 2.   It is very useful to carry a pocket dictionary with you.

The actual subjects of these sentences are *to go out now* and *to carry a pocket dictionary.* Here, you may reverse the order and say, "To go out now is very dangerous," and "To carry a pocket dictionary is very useful." However, English speakers do not prefer this structure.

Noun Phrases

The nucleus of a noun phrase is a *noun,* which can be modified by adjectives and articles, both of which precede the noun nucleus. Nouns can fill either the subject or object position. Many ESL speakers have difficulty in the use of singular and plural numbers of nouns and of count/non-count nouns.

Number

Remember : The plural noun usually ends in *-(e)s.*
   Some exceptions are :

sing.	*pl.*	*sing.*	*pl.*
child	children	deer	deer
foot	feet	louse	lice
means	means	mouse	mice
ox	oxen	people	people
sheep	sheep	species	species
series	series		

Count and Non-count Nouns

Count nouns refer to persons, things, or events which are countable (two books, three children, etc.), and non-count nouns refer to persons, things, or events which are not countable. Remember: Only count nouns take the plural form -(e)s.

Non-count nouns belong to categories like the following:

1. Abstractions

   Examples:
   honesty/dishonesty   beauty/ugliness
   happiness/unhappiness   wisdom/stupidity
   love/hatred   poverty/richness/wealth
   truth/falsehood/knowledge   literacy/illiteracy/information

2. Metals or solids

   Examples: gold, silver, diamond, sand, silk, dirt, dust

3. Liquids

   Examples: water, gasoline

4. Gases

   Examples: air, gas, oxygen, hydrogen

5. Food

   Examples: salt, coffee, tea, sugar, butter, bacon, flour, rice, corn

6. Fields of study or activity

   Examples: mathematics, science, agriculture, linguistics, history, swimming, volley ball, shopping, farming

7. Languages

   Examples: English, Russian, Japanese, Chinese, Spanish

   Note: Do not add -(e)s when you use non-count nouns even when the meaning is plural. Such nouns are made plural by adding quantitative modifiers:

Examples: *fields* of knowledge, *two ounces* of gold, *two bags* of sand, *two cups* of coffee, *three bottles* of water

Pronouns

Pronouns are substitutes for nouns, and like nouns, they can fill both the subject and object positions.

Three problems you have to watch out for when editing are:

1. Shift in number, person, or gender.

    Ex. 1. Incorrect: When we edit your essays we should correct mistakes in grammar.

    Rewrite: When *you* edit your essays *you* should correct mistakes in grammar.

    Or: When *we* edit *our* essays we should correct mistakes in grammar.

    Ex. 2. Incorrect: My friend's parents moved to his new retirement house yesterday.

    Rewrite: My friend's parents moved to *their* new retirement house yesterday.

2. Unclear pronoun reference. A pronoun should refer back clearly to the noun it stands for. Otherwise ambiguity will result.

    Ex. 1. Incorrect: When the Mayor talked to the City Council Chairman, he complained about the lack of funding for the project.

The pronoun, *he,* in this sentence may refer to either *Mayor* or *Councilman* so that the answer to, "Who complained?" is unclear. Correct the sentence by repeating the noun to which *he* refers, or change the sentence structure:

    Rewrite: While talking to the Mayor, the City Council Chairman complained about the lack of funding for the project.

    Ex. 2. Incorrect: On Friday evenings my mother did jigsaw puzzles with my little brother and read short stories to him. This was a good mental exercise for him.

What does *this* stand for — jigsaw puzzles or short stories or both? If it is the puzzles, rewrite the sentence:

Rewrite: On Friday evenings my mother did jigsaw puzzles with my little brother and read short stories to him. The puzzles provided him with good mental exercise.

If *this* refers to *stories*, rewrite the second sentence:

Rewrite: The stories provided him with good mental exercise.

Or, if *this* refers to both, rewrite the second sentence:

Rewrite: These puzzles and stories provided him with good mental exercise.

Adjectives

Adjectives and adjective phrases can make up a noun phrase, which can fill the subject or object position of a sentence.

Some common errors ESL speakers make with adjectives are:

1. Incorrectly pluralizing adjectives to make them agree with the nouns they qualify. *In English, adjectives are not pluralized as in some other languages, such as Spanish.*

    Ex. Honesty and sincerity are the most importants values in my life.
    Rewrite: Honesty and sincerity are the most important values in my life.

2. Incorrect use of comparative and superlative forms. Remember: In English there is no double comparative or superlative form. When you use *more/most* with long adjectives, you cannot also use *-er/-est.* Also, remember that short adjectives take only *-er/-est.* not *more/most.*

    Ex. Yesterday's test was more easier than today's.
    Rewrite: Yesterday's test was easier than today's.

    Some troublesome adjectives:

positive	*comparative*	*superlative*
good	better (than)	the best
bad	worse (than)	the worst
little	less (than)	the least

3. Wrong use of present and past participles as adjectives:

    Ex. 1. I found the movie interested.
    Rewrite: I found the movie *interesting*.

4. Misplacement of adjectives. In English, adjectives go before the noun.

    Ex. Marie was the girl most beautiful in that group.
    Rewrite: Marie was the most beautiful girl in that group.

5. Unclear or dangling modifiers.

    Ex. 1. The librarian handed Gary a book across the desk *that was old and fragile*.[1]

The adjective clause *that was old and fragile* modifies *book*. However, in the sentence it appears to modify *desk*, which gives the sentence an awkward meaning.
The corrected sentence is:

    Rewrite: Reaching across the desk, the librarian handed Gary a book that was old and fragile.

    Ex. 2. Sitting in the garden, a dog bit me.

The modifier *sitting in the garden* is without a subject. According to the rule that applies to the use of the participle, the subject of the sentence is also the subject of the participle. As it stands, this sentence means: "The dog was sitting in the garden and bit itself." This is unlikely to be what the writer meant.

    Rewrite: While I was sitting in the garden, a dog bit me.

6. Incorrect use of *only*. Notice the difference in meaning in the following sentences:

    Ex. 1. Only she marked the grammar mistakes. (Means: Nobody else marked the grammar mistakes.)

---

[1]This example is taken from Robert Miles, *First Principles of the Essay* 2nd ed. (New York: Harper & Row Publishers, 1975) p. 225.

Ex. 2.   She only marked the mistakes. (Means: She marked them, but did not correct them.)

Ex. 3.   He marked only the grammar mistakes. (Means: He didn't mark any other mistakes.)

Remember: Put *only* before the noun or noun phrase it modifies. If *only* modifies a final noun or noun phrase, it can be placed either before or after the word(s) it modifies. For example, the following two sentences have the same meaning:

Ex. 1.   The city school system hires *only* licensed teachers.

Ex. 2.   The city school system hires licensed teachers *only.*

Articles

An article, like an adjective, goes before a noun to make up a noun phrase. Most ESL speakers have problems with articles. Errors fall into three categories.

1.   Omission of articles
2.   Wrong use of articles
3.   Using the indefinite article *a* before a non-count noun

The following is a summary of the general rules that apply to the use of articles in English:

1.   An article (either definite or indefinite) always goes before a singular count noun, unless it is preceded by another determiner.

Ex. 1.   We need *a* blackboard in this classroom.
Ex. 2.   We need *another* blackboard in this classroom.

2.   The indefinite articles *a* and *an* never go before a noun used in its non-count meaning. However, when it is used in a countable context, *a* or *an* can be used before it. Meaning and context determine the use.

Ex. 1.   My sister-in-law has long hair.
Ex. 2.   Yesterday my baby sister didn't drink her juice because she found *a* hair in the juice bottle.
Ex. 3.   Life is a mysterious journey.
Ex. 4.   She had *a* terrible life because her husband was abusive.

Specific Rules

INDEFINITE ARTICLE: *A/AN*

Use *a* before:

1. A noun beginning with a consonant sound:

   Examples: *a* house, *a* desk, *a* book, *a* pen

2. Certain ailments (not diseases), such as toothache, headache, cold.

   Ex. 1. I have *a* terrible headache.
   Ex. 2. I catch *a* cold every winter.

Use *an* before a noun beginning with a vowel *sound* (not *letter*):

   Examples: *an* umbrella, *an* honest man

   Certain idiomatic expressions require the indefinite article:

   Examples: in *a* hurry, all of *a* sudden, *a* couple of, *a* hard/good/
   long time, *a* great deal, *a* lot of

Note: In some expressions, the presence or absence of *a* makes a difference in meaning. Many ESL speakers have problems with these expressions. Some of these are:

1. Few; a few (used only with count nouns). The two phrases convey opposite meanings.

   Ex. 1. My school has *few* international students. (Meaning: practically no international students.)
   Ex. 2. My school has *a few* international students. (Meaning: some international students.)

2. Little; a little (used only with non-count nouns).

   Ex. 1. I have *little* money left in my wallet. (Meaning: practically no money.)
   Ex. 2. I have *a little* money left in my wallet. (Meaning: some money.)

THE DEFINITE ARTICLE : *THE*

Use the definite article *the* before :

1. Certain words to point out specifically which previously mentioned person or thing the speaker is talking about

   Examples :   *the* former, *the* latter, *the* same, *the* rest, *the* remainder, *the* last, *the* first

   In context :   When I went to the tutoring lab yesterday, I met two tutors, Miss Peters and Mr. Rowley. *The* former is an English tutor and *the* latter, a Math tutor.

2. A noun which the listener or reader recognizes as specific (as distinguished from others of the same species)

   Ex. 1.   On my way to school this morning I encountered *a* shaggy looking man walking with *a* pretty young woman. Later on I learned that *the* man was *the* woman's boyfriend.

   By the second time the speaker talks about the man and woman, the listener knows what *particular* man and woman are being referred to.

   Ex. 2.   I am an international student at Columbia University. I want to open an account at this bank. Should I speak with *the* bank manager or *the* customer service representative ?

   Here *the* is used because the listener understands which people the speaker is talking about, not because there is any previous reference to them.

3. A noun which has a modifying noun, phrase, or clause

   Ex. 1.   *The* man in *the* blue uniform was carrying a pistol with him.
   Ex. 2.   The lady who lives in *the* blue house is sick.

4. Ordinal numbers

   Examples :   *the* first, *the* second, *the* tenth

5. Transition words indicating order

   Examples :   *the* next, *the* last

6. Superlative adjectives

   Examples : *the* most important, *the* best

7. Parts of body in a general sense

   Ex. 1. In some cultures *the* head is considered the most important part of the body.

   Note : When reference is made to a specific person's body parts, use a possessive adjective :

   Ex. 1. I feel like *my* head is spinning.

8. Nouns referring to means of communication

   Examples : *the* radio, *the* news, *the* telephone

   Note : *TV* and *television* do not take *the* before them, unless you mean a specific television.

   Ex. 1. I watch my favorite program on television at five o'clock in the evening everyday. However, I couldn't watch it yesterday because my sister took *the* television to her house.

   Note : Do not use *the* with the preposition *by.*

   Ex. 1. The news about the hurricane was spread around the town by radio.

9. Certain activities

   Ex. 1. I cannot play *the* piano, but I can play *the* violin very well.

10. Names of languages followed by the word *language*

    Examples : *the* French language, *the* Spanish language, *the* English language (but : a book written in French)

11. Nouns referring to people of specific nationalities

    Examples : *the* English, *the* French, *the* Spanish

12. Unique (one of a kind) things

      Examples: *the* sun, *the* moon, *the* Bible, *the* Koran

13. A family name when its members are referred to collectively

      Examples: *the* Smiths (means: every member of the family with the last name *Smith*)

14. The name of a geographic family or group

      Examples: *the* Philippines, *the* Netherlands, *the* Rocky Mountains, *the* Far East, *the* Near East, *the* United Nations

15. Place names which are descriptive in meaning

      Examples: *the* Dominican Republic, *the* Punjab

16. Place names which contain the word *United* or *Union*

      Examples: *the* United States of America, *the* Union of Soviet Socialist Republics (the U.S.S.R. or *the* Soviet Union), *the* United Kingdom

17. Class names

      Examples: *the* State of New Jersey
                  the People's Republic of China
                  the Muslim Kingdom

18. The name of a religion or race followed by the word *religion* or *race*

      Examples: *the* Hindu religion, *the* Christian religion, *the* Jewish religion

19. Names referring to races

      Examples: *the* whites, *the* blacks, *the* Jews

20. Followers of a religion

      Examples: *the* Christians, *the* Hindus

21. Names of oceans, seas, rivers, canals, peninsulas, deserts, monuments, buildings, forests, groups of islands, groups of lakes, gulfs, tunnels, gardens, zoos, ships, newspapers

Examples:

the Pacific Ocean	*the* West Indies
the Arabian Sea	*the* Finger Lakes
the Nile	*the* Persian Gulf
the Panama Canal	*the* Holland Tunnel
the Balkan Peninsula	*the* Hanging Gardens
the Sahara Desert	*the* Bronx zoo
the Lincoln Memorial	*the* Titanic
the Empire State Building	*The* New York Times
the Black Forest	

22. Names of mountain ranges

Examples: *the* Himalayas, *the* Rocky Mountains

23. Names of colleges and universities when they are specified by *of*

Examples: *The* City University of New York
The City College of New York
The University of Pennsylvania

24. Names of companies when *the* is part of the company's name

Examples: *The* New York Telephone Company
The IBM Corporation

25. Titles of officials when specified by *of*

Examples: *the* president of the United States
the prime minister of India

26. Periods of history

Examples: *the* Dark Ages, *the* Victorian Age, *the* Middle Ages

Do not use *the* before:

1. Personal names

Examples: Mary, Anna, Carmen, James, Yi Ping, Ram

Note: You can use *the* to distinguish between two persons with the same name.

Ex. 1.   *The* Josephine who got married yesterday was not *the* same Josephine who is my sister's friend.

2.   Names of individual countries, continents, states, cities, boroughs, streets, avenues, lakes, parks and squares, mountains, islands, halls, falls, beaches

Examples: India, China, Russia
Asia, Europe, Australia
New York State, Virginia, California
New York City, Delhi, Tokyo
Brooklyn, Manhattan, Queens (but *the* Bronx)
Mott Street, 10th Street, 42nd Street
Broadway, Atlantic Avenue, Convent Avenue (but *the* Avenue of the Americas)
Lake George, Lake Periyar, Lake Erie
Central Park, Alley Pond Park, Hudson Park
Times Square, Tiannamon Square, Washington Square
Mount Everest, Mount Helen, Mount Kilimanjaro
Roosevelt Island, Greenland, New Zealand
Victoria Town Hall, Whittier Hall, Johnson Hall
Niagara Falls, Victoria Falls
Miami Beach, Rockaway Beach, Jones Beach

3.   Plural nouns used in a general sense

Examples: people, men, women, ladies, politicians, social workers

4.   Names of colleges and universities

Examples: Columbia College, Smith College, Long Island University, Columbia University

5.   Titles of officials when used with personal names

Examples: President Bush
Prime Minister Bhutto
Chairman Mao

6. Non-count nouns unless followed by a modifying phrase

    Examples: money, dust, tea (but *the* money in my wallet, *the* dust on my glasses, *the* tea I make)

7. *Man* or *mankind*, even when modified

    Ex. 1. Primitive man did not have the need to save for the future.
    Ex. 2. Mankind will always have social problems.

    Note: Use *the* with *human race*.

8. Collective nouns like *society, civilization*, when used in a collective sense

    Ex. 1. Society needs children.
    Ex. 2. Civilization is a result of man's progress in the world.

9. Abstract nouns unless used with a specific reference

    Ex. 1. Marriage is a social custom. (general)
    Ex. 2. *The* marriage between the two prisoners made headlines in the newspapers. (specific)
    Ex. 3. Death is very hard to take. (general)
    Ex. 4. *The* death of my uncle last week was very hard to take. (specific)

10. Activities, when used in a general sense

    Ex. 1. Running is good exercise.
    Ex. 2. Some people have a talent for writing.

11. Fields of study

    Ex. 1. My major is economics.
    Ex. 2. Mathematics is difficult for me.

12. Places of activity when the reference is to the activity

    Ex. 1. I went to church last Sunday. (Meaning: I worshipped last Sunday)
    Ex. 2. I went to *the* church last Sunday. (Meaning: to visit, not to worship)

Some other nouns of this category are *court, school, chapel, prison.*

Note: In English, *university* is not considered a place of activity, so it is always used with an article.

13. Religious place names

    Examples: heaven, hell, paradise, purgatory, Hades

14. Activities (idiomatic)

    Examples: go to bed, go shopping, on vacation, at work

15. Names of companies, especially in the possessive

    Examples: Macy's, Sears Roebuck's, Lord and Taylor's

16. Names of magazines and periodicals

    Examples: *Time, Psychology Today, Life*

17. Names of days of the week, months, holidays

    Examples: Monday, Tuesday, April, May
    Halloween, Christmas, New Year's Day (but *the* third of September, *the* Fourth of July)

18. Directional nouns

    Examples: east, west, south, north

19. Names of diseases

    Examples: measles, pneumonia, typhoid

20. Games and sports

    Ex. 1. My brother plays basketball.
    Ex. 2. My husband hates skiing.

THE VERB PHRASE

The second position in an English sentence is that of the *verb phrase,* which comprises two slots, namely:

1. An X-word slot
2. A verb slot, which is usually filled by an action word, like *cry*

x-words are of two kinds, *auxiliary* and *modal*

Auxiliaries

The *auxiliaries* are:

1. The *be* set: *am, is, are, was, were*
2. The *do* set: *do, does, did*
3. The *have* set: *have, has, had*
4. Special auxiliaries: *dare, need to, ought to*

X-words belonging to groups 1–3 above help to form negatives and questions. In addition, they help to mark the verbs for agreement with the subject and tense forms.

Ex. 1.   I *am* an international student.
Ex. 2.   *Is* your friend an international student?
Ex. 3.   I *am not* a native speaker of English.
Ex. 4.   We *are* international students.
Ex. 5.   I *am* watching TV now.
Ex. 6.   I *was* watching TV when you came in.
Ex. 7.   She watch*es* TV every Friday evening.
Ex. 8.   *Does* your friend watch TV on Fridays?
Ex. 9.   My friend *does not* watch TV on Fridays.
Ex. 10.   She *watched* TV last Friday.
Ex. 11.   *Did* your friend watch TV last Friday?
Ex. 12.   My friend *did not* watch TV last Friday.
Ex. 13.   She *has* watched that show several times.

While you are editing your essay it is very important to remember that usually *it is the x-words that mark the subject-verb agreement and verb tense forms* and not the verbs. (Study the examples above.)
    These x-words can also function as main verbs.

Ex. 1.   I *am* a student.
Ex. 2.   She *is* beautiful.
Ex. 3.   I *have* two daughters.
Ex. 4.   I *did* something wrong yesterday.

Modals

The *modals* are of two kinds:

1. Those which are *always followed by the simple form of the verb*:

    -   shall, will, should, would
    -   can, be able to, could
    -   may, might
    -   must
    -   have to, have got to, had to
    -   would like to, would rather, had better
    -   be supposed to, used to, got to

2. Those which are *always followed by the past participle of the verb*:

    -   may have, might have, must have
    -   should have
    -   would have
    -   could have
    -   might have

The use of modals is so natural to native speakers that they do not have to remind themselves about their meanings when they use them. However, for learners of English, modals pose problems.

The following is a summary of the uses and meanings of modals. Some of these have already been discussed in preceding chapters.

Modal	Meaning	Examples
shall	polite question (requesting consent); first person; present/future	Shall we close the door now?
will	(1) future: all three persons	The committee will meet next week.
	(2) polite request	Will you please do me a favor?
	(3) promise (usually with stress on *will*) or agreement	I will do what I can to help you.
	(4) willingness: all three persons	They will do it for you.

should	(1)	obligation or likelihood	I should pass the final test.
	(2)	advisability	You should edit your essay before you hand it in.
	(3)	necessity	I should write the placement test in April to begin school in the fall.
would	(1)	polite question	Would you mind erasing the blackboard for me?
	(2)	repeated action	When I was in my home country, I would walk to school, but here I take a bus.
	(3)	willingness (See *will* above)	I would gladly go with you to the movie tonight.
	(4)	polite statement	I would like to stay home tonight.
	(5)	past tense of *will*	She says Bill will go to the movie with her. She said he would go to the movie with her.
	(6)	unreal condition (present and future)	If I worked in the summer, I would buy a car.
can	(1)	ability (present and future)	I can swim very well.
	(2)	possibility	You can learn a lot about other cultures in an ESL class.
	(3)	permission (informal)	Can I go out with my friend tonight? Yes, you can.
be able to		ability (See *can* above)	I am able to speak French, Spanish, and Russian fluently. I will be able to speak English in a year.

could	(1)	ability in the past[a]	My mother could knit well when she was young.
	(2)	past tense of *can* (in reported speech)	My mother said that she could knit well. (reported speech)
	(3)	polite question	Could you please explain it once again?
	(4)	possibility	If it doesn't rain, we could go out today.
	(5)	unreal condition	If I won the lotto, I could stop working. (pres. and fut.)
may[b]	(1)	permission (formal)	You may use your text-book to answer this test. May I take the test home?
	(2)	polite question (formal)	May I bring you a cup of coffee?
	(3)	guess based on possibility	It may snow tomorrow.
	(4)	possibility	I may give you a make-up test.
might[b]	(1)	past tense of *may* (in reported speech)	Mary says her father may call her tomorrow. Mary said her father might call her the next day.
	(2)	polite request (very rare)	Might I take the test tomorrow?
	(3)	remote possibility	It might snow tomorrow. (not very possible)

[a]With this meaning *could* is interchangeable with *was able to*. However, English speakers usually use *able to* when talking about a specific accomplishment or event and in this sense it is not substituted for *could*.

Ex. 1. When my mother first arrived in the United States, she *could* not speak English. However, after attending adult English classes for a year, she *could* at least understand English even though she *was not able to* speak it.

[b]*May* and *might* are never used in contraction form in the negative.

	(4)	unreal conditional possibility (pres. and fut.)	If I shopped around, I might get a better buy.
must[c]	(1)	necessity or obligation (interchangeable with *have to*)	We must eat balanced meals everyday.
	(2)	guess (especially with certain verbs[d])	He was absent the whole week. He must be sick.
	(3)	order	You must come home exactly at 10 o'clock tonight.
ought to		advisability or expectation (see *should* above)	I ought to do my homework tonight.
have to/have got to		necessity or obligation (present and future) (See *must* above)	I have to pass this test. I have got to pass this test.
had to		necessity or obligation in the past	I had to take this test last April, but I didn't.
would like to	(1)	polite way to say *want*	I would like to see you this afternoon.
	(2)	polite order	I would like you to be seated.
	(3)	polite invitation	Would you like to start eating now?
would rather		preference	I would rather buy a house because it is cost-effective.
had better		advisability (stronger than *should*)	You'd better stay home on this rainy day.
be supposed to		unfulfilled expectation	My brother was supposed to call me last night. I wonder what happened.

[c]*Must* is not usually used to make questions. *Have to* is generally preferred in questions.

    Ex. 1. Do we *have to* go out in this rain today?

[d]For example: *be, seem, appear, want, need, believe, walk, run, drive*

used to	habit	I used to go out a lot. before I got married.
may/might/ must + have + past participle	These carry the same meaning as their simple forms, except that the time of action is in the past.	
should/ ought to + have + past participle	advisable, necessary, or obligatory action in the past, but not done	She should have written the placement test in April.
could have + past participle	possible but unfulfilled action in the past	You could have bought that blouse at a cheaper price.

Verbs

Examples of verbs are :

- *Run, walk, cry, play,* etc.
- *Seem, appear, taste, smell, sound,* etc.

Remember : When the verb is *not* preceded by an X-word (this includes both auxiliary and modal) :

1. The verb should agree with the subject in number and person.
2. The form of the verb should express the time of action (tense).

Also remember : When the verb *is* preceded by an X-word :

1. The verb that follows the X-word is usually in the simple (basic) form. Some exceptions are the continuous tense verbs and present and past participles.
2. The tense form is added to the X-word, not to the verb.
3. It is the X-word that agrees with the subject in number and person, not the verb.

In some cases the tense form is hidden, as in :

Ex. 1.   My sisters watch TV with me everyday.

The hidden X-word *do* in this sentence comes out of its "hiding place" when it is changed into the question and negative forms, as shown below :

Ex. 1.   *Do* my sisters watch TV with me everyday ?
Ex. 2.   My sisters *do* not watch TV with me everyday.

Special Uses

Some verbs expressing communication and mental states may be followed by noun clauses as their objects.

Ex. 1.   The students complained that the course requirements were too demanding.
Ex. 2.   I feel that I should take a few days off.

Some other verbs belonging to this category are :

Communication

acknowledge	confess+	persuade°	state
admit+	deny+	promise°	suggest
advise°	hear	propose	urge°
argue	infer	recommend	warn°
command/order°	mention	request°	hear

Mental states

anticipate	dream	judge	resolve+
assume	expect°	know	see
believe	find	notice	speculate
bet	grant	perceive	trust
conclude	guess	prefer+	wish+
conceive	hope	recognize	wonder
decide+	imagine		

*These verbs may be followed by indirect objects plus infinitives / infinitive phrases

Ex.   I commanded him to get out of the house immediately.

+Those verbs marked with plus may be followed by infinitive phrases.

Ex. 1.   I decided to write my test in April.
Ex. 2.   The robber admitted to having stolen the money from the bank. (very rarely used)

Some other verbs that are followed by noun or pronoun plus infinitive as objects are :

Ex. I advised my daughter to major in mechanical engineering.

allow	cause	get	teach
advise	encourage	oblige	tell
ask	force	remind	want
beg			

Verbs that may be directly followed by infinitives as objects:

Ex. I plan to visit my aunt this summer.

begin	endeavor	like	remember
care	forget	mean	start
cease	intend	neglect	try
continue	learn	plan	want
decide			

Verbs usually followed by gerunds, if not followed by nouns/noun clauses:

Ex. The robber admitted stealing the money.

anticipate	discuss	postpone	remember
avoid	enjoy	practice	resist
can't help	finish	quit	risk
complete	keep	reason	stop
consider	mention	recall	suggest
delay	mind	recommend	tolerate
deny	miss	regret	understand

Verbs followed by infinitives:

Ex. I hope I pass the course.

afford	fail	offer	struggle
agree	forget	plan	swear
appear	hesitate	prepare	threaten
arrange	hope	pretend	volunteer
consent	learn	promise	wait
decide	manage	refuse	want
deserve	mean	remember	wish
expect	need	seem	

Verbs followed by nouns/pronouns plus infinitives:

Ex. I expect you to pass this course with honors.

advise	challenge	instruct	remind
allow	expect	need	teach
ask	forbid	order	urge
beg	force	permit	want
cause	hire	persuade	warn

Using Verbs Correctly

Some common errors in the use of verbs are:

1. Not using the proper tense forms.
2. Not making the verb agree with the subject in number and person.
3. Not using the correct verb form.
4. Unnecessary shifting of tenses.

1. THE USE OF CORRECT TENSE FORMS

The most commonly used tenses and their forms have already been explained in the previous chapters of this book. Review them.

2. SUBJECT-VERB AGREEMENT

ESL speakers often make errors in this area not because they do not know the rules, but because they are careless, and carelessness deserves no excuse. Therefore, carefully edit your essay to check whether:

1. The third person singular auxiliary (if one is used in the sentence) or the base verb (if no auxiliary is used) has the -s ending in the present tense. Remember the formula:

> *does* + base verb = third pers. sing. pres.;
> or: base verb + -s = third person sing. pres.

Ex. 1. My neighbor *does* not *speak* English.
Ex. 2. Codeine often *controls* attacks of severe pain.

2. The plural subject noun or pronoun is followed by the no -es verb form in the present tense (or, with an auxiliary: *do* + base v. = pl. pres. v.) where the *do* becomes a $\emptyset$ when added to the verb)

Ex. 1.   Doctors often *recommend* soda for patients with upset stomach.

3.   The subject pronouns, *I, you, we, they,* have the plural X-word forms and verb forms.

Ex. 1.   I *have* improved my writing a lot.
Ex. 2.   I *write* two essays a week for practice.

4.   The *be, do,* and *have* auxiliaries have the correct form for singular and plural subjects.

Ex. 1.   I *am* very hopeful about this class.
Ex. 2.   They *were* very anxious about the result of their placement exams.
Ex. 3.   We *do* not have to look for errors while we are writing.
Ex. 4.   We *do* it after we finish writing.
Ex. 5.   She *has* done it already.

Some subject nouns or pronouns give problems in subject-verb agreement:

1.   A singular subject noun/noun phrase or clause with a plural noun immediately preceding the verb, or a plural subject noun/noun phrase, or clause with a singular noun immediately preceding the verb. This confuses beginning writers especially if the subject is long.

Ex. 1.   A problem that bothers some writers, especially beginning writers, *is* what is called writer's block.
Ex. 2.   The implications of the new view of creative writing on a word processor *are* very encouraging.

A simple test of the grammaticality of such a sentence regarding subject-verb agreement is to replace the noun nucleus in the whole phrase or clause to which the verb refers by an appropriate pronoun, and find the appropriate verb form. For example, in the examples above, the noun nuclei are *problem,* and *implications.* Replacing them with pronouns, we get *it* (sing.), and *they* (plural), respectively.

2.   *There*-subjects. The verb should agree with the subject that follows, not with *there.*

Ex. 1.   By 1849, there were sixty-four soda bottling plants in the United States. Today, there are more than 3,000 plants involved in the manufacturing of soda, with more than 200 brands on the market.

Ex. 2. There has been tremendous improvement in soda manufacturing recently.

Ex. 3. There have been tremendous changes recently.

3. Subject, nouns, or pronouns combined with *nor, or.* The verb agrees with the noun or pronoun nearest the verb.

Ex. 1. Neither the typewriter nor the word processors are substitutes for your learning the discipline of writing.

Ex. 2. A fork or two chopsticks are to be placed on the table.

Ex. 3. A fork or two chopsticks or both are to be placed on the table.

Ex. 4. There is a fork or two chopsticks to choose from.

4. *One of* as subject. This is always followed by a plural noun and a singular verb.

Ex. 1. *One* of the *advantages* of a word processor *is* that it speeds up the editing process.

5. *Each, every, any,* and combinations with these as subjects. These take only singular verbs (even when they are joined by the coordinating conjunction *and*).

Ex. 1. *Each* kind of ants *has* its own survival techniques.

Ex. 2. Not *everybody is* talented enough to be a musician.

Ex. 3. *Each girl and boy* in this country *is* entitled to enjoy freedom in every sense of the word.

Ex. 4. *Anybody* is welcome to speak up.

6. Collective nouns as subjects. When referring to members, use a plural verb; when referred to as one unit, use a singular verb.

3. VERB FORMS

The main things to look for when checking verb forms are:

1. Do your simple present tense verbs have the *-(e)s* endings?
2. Do your regular past tense verbs have their final *-(e)ds*?
3. Do your irregular past tense verbs have their correct past tense forms (*-(e)d* for regular verbs and correct past tense forms for irregular verbs)?

4. Do your continuous verbs have the *-ing* forms?
5. Do your perfect tense verbs have the appropriate *have* forms followed by *ed -t* or *-en*, depending on whether the verb is regular or irregular?
6. Do the auxiliary and modal verbs used in your sentences have the correct tense form? Do they agree with the subject in number and person (see p. 282, 1–3).

4. VERB TENSE SHIFT

Ex. 1. I went out shopping yesterday. All I want to buy is a pair of blue shoes to match my blue suit. Finally, going from one store to the other, I spent almost six hours, but cannot find the kind I was looking for. I come home with a pair of blue jeans, and to add to my disappointment, I find the zipper broken!

There are two kinds of tense shift in this short paragraph.

1. Shifting tenses in the same sentence.
2. Shifting tenses in the paragraph unnecessarily.

The writer begins the narration in the past tense, as the first sentence shows. Then there is a tense shift in the second sentence — from the past to the present. Correct the sentence, changing the tense to the past. There are two different tenses used in the third sentence. Preserve the sequence of time by changing *cannot* into *could not*. The last sentence shifts to the present time again. Put it in the past tense.

Corrected Version: I went out shopping yesterday. All I wanted to buy was a pair of blue shoes to match my blue suit. Going from one store to the other I spent almost six hours, but could not find the kind I was looking for. Finally I came home with a pair of blue jeans, and to add to my disappointment, I found the zipper broken!

Middle Adverb

The position in an English sentence right before the verb can be taken by the middle adverb. Words or phrases showing negation, for example, *not, never, (very) seldom, hardly,* and frequency adverbs, when used in the middle of the sentence (not in the beginning or in the end), for example, *always, usually, often, frequently,* go in this position.

Ex. My mother *can* never speak English. She *hardly* makes an effort to learn English. I *often* tell her that she should go to an adult evening school, but she *never* listens to me.

THE OBJECT

The object position is the third basic position in an English sentence. Remember : Only transitive verbs take objects after them. The traditional definition of an object is : it answers to a *what, whom* question after the verb. All the constructions that go in the subject position (nouns, noun phrases, gerunds and infinitive phrases, and noun clauses) can also fill the object position.

ADVERBS AND ADVERBIALS

The last position in a basic English sentence is that of an adverb. Single words like *successfully,* time words or phrases, (for example, *yesterday, in the evening*) can go in this position. They usually show time, place, manner, or purpose.

Ex. 1. I called my uncle *yesterday.* I told him I wanted to see him. He said he would be home *at 6 o'clock in the evening.* He talked to me very *nicely.*

Common errors in the use of adverbs may be categorized as follows :

1. Not using the correct form.
2. Not placing it in the right position in the sentence.

1. Form

Many ESL speakers leave out the *-ly* ending.

Ex. 1. He spoke to me very angry. (correct *angry* to *angrily*)

2. Position of Adverbials

The adverbials are the most moveable element in an English sentence. They can be placed in the beginning, middle, or end of a sentence. However, they can never come between a verb and its object. For example, you can never write :

I watch everyday at 8 o'clock in the evening my favorite program on TV.

Corrected version : I watch my favorite program on TV everyday at 8 o'clock in the evening.

Frequency adverbs are usually placed before the verb. Examples are *usually, frequently, seldom, always, often, almost, never, ever,*

PREPOSITIONS

Prepositions are an important element that makes up an English sentence. Prepositional phrases can go in the subject, object, and adverbial positions. Most ESL speakers have problems finding the correct preposition. Some basic prepositions and their uses are given below.

TIME

on

Examples :   on September
            on my wedding anniversary
            on time
            on Sunday
            on New Year's Eve

in

Examples :   in 1999
            in the morning/evening
            in the spring
            in May
            in a couple of days

during

Examples :   during the weekend
            during the year
            during the month of May
            during the winter season

by

Examples :   by evening tomorrow
            by 6 o'clock
            by 12 midnight

for

Examples :   for a year
            for two hours

from ... to

Examples :   from July 2nd to August 14th
            from 6 o'clock to 10 o'clock at night

PLACE OR DIRECTION

to

Examples :   to the hospital
            to his school
            to his office

from

Examples :   from my school
            from your house

toward

Examples :   (point) toward something/someone
            (walk) toward the building

into

Examples :   into the swimming pool
            into the river

on

Examples :   on the river
            on the beach

at

Examples :   at the Mayor's office

MANNER, INSTRUMENT, OR AGENT

with

Examples: with a gun
with my brother
with an angry look

in

Examples: in slow motion

by

Examples: by myself
by my brother

PURPOSE

for

Examples: for the house
for my brother

to

Examples: to buy
to work hard

Idiomatic Uses of Prepositions

The idiomatic use of prepositions can be mastered only by extensive reading. Some verbs followed by specific prepositions are given below.

account for (something)
accuse (somebody of something)
agree on (something)
agree with (somebody)
apologize to (somebody for something)
apply to (a school, etc., for something)
argue with (somebody)

believe in (something)
belong to (something/somebody)
borrow (something) from (somebody)
call back (somebody)
call in (someone, for a visit, etc.)
call off (a meeting, etc.; meaning: cancel)
care for (somebody)
call (somebody) up (on the telephone)
call on (somebody, to speak, etc.)
catch up with (something/somebody)
check into (something; meaning: investigate)
check into or check in at (a hotel)
check out (a book, etc.)
check out of (a hotel, etc.)
cheer (somebody) up
clean up (something)
come across (somebody/something)
complain to (somebody) about (something)
compliment (someone) on (something)
consent to (something)
consist of (something)
contribute to (something)
count upon or on (somebody)
convince (someone) of (something)
cross out (something)
decide on (something/somebody)
depend on (something/somebody)
drop off (somebody) at (some place)
drop out of (school, etc.)
escape from (somebody/something)
excel in (something)
excuse (somebody) for (something)
figure out (something)
fill out (something)
find out (something)
get along with (somebody)
get back from (some place)
get off (a bus, etc.)
get on (a bus, etc.)
get over (a problem, etc.)
get rid of (something/somebody)
get through (something, meaning: finish)

give up (something; meaning: stop doing something)
go over (something; meaning: review)
hide from (somebody)
hope for (something)
insist on (something)
invite (somebody) for (something)
laugh at (somebody/something)
listen to (somebody/something)
look for (somebody/something)
look forward to (doing something)
look (something) over (meaning: review)
look (something) up in (a dictionary, etc.)
object to (something)
participate in (something)
pass away (meaning: die)
pass out (something; meaning: distribute)
pass out (with no object following; meaning: faint)
pick out something (meaning: select)
pray for (something/somebody)
prohibit (somebody) from (doing something)
protect (somebody) from (something)
provide for (somebody)
provide (somebody) with (something)
put away (something)
put off (something; meaning: postpone)
put out (cigarettes, etc.)
put up with (somebody/something)
recover from (a shock, etc.)
rely on (somebody/something)
remind (somebody) of (something)
rescue (somebody) from (something)
respond to (somebody/something)
run into/across (somebody)
run out of (something)
show up (with no object)
shut off (something)
stare at (somebody/something)
stop (somebody) from (doing something)
subscribe to (something)
substitute (somebody/something) for (somebody/something)
succeed in (something)
take advantage of (something/somebody)

take after (somebody)
take over (something)
take up (something)
tear down (something)
wait on (somebody)

SOME OTHER PREPOSITION COMBINATIONS

be accustomed to (doing something)
be acquainted with (somebody)
be capable of (doing something)
be committed to (doing something)
be dedicated to (something)
be devoted to (something/somebody)
be disappointed in/with (somebody/something)
be envious of (somebody)
be familiar with (something)
be finished with (somebody/something)
be fond of (somebody/something)
be friendly with (somebody)
be guilty of (something)
be innocent of (something)
be interested in (somebody/something)
be jealous of (somebody)
be known for (something)
be proud of (somebody/something)
be responsible for (somebody/something)
be scared of (somebody/something)
in accordance with (something)

Part 2: RECOGNIZING MEANING RELATIONSHIPS IN SENTENCES

There are certain expressions used in showing meaning relationships in sentences, especially among two or more sentences. These expressions may be transition words, coordinators, subordinators, or phrases.

Meaning	Transition Words	Coordi-nators	Subordina-tors	Phrases
Addition	additionally in addition also besides furthermore moreover	and as well as		chiefly especially in particular let alone not to mention notably particularly specifically to say nothing of
Definition	in other words that is that is to say			to define
Intensification	as a matter of fact in fact indeed			
Repetition				it is important to make clear to repeat
Choice	otherwise	or	as long as if provided (that) unless	
Clarification	For example For instance			to illustrate

Chronology/
  time
	after that
	at the same time
	before that
	first ... second
	first of all
	next ...
	  last/finally			

Meaning	Transition Words	Coordinators	Subordinators	Phrases
Chronology/ time	previously then			
Explanation	that is that is to say			to clarify to explain
Similarity	similarly likewise	as	as just as	
Contrast	conversely however in contrast nevertheless nonetheless on the contrary on the other hand still	but yet	although even though though whereas	despite in spite of
Cause/effect	accordingly as a result because of this consequently for this reason hence therefore thus	for since so	as because since so that	because of
Summing up	after all in brief in conclusion in short to sum up to summarize summarizing			

Part 3: PARALLELISM

Parallelism is a grammatical term applied to combining words/phrases/ clauses of the same grammatical structure with coordinating conjunctions. Examples of conjunctions are *and, but, as well as, or, not, neither ... nor, either ... or, both ... and, not only ... but (also), rather ... than.* In English, these coordinating conjunctions can be used to join only the same kind of grammatical structures: clauses with clauses, phrases with phrases, nouns with nouns, adjectives with adjectives, adverbs with adverbs, infinitives with infinitives, gerunds with gerunds, participles with participles, and so on. Examples from your readings are:

Ex. 1. For the rest of the eighteenth century *and* early into the next century, scientists in England and abroad worked at perfecting Priestley's apparatus. (Chapter 1, Rdg. Par. 2)

Ex. 2. Across the Atlantic, researchers in the U.S. followed Priestley's example *and* began devising their own methods for making carbonated drinks. (Chapter 1, Rdg. Par. 3)

Ex. 3. Profits increased steadily, *but* slowly. (Chapter 1, Rdg. Par. 3)

Ex. 4. Most modern plants do not make their own syrup on the premises, *but* rather purchase it from wholesalers. (Chapter 1, Rdg. Par. 8)

Ex. 5. Day and night certain nitrogen-containing compounds, *or* alkaloids, are produced by the plant.

Ex. 6. Taking drugs for kicks *and* taking them to control pain are entirely different things. (Chapter 2, Rdg. Par. 2)

Ex. 7. The differences between writing longhand, typing *and* word processing are obvious. (Chapter 3, Rdg. Par. 3)

Ex. 8. Good prose is not just a collection of neatly displayed *and* properly constructed sentences. (Chapter 3, Rdg. Par. 6)

Ex. 9. Later, they can instruct the word processor to locate each "XXX" *and* (to) display the surrounding text, *and* then (to) develop *and* (to) insert the needed transition. (Chapter 3, Rdg. Par. 9)

Ex. 10. Word processors make an important contribution, improving motivation *not only* during revision *but also* during the entire writing process. (Chapter 3, Rdg. Par. 11)

Ex. 11. Even though the mechanical *and* motivational effects of the word processor are powerful. ... (Chapter 3, Rdg. Par. 31)

Ex. 12. Because a word processor makes it easier both to produce *and* to modify our writing. ... (Chapter 3, Rdg. Par. 16)

Part 4: FRAGMENTS

Grammatically, a fragment means a piece of a sentence, not a complete sentence. Inexperienced writers, both native and nonnative, tend to write sentence fragments.

A simple test to find a fragment is to try to change it into a yes/no question. In doing this, you may have to move the front adverbial (adverbial that begins the sentence) and transition word to the end of the sentence. Remember, a yes/no question begins with an auxiliary, X-word, or modal verb. If you cannot make a yes/no question out of the "testing sentence" without adding something, you have a fragment. Example from your reading:

Ex. 1. Although the name soda was born in the early nineteenth century, the product's true beginnings go back several centuries. (Chapter 1, Rdg. Par. 2)

Step 1. Move the front adverbial, "Although ... century" to the end of the sentence.

Step 2. Find the X-word equivalent of *go* in this context.

Step 3. Put the X-word equivalent at the beginning of the question.

Yes/no question: Do the product's beginnings go back several centuries although the name soda was born in the early nineteenth century?

Since the sentence can be changed to a yes/no question without adding anything, it is a complete sentence.

Examples of fragments from students' writing are:

Ex. 1. Today, I got home very sick. My mother got sick. *Waiting for me.*

Ex. 2. Last weekend we went to Florida. My father got tired. *Having driven more than 300 miles.*

Ex. 3. *When my cousin said he would like to go to college in New York City.* I told him how hard it is to understand lectures in English.

Ex. 4. *I always tell my friends is not easy to learn to write in English.*

Ex. 5. *Professionals sent to America to be trained in computer science.*

Can you change the italicized "sentences" to yes/no questions? What is the problem? In each of these sentences at least one basic position of an English sentence is missing. The missing positions in each of these are sentences are:

1. Subject and X-word
2. The whole sentence unit (what you have here is only a participle)
3. The whole sentence unit (what you have here is only a time clause)
4. Subject (anticipatory *it*)
5. Verb

How do we correct these sentences?

1. Supply the subject she and the X-word *was*: She was waiting for me.
2. Combine the second sentence with the fragment: My father got tired after having driven more than 300 miles.
3. Combine the fragment to the sentence that follows: When my cousin said he would like to go to college in New York City I told him how hard it is to understand lectures in English.
4. Supply *it*: I always tell my friends it is not easy to learn to write in English.
5. Supply *are*: Professionals are sent to America to be trained in computer science.

Part 5: RUN-ON SENTENCES

A run-on sentence, as the term implies, is that kind of a sentence which runs on to another sentence without stopping. In other words, the writer is running, not taking any "deep breaths" between complete sentences. The "deep breath" the writer is supposed to take is to put a "full stop" — a period after each sentence.

You can identify a run-on sentence by changing the "testing sentence" into a yes/no question. If it makes more than one complete sentence, you have a run-on sentence.

Examples of run-on sentences from students' writings:

Ex. 1. My hometown is different from New York City it is situated in the northern part of Haiti.

Ex. 2. In New York you cannot make friends you try to help they will beat you up.

The above "sentences" can be changed into more than one yes/no question. Therefore, they are run-on sentences.

Corrected versions:

1. My hometown is different from New York City. It is situated in the northern part of Haiti.
2. The second student sample is actually made up of three sentences. To be idiomatic, it is better to combine all three into one:

In New York you cannot make friends because even when you try to help you might get beaten up.

A N S W E R · K E Y

CHAPTER 1

Grammar

VERB TENSES

Simple Present vs. Simple Past

For Your Critical Thinking (p. 6)

1. In Par. 1 the writer talks about some facts relating to soda as they exist now and in Par. 2, some past history.
2. Simple past; because the sentence talks about some past history about soda.
3. Simple present.
4. In these two sentences the writer is talking about some *facts* in the history of the development of soda industry (using simple present tense) and in the other sentences he or she is *narrating* some past historical events (using simple past tense).
5. Par. 11

Present Perfect vs. Simple Present

For Your Critical Thinking (p. 7)

1. S1. "In recent years" introduces the idea that the controversy began some time before the present and continues to the present. This idea cannot be conveyed if the simple present tense is used in the sentence. (See Chapter 1, p. 7, Note.)
   S2. As in S1, "long" conveys the idea that the fact that "man can exist sixty days without food" began to be known some time in the past and is still known in the present. If the sentence was written in simple present, it would simply mean, "Now we know that 'man can ... food.'"
   S3. The writer may not know when exactly the soda industry set up its standards. (See Chapter 1, p. 8, no. 3.)

2. See Chapter 1, p. 9.

Simple Past vs. Past Perfect

For Your Critical Thinking (p. 9)

1. The time before the invention and the time when Painter invented the Crown Cap (both of which took place in the past.)
2. S1. Before Painter invented the Crown Cap, more than 1,500 stoppering bottles were (had been) tried with little success.

     The two times of action are before the invention and at the time of the invention. (See Chapter 1, pp. 9–10.)

PASSIVE VOICE

Problems for You to Solve (pp. 10–11)

1. The passive voice verbs are :

    - Par. 1. has been known, to be called, is found
    - Par. 2. was born, (was) identified
    - Par. 3. is recognized, was granted, (are) involved
    - Par. 4. was filtered, were put
    - Par. 5. had been tried
    - Par. 6. could be standardized, could be produced
    - Par. 8. is made, are used, (is) used
    - Par. 9. must be purified, are used
    - Par. 10. is released, is exposed, is packaged, (is) inspected, (is) dissolved, (is) needed
    - Par. 11. were perfected, is packaged
    - Par. 13. is comprised, (are) approved
    - Par. 14. has (long) been known, is (highly) purified, (is) used

2. See Chapter 1, p. 11.

For Your Critical Thinking (p. 11)

S1. Q1. See Chapter 1, p. 11.

S2. Q1. People in general.
    Q2. See Chapter 1, p. 11.

S3. Q1. Probably *he/she* does, but *he/she* is talking about Hawkins, not about the agency which granted him the patent. That is why *he/she* prefers passive to active voice.

Adjectives: Degrees of Comparison — Positive Degree

For Your Critical Thinking (p. 12)

Water used for soft drinks internationally and water used for soft drinks in the U. S. are being compared.

Sentence Combining

Problems for You to Solve (pp. 13–14)

See the sentences in the reading passage (pp. 3–5). Follow the paragraph numbers indicated in parentheses.

Vocabulary and Word Forms

FILL-INS (p. 17)

1. (1) began (2) produced (3) ago
2. (4) ancient (5) enjoyment (6) bubbles (7) came out
3. (8) attempts (9) reproductions (10) effervescence
4. (11) experimenting (12) simulating
5. (13) reported (14) four times
6. (15) filtering (16) primitive
7. (17) introduction (18) results (19) way (20) stoppered
8. (21) Before (22) devise (23) did not succeed
9. (24) standardization (25) together (26) finally
    (27) production (28) quicker (29) efficient
10. (30) operates (31) produces (32) while
11. (33) recently (34) disagreement (35) with respect
12. (36) necessarily (37) biological

CHAPTER 2

Grammar

VERB TENSES

Present Perfect

For Your Critical Thinking (p. 27)

1. Yes, they are. The verb form *have treated* and the preposition *since* tell the reader that the action (treating the drug addicts), which started in 1959, still continues. (See Chapter 1, p. 8, no. 1.)
2. The writer does not say when exactly the parties agreed. The exact date when the parties agreed is not important to the writer. (See Chapter 1, p. 8, no. 3.)

Present Continuous vs. Present Perfect Continuous

S1. The action, that is, *changing*, which began some time in the past, is still continuing, and may continue into the future.
S2. The action, that is *trying*, did not start in the past. At present the action is in progress and it may or may not continue into the future. (See Chapter 2, pp. 27–28.)

Passive Voice: Review (p. 28)

For Your Critical Thinking (p. 27)

1. See Chapter 1, pp. 11–12.
2.

S1a. You dissolve opium in alcohol.
S1b. You know the mixture as laudanum.
S1c. People say it was an essential item in most medicine chests during the Middle Ages. (active voice)

S2. People report that the spectacular treatment of addicts at Tham Krabok Monastery results in 70 percent success. (active voice)

In expository writing, the impersonal *you* should be avoided since it is considered too informal. Also, whenever the actors are the impersonal *people*, the passive voice is used.

Modal Verbs: *Should, Must Have*

For Your Critical Thinking (p. 28)

See Chapter 2, Note, p. 29.

The *-ing* Forms of Verbs

Application (p. 29)

S1. Taking drugs for kicks and taking them to control pain (subject)
S2. Giving drug addicts inexpensive daily doses of the synthetic drug methadone (subject)
S3. substituting one addiction for another (complement of the verb is)

Sentence Combining

CLAUSE MARKERS

Who, Which, That (Review); *Where, Because*

Problems for You to Solve (p. 30)

Check your answers against the sentences in the reading passage.

PAST AND PRESENT PARTICIPIAL PHRASES

Application (p. 32)

Your answers might vary. Some possible responses:

1. Written for ESL students, this book is very helpful for me.
2. Printed in the United States, this magazine sells well.
3. Sung by trained student groups, this opera had a lot of publicity.

4. Watching TV last night, I fell asleep.
5. Crying so loudly, the baby got what it wanted.

REDUCTION OF ADJECTIVE CLAUSES

Application (p. 33)

1. Students waiting in line for registration are getting tired.
2. The teenager driving a blue car got a ticket for speeding.
3. My friends taking Professor Carlton's class have a hard time getting good grades.
4. Foreigners touring New York City during the summer time have to stand in long lines to see the Statue of Liberty.
5. The news about student strikes published in the newspaper was exaggerated.

Sentence Relating

IN FACT, HOWEVER, FOR EXAMPLE, BUT

For Your Critical Thinking (p. 33)

The sentences in each set are related to each other by the transition words:

S1. *In fact, For example*
S2. *However*
S3. *But, Now*

Application (p. 34)

Answers may vary. Here are some examples.

1. My writing has improved a lot recently. In fact, I have very few mistakes marked when I get back my compositions.
2. The computer industry has revolutionized the life of modern people. In fact, computers are playing such an important role in every field that it seems people cannot carry out their daily activities without them.
3. English is very difficult to learn. However, I am making good progress in learning it.
4. Yesterday's test was very difficult. However, I think I am going to get at least 80 on it.

Vocabulary and Word Forms

FILL-INS (p. 34)

1. (1) smuggling   (2) almost   (3) part   (4) addicted
   (5) miserable
2. (6) examining   (7) reasons   (8) Constantly   (9) some
   (10) contain   (11) store   (12) swollen   (13) shallow
   (14) incision   (15) come out   (16) dried   (17) resembling
3. (18) dissolving   (19) basic
4. (20) Even though   (21) treatment   (22) carefully   (23) like
   (24) counteracted   (25) mixed   (26) gradually
   (27) decreasing   (28) aware   (29) addicted
5. (30) prescribe   (31) suffer   (32) intense
   (33) specifically   (34) adjusted   (35) diabetes   (36) lessens
   (37) intensity   (38) also   (39) relief   (40) experience
   (41) reconciled   (42) resolved   (43) peaceful death.
6. (44) report   (45) begun   (46) abstain   (47) using   (48) induces
   (49) immediate   (50) vomiting   (51) clear   (52) helping
   (53) eliminating   (54) includes   (55) constantly
   (56) counseled

CHAPTER 3

Grammar

VERB TENSES

For Your Critical Thinking (p. 51)

1. Two tenses are used: simple past and present.
2. As the word *Now* indicates, the writer is talking about the present time
3. The simple present tense is mostly used, because the writer is talking about facts relating to the use of word processors as they exist now.

MODAL VERBS

For Your Critical Thinking (p. 52)

See Chapter 3, p. 52, Note.

COMPARISON: COMPARATIVE DEGREE

For Your Critical Thinking (p. 52)

S1. Points of comparison : the process of composing with pen, pencil, and typewriter, and the process of composing with a word processor. Vocabulary : *less convenient than*

S2. Points of comparison : a word processor screen and a blank piece of paper. Vocabulary : *less than terror*

S3. Points of comparison : filling a word processor screen, and filling an entire 8½-by-11-inch page. Vocabulary : *faster than*

S4. Points of comparison : producing, modifying, and finding out what we think, when we use paper, pencil, and typewriter, and doing all three using a word processor. Vocabulary: *easier (than)*

Problems for You to Solve (p. 53)

1. The use of *-er ... than* and *more ... than* :

    * Most one-syllable words add *-er*, followed by *than*. Ex. *harder than, wider than*.
    * Two-syllable words ending in *-y* or *-ow* add *-er*. (Change *y* to *i* before adding *-er*, if it is preceded by a vowel.) Ex. *easier than, narrower than*.
    * Most adjectives longer than two syllables take *more ... than*. Ex. *more beautiful than, more hardworking than*.

GERUNDS AND PARTICIPLES

Problems for You to Solve (p. 54)

See Chapter 3, *Note*, pp. 55–56.

Sentence Combining

CLAUSE MARKERS
Who, Which, etc.

Problems for You to Solve (p. 57)

1a. *Many people* are inexperienced in the word processor.
  b. The differences between writing longhand, typing, and word processing are obvious even to those *inexperienced people.*

2a. Beginning writers in a second language may or may not revise.
  b. *Suppose* they revise.
  c. *Still,* all they do is correct basic mistakes.

3a. The writer can mark each place.
  b. *At this place* a transition word might be needed.

4a. Many people compose with pen, pencil, or typewriter.
  b. *At that time* they may do the same thing.
  c. *However,* the whole process is less convenient than it is with a word processor.
  d. *For this reason,* this is less likely to get done.

5a. Clean copies offer positive psychological benefits.
  b. *The reason is* they promote the writer into reviewing the material.

6a. Word processors eliminate one of the more perplexing obstacles for many writers.
  b. *This perplexing obstacle* is the blank sheet of paper.
  c. *This blank sheet of paper* seems to stare back reprovingly.

7a. Writers can fill a screen faster than they can fill a sheet of paper.
  b. *The reason is* few word processor screens display the equivalent of an entire 8½-by-11-inch page.

8a. A word processor helps writers to detour to another part.
  b. *This part* will be easier to complete.

9a. The mechanical and motivational effects of the word processor are powerful.

b. *However,* they may prove minor compared to one potential effect of this new technology.

10a. This view encourages an idea.
  b. *The idea is* that writing can be taught and learned in simple and convenient chunks.
  c. *However,* many writers have a different understanding of the writing process.

11a. Writers review the text.
  b. At the time, they may feel *something.*
  c. *This something is* that a change is needed at a particular place.
  d. They may not know precisely what that change should be.

Note on Adjective Clauses
Problems for You to Solve (p. 58)

1. 1, 6, 8. (In 10 and 11, *that* is not an adjective clause marker, but a noun clause marker.)
2. All of them.
3. None of them.

When, Once, So That

Problems for You to Solve (p. 59)

1a. and b. When the initial copy is made, writers can concentrate on the content. For answers to 2a, b, c; 3a, b. check your answers against sentences in the reading passage. Follow the paragraph numbers given in parentheses. Also, see the Note given in the text, following each group.

NOT ONLY ... BUT ALSO

Application 1 (p. 60)

1. This book helps me improve not only my writing but also my reading.
2. My father works not only during the day but also during the night.
3. Not only did I have to pick up my brother from the airport but I also had to take my mother to the hospital.

REDUCTION OF ADVERBIAL CLAUSES

For Your Critical Thinking (p. 60)

See Chapter 3, pp. 60–61.

Application (p. 61)

1. Watching the movie, I fell asleep.
2. Having handed in the test, I discovered that two of the answers were wrong.

Sentence Relating

TRANSITION MARKERS

Application (p. 63)

1. Professor Peters' classes are very interesting. But his homework assignments are very demanding.
2. Writing in English is very difficult for me. However, I am getting good grades in my writing class.
3. Textbooks are very expensive. For example, my chemistry textbook cost me $40.00.

Word Forms, Vocabulary, and Idioms

FILL-INS (p. 63)

1. (1) differs   (2) clear   (3) do not know
2. (4) emphasis   (5) revision   (6) important
3. (7) However   (8) particularly   (9) strongly   (10) hate
4. (11) provided   (12) led   (13) another   (14) with no
5. (15) more difficult
6. (16) Besides   (17) help   (18) getting cleanly
7. (19) more terrifying
8. (20) nevertheless   (21) less   (22) comparison with
   (23) potentiality   (24) modifying

9. (25) review (26) specific (27) not know (28) exactly
10. (29) entrance (30) obsessed

Punctuation

See Notes for answers to questions in this part.

Writing

THE EXPOSITORY ESSAY: FORM

For Your Critical Thinking (p. 71)

1. Three paragraphs are used for the introduction.
2.

Advance in technology and creativity
Ex. 1. Improved fabrication of steel and architecture
2. Developments in electronics and music
3. Word processing and writing
Word process: Definition
electronic devices allowing you
to type, modify and print text
word processing compared
with writing longhand
and typing.
Does everything
electronically
plus
↓

1. Eases mechanical drudgery
2. Enhances motivation
3. Helps in thinking process

3. The writer is going to use comparison and contrast to explain his or her views.

4. The writer locates the thesis statement for the whole essay in Par. 4. This is the neck part, which connects the introduction to the body of the essay, namely, the developmental paragraphs.

5. The three controlling ideas are:

    a. The word processor can ease the mechanical drudgery of writing.

    b. It can enhance our motivation and willingness to spend time going through the entire process of writing.

    c. It can bring about qualitative changes in the writing product, helping the writer in his or her thinking process.

6. Par. 5–10 discuss subpoint a, 11–12, subpoint b, and 13–21, subpoint c.

7. Key words: *revising, revision, revise, review.* (The words *revision* and *revise* are used several times in Par. 5. Also, Par. 9. ends with *revision.*) Substitutes: *repairs, clean copy, reviewing,* cleaning up.

8. *Revision, review.*

9. By comparing the process of revision with a word processor to that with pen, pencil, and typewriter (last two sentences in Par. 9), the writer connects the paragraph to the first subpoint introduced in Par. 5, namely, motivating and promoting revision, easing the drudgery of writing.

10. Repetition of the words *motivation* and *revision* in the first sentence of the paragraph and the use of *not only ... but also* link Par. 11 to previous paragraphs.

11. It means "one reason" and serves as a transition word, introducing one example of the "several reasons" mentioned in the previous sentence.

12. One subtopic, namely: Word processors can make writing bearable for several reasons. Par. 12 is written separately because the reason discussed is different from the one discussed in Par. 11.

13. The subtopic c is discussed in Par. 13.

14. The key words in the opening sentence of Par. 13, namely, "the mechanical and motivational effects," summarize the first two subpoints already discussed and relate the paragraph to the ones preceding.

15. The writer concludes by making a suggestion and advising.

CHAPTER 4

Grammar

VERB TENSES: REVIEW

Problems for You to Solve (p. 80)

S1. The present perfect tense. If *have evolved* were changed into *evolved* (simple past), the writer would have to specify the time of evolution. The simple past is wrong in the context because the evolution must have taken place, and continues to take place, over a period of time which cannot be specified.

S2. The present perfect tense, for the same reasons as in S1.

PRESENT AND PAST PARTICIPLES AS ADJECTIVES

For Your Critical Thinking (p. 81)

present participle	past participle
laying	highly developed
living	self-contained
protruding	specialized

The present participles end in *-ing* and the past participles here end in *-ed*. Since both are being used before nouns, they occupy the adjective position. (See Chapter 4, pp. 81–82 for further explanation.)

Application (p. 82)

1. Present and past participles: <u>annoying, annoyed</u>
   actor: <u>children</u>   experiencer: <u>mother</u>
   the <u>annoying</u> children   the <u>annoyed</u> mother

   Sentences:

   - The <u>annoying</u> children bother their mother.
   - The <u>annoyed</u> mother scolded her children.

2. Present and past participles : answering, answered
   actor : machine   experiencer : questions
   the answering machine   the answered questions

   Sentences :

   • My answering machine is broken.
   • I crossed out all the answered questions.

3. Present and past participles : cleaning, cleaned
   actor : lady   experiencer : floor
   the cleaning lady   the cleaned floor

   Sentences :

   • The cleaning lady cleaned the floor very well.
   • The cleaned floor shines like a mirror.

4. Present and past participles : astonishing, astonished
   actor : news   experiencer : mother
   the astonishing news   the astonished mother

   Sentences :

   • They watched the astonishing news on TV.
   • The astonished mother could not talk for a while.

5. Present and past participles : invigorating, invigorated
   actor : exercise   experiencer : athletes
   the invigorating exercise   the invigorated athletes

   Sentences :

   • The invigorating exercise activated the athletes' muscles.
   • The invigorated athletes were ready to run the race.

6. Present and past participles : depressing, depressed
   actor : test results   experiencer : counselor
   depressing test results   the depressed counselor

Sentences:

- The depressing test results displeased my counselor.
- My depressed counselor got mad at me.

7. Present and past participles: offending, offended
   actor: girlfriend   experiencer: Fred
   offending girlfriend   the offended Fred

   Sentences:

   - Fred's offending girlfriend has to be taught a lesson.
   - The offending Cathy should apologize to her offended boy-friend, Fred.

8. Present and past participles: confusing, confused
   actor: lesson   experiencer: students
   the confusing lesson   the confused students

   Sentences:

   - The confusing lesson should be taught once more.
   - The confused students asked for more explanations.

9. Present and past participles: interesting, interested
   actor: movie   experiencer: audience
   the interesting movie   the interested audience

   Sentences:

   - The audience watched the interesting movie without even taking a break.
   - The interested audience wanted to watch the movie over again.

10. Present and past participles: fascinating, fascinated
    actor: clown   experiencer: guests
    the fascinating clown   the fascinated guests

    Sentences:

    - The fascinating clown amused the guests with his jokes.
    - The fascinated guests gave the clown an award.

11. Present and past participles: <u>shattering, shattered</u>
     actor: <u>earthquake</u>   experiencer: <u>buildings</u>
     the <u>shattering</u> earthquake   the <u>shattered</u> buildings

     Sentences:

     • The <u>shattering</u> earthquakes caused a lot of damage.
     • To replace the <u>shattered</u> buildings requires time and money.

ADVERBS

All the questions in this section are answered and explained in the Notes.

Vocabulary, Word Forms, and Idioms

FILL-INS (p. 92)

1. (1) highest rank/order (2) homo sapiens (3) In spite of the fact (4) totally (5) overcome (6) during (7) process (8) Struggling (9) survival (10) In comparison (11) overcoming (12) related to
2. (13) typical characteristic (14) advanced (15) millions (16) only (17) operates (18) fixed (19) divided (20) serving (21) cooperatively (22) advancement (23) made possible (24) very clever (25) However (26) characteristics (27) dominates
3. (28) most important (29) carried out (30) chief (31) Therefore (32) understandable (33) placed (34) and (35) promotes
4. (36) highly influential (37) assuring (38) unity (39) keeps (40) dominant (41) crushing (42) rapidly effective (43) found
5. (44) achieve/accomplish (45) effective cooperation (46) require (47) at the minimum (48) distinguish (49) met (50) mainly (51) constant production (52) collection (53) Serving (54) medium (55) range (56) locating (57) dangerous (58) also (59) varied (60) looking after

Writing

ESSAY DEVELOPMENT AND PARAGRAPH STRUCTURE

For Your Critical Thinking (p. 103)

COHESION

1. Highly developed social behavior.
2. Par. 2, sentence 1.
3. Key words are: "programmed," "division of labor," "cooperative work," "society."
4. Par. 2.
5. By cooperative work effected through division of labor and by a communication system based on scents and body language.
6. The unity displayed by each ant colony. The colony is compared to an extended family with many members, but one head.
7. Working together as a unit for a common purpose requires not only cooperation but even sacrifice. To make this idea clear to the reader, the writer gives two examples — one, about female worker ants, and the other, about soldier ants.
8. Cooperation works through the system of division of labor, practiced by the members of each ant colony.
9. The writer has used the term "division of labor" in Par. 4-6, and the word "cooperation" is used in Par. 5. These words are put toward the beginning of these paragraphs to let the reader know that the writer is staying with the same idea in these three paragraphs.
10. The second part of S1 is meant as a definition of the caste system to distinguish it from the system of division of labor, according to which work duties can be shifted from one member or group to another, depending on the nature of the work. In a caste system each member or group is specialized to do a certain kind of work.
11. The division of labor or the caste system by which specific workers are assigned to perform assigned duties.
12. The writer explains in Par. 4 how ant colonies practice a division of labor by *giving an example from weaver ants*.
13. Words used: "cooperation," "division of labor."
14. How their construction of nests is a good example of their cooperation and division of labor.
15. By describing each process of nest construction in which each specific group of ants has a specific role to play.

16. The queen ant's unique role in reproduction and how the other members cooperate with her in carrying out this common cause.
17. The word "queen" and the pronouns "she" and "her" are repeated several times in all three paragraphs.
18. No, the writer does not. The word "cooperate" given in the first sentence of this paragraph tells the reader that she is staying with the main idea.
19. No new information is conveyed in the last paragraph. The writer ends the essay with the same kind of comparisons given in the first paragraph, namely, comparing ant colonies to human societies.
20. The writer appeals to the reader by the philosophical conclusion she derives, namely, "nature's own power," as displayed in ants' social behavior, sometimes surpasses human intellect.

COHERENCE

1. Because the writer differentiates between "instinct" as seen in insects and man's powers of "emotion" and "reasoning." Whatever things the insect world accomplishes is through instinct, not by reasoning. The writer introduces the reader to this contradictory idea, using the transition word "yet." Some synonyms are *however, nevertheless, nonetheless*.
2. The pronoun *this* here stands for the whole idea explained in the previous sentence, namely, that the members work together for a common purpose. To avoid repeating the idea and also to keep the unity of the paragraph, the writer uses this device of *pronoun reference*.
3. The same idea. *Likewise.* This word may be replaced by *similarly, in a similar way, also*, etc. (see answers to Question 7 above.)
4. This transition word introduces the reader to the example the writer gives from weaver ants, to illustrate the system of division of labor practiced by most ant colonies. (See answers to Questions 11 and 12 above.)
5. Transition words: "Another example."
6. Transition words: "first," "one," "then" (used twice), and "next."
7. To tell the reader that this is another role that the queen plays in the colony. *In addition, besides, furthermore, also*, etc., give the same idea of "addition."
8. The word "This" in the sentence, "This communication is carried out largely through chemistry," relates the whole sentence to the previous sentence, which introduces the idea of the communication system among ants. The transition word *in fact* repeats the same idea in a different, but emphatic way.

TOPIC SENTENCE AND PARAGRAPH DEVELOPMENT
BY GIVING EXAMPLES

1. The first sentence gives the key idea of the whole paragraph (the topic sentence), and the rest of the sentences are just a development of this key idea.
2. "This demands not only cooperation but altruism."
3. This sentence explains the idea expressed in the previous sentence, namely, "This demands not only cooperation but altruism."
4. The first sentence of the paragraph is the key statement.
5. By giving examples from the actual life of weaver ants.
6. This paragraph is a continuation of the previous paragraph, in which the writer illustrates the division of labor practiced by the ants by giving examples from the life of weaver ants. In Par. 5 the writer gives another example of the ants' cooperative life, and the first sentence introduces this example.
7. The rest of the sentences are "tied" together to this first sentence by transition words like "first," "next," etc.

Note

For beginning writers, it is advisable to start each paragraph with a topic sentence, as shown by the reading passage in this chapter. The topic sentence should be supported by detailed explanations, examples, data, etc. In this section you have learned how to develop the topic sentence by giving examples.

The Expository Essay: Process

Problems for You to Solve (p. 107)

Note: For the answers in this section the titles of the four reading passages are abbreviated as follows:

- "From Quill to Computer": Quill
- "The Ant and Her World": Ant
- "Caffeine": Caf
- "The Awesome Power of Being Ourselves": Power

1. Quill: 4; Ant: 2; Caf: 7; Power: 5.
2. Quill: #4; Ant: #2; Caf: #7; Power: #5.

3. Quill: at the end of Par. 4.
   Ant: at the beginning of the second introductory paragraph.
   Caf: at the end of the last introductory paragraph.
   Power: implied in the short Par. 5, which has only two sentences.
4. Quill: The word processor accomplishes these and several other tasks electronically, and consequently can transform writing in three distinct ways: It can ease the mechanical drudgery of writing; it can enhance our motivation and willingness to spend time going through the entire process of writing; and it can bring about qualitative changes in the writing product, helping writers in their thinking process. (Par. 4)
   Ant: "The hallmark of ants is their highly developed social behavior." (Par. 2)
   Caf: "Here are some of the questions that have been raised and what scientific studies have found so far." (Par. 7)
   Power: "Being oneself is power." (Par. 5)
5. Your answers may vary; however, the outlines should have the thesis and controlling ideas — the subpoints for the developmental paragraphs. An outline for Quill is given below.

   OUTLINE

Introduction

   • Differences: writing long hand, typing, and wordprocessing.

Thesis

   • Word processor can transform writing in three different ways.

Subpoints:

   1. Eases the mechanical drudgery of writing
   2. Enhances motivation and willingness to spend time going through the process of writing
   3. Helps writers in their thinking process

Developmental Paragraphs

1. No need of erasers, scissors, correction tapes; easy to make revision by adding, deleting; clean copies made
2. Screens shown in small chunks; can be filled much faster than an 8½-by-11-inch sheet of paper; writer's block can be overcome by

detouring to wherever the writer feels comfortable and whenever s/he gets ideas to develop
3. Helps find out the writer's thinking process and product by asking questions, like, "How would it read if I change it this way/that way?"

Conclusion

• A valuable tool for writers; however, use it with moderation

CHAPTER 5

Grammar

VERB TENSES

Unreal Conditions in the Past

Application (p. 116)

1. If I had not been sick I would not have failed the test.
2. If he had been nice to his wife she would not have divorced him.
3. The boy could have been saved if the paramedics had been available.
4. If my father had not wanted me to be a professional he would not have sent me to college.

Passive Voice

For Your Critical Thinking (p. 116)

The passive verbs are:

S1. *are outnumbered*
S2. *is said*
S3. *being eaten*
S4. *was characterized*
S5. *to be carried*
S6. *were used*

S7. *may not have been used*
S8. *has been reported*
S9. *is said, were forbidden, were regarded*
S10. *is reported*

Review Chapter 1, pp. 11–12 and Chapter 2 (text) and the relevant answer keys to these problems to see why the writer preferred to use passive verbs in the above contexts.

Comparison of Adjectives

For Your Critical Thinking (p. 117)

1. S1–S4: The definite article *the* should always be used with the superlative degree.
2. There need be at least three people, things, or groups for the use of the superlative degree to be possible.
3. All the adjectives used in S1–S4 are short adjectives. The following formulas apply for the comparative and superlative forms of short adjectives:

    adj + -er + than = comp. degree
    the + adj + -est = sup. degree

4. Some words have irregular comparative and superlative forms. Like the irregular verb forms, these are memorized by most learners of English. However, it is always better to learn their use from your reading. The word *best* is the irregular superlative form of *good*. Following is a list of irregular comparative forms of some adjectives and adverbs.

Base Form	Comparative	Superlative
bad	worse	worst
badly	worse	worst
little	less	least
good	better	best
well	better	best
many	more	most
much	more	most
far	farther/further	farthest/furthest

Sentence Combining

CLAUSE MARKERS

Problems for You to Solve (p. 118)

Check your answers against the writer's sentences in the text. If your answer is different, discuss it with your instructor. There are different correct ways of combining some of these sentences.

PREPOSITIONAL PHRASES

Problems for You to Solve (p. 119)

Because of is not a clause marker like *because* that requires a clause (with a complete verb) to follow it.

Vocabulary, Word Forms, and Idioms

FILL-INS (p. 119)

1b. (1) basis (2) classified (3) categories
     (4) mysteriously (5) systems (6) although (7) exist
     (8) thorough (9) how (10) put (11) controversy
     (12) settle (13) chauvinistic (14) topic
2b. (15) Americans (16) predominantly (17) almost all
     (18) East
     (19) Africans (20) which (21) fork-feeders (22) majority
3b. (23) history (24) because (25) invented (26) earliest
     (27) China (28) dated (29) even though (30) utensils
     (31) earlier
4b. (32) advantage (33) deal with (34) appearance (35) except
     (36) used (37) needed (38) since (39) pieces (40) cooked
5b. (41) three groups (42) militantly (43) defensive
     (44) utensil/tool (45) uses (46) instance (47) famous
     (48) non-finger feeders

Writing

THE EXPOSITORY ESSAY: CLASSIFICATION

For Your Critical Thinking (p. 128)

1. Classification is the style used.
2. The essays, "The Technology of Eating," and "College Teachers," are the best. Analysis follows:

"The Technology of Eating"

- Basis of classification: single principle applied, namely, the technology of eating solid food
- Classification: finger-feeders, chopstick-feeders, and fork-feeders; classification complete (doesn't exclude any category)
- Specific topic of discussion: the controversy over which of the three is the best way to eat solid food
- Development of topic: the origin of each the three traced, using examples; comparative method applied to explain the use of each of the three
- Writer's own conclusion given in the last paragraph

"College Teachers"

- Basis of classification: teaching effectiveness (single basis).
- Classification: positive, neutral, and negative teachers.
- Development: Each category defined, explained, and compared with good, personal examples.
- Writer's own conclusion (last paragraph), given as a suggestion to college administration.

Note: In comparing these two essays, bear in mind that "College Teachers" is a very personal topic, whereas "The Technology of Eating" is a scientific essay, based on research information. In an advanced level of writing, you should try to incorporate into your essays information from your reading, if not from your research.

"Herbs"
This essay is not expository, but descriptive, even though it adopts the technique of classification in developing the topic. Reasons:

- Classification not complete : excludes herbs used for (1) fragrance, (2) dyeing (these are just mentioned in the definition given in the introductory paragraph).
- No stand taken by the writer ; no comparison of one to the other.
- Paragraphs not expository ; no topic sentence developed in any paragraphs ; example given, not to prove any points, but merely to explain.

Note : This essay is a good example of how you can do research on a certain topic and summarize the information you receive from this research, which skill you need in many of your content area courses.

3. Thesis Statement :

- "The Technology of Eating" : "Why people fall into these categories is a mystery and there is no comprehensive account of the ways of putting solid food into the mouth." (Par. 1)
- "Herbs" : no thesis statement
- "College Teachers" : "In fact, I have found that most professors at state fall into three categories : the positive teachers, the neutral teachers ... and the negative teachers." (Par. 1)

Note : It will be helpful for you to note here that the patterns of classification and comparison/contrast overlap. In essays of classification, the technique used to explain each category is usually comparison and contrast. Of course, examples belong in any expository essays and they are appropriate in classification essays, too.

4. (a)

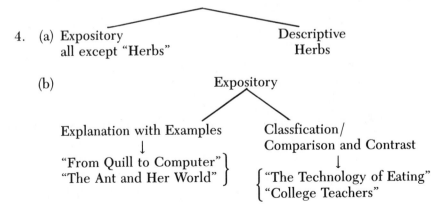

Expository
all except "Herbs"

Descriptive
Herbs

(b) Expository

Explanation with Examples
↓
"From Quill to Computer"⎱
"The Ant and Her World"⎰

Classfication/
Comparison and Contrast
↓
⎧ "The Technology of Eating"
⎩ "College Teachers"

(c)

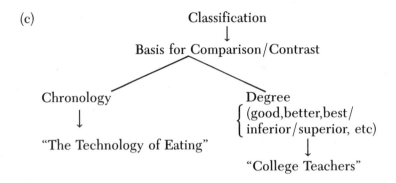

5. Basis for Classification:

  • Whether the writer has a point of view or not.
  • Specific rhetorical styles used to explain the writer's point of view.
  • Techniques used to distinguish one category from the other.

6. Distinguishing characteristics: In the descriptive essay ("Herbs") the writer does not take a stand. Neither does any of the developmental paragraphs have a topic sentence. Examples are given in most paragraphs. However, they do not prove any point, but merely describe the items under each category.

  (a) In each of the four expository essays the writer takes a stand in the introductory paragraph, which he or she explains in the developmental paragraphs. Each developmental paragraph begins with a topic sentence, which is explained by giving supporting details.

  (b) In the two classification essays the writers classify the topic, applying a single principle. Using the technique of comparison/contrast, each category is further explained in the developmental paragraph and is distinguished one from the other.

  In the two essays of explanation the writers' points of view are explained in the developmental paragraphs, giving supporting details and examples.

  (c) In "The Technology of Eating," each classified group is chronologically compared and contrasted.

  In "College Teachers," the basis of comparing and contrasting each category is the degree of each teacher's effectiveness in teaching, with special reference to his or her relationship with students.

7. You should have your own preferences. Defend your preference, giving sound reasons.

CHAPTER 7

Grammar

MODAL VERBS

For Your Critical Thinking (p. 171)

S1. obligation/advisability
(It is *strongly advisable* that you check with your doctor.)
S2. expectation
(How much are you *expected* to spend?)
S3. obligation
It is *obligatory* that a sport-touring bike has a one- to-two-inch ... bar.
S4. expectation
(and turn ... what is *expected* to be a pleasure into a chore.

Sentence Combining

IF-CLAUSES:

Problems for You to Solve (p. 172)

1. S1. Suppose your idea of exercise as been stepping out on the porch and stooping over to pick up the morning paper. Then (in that case) don't expect cycling to be easy on your body.
   S2. Suppose you are over thirty-five. Then the first thing you should do is to check with your doctor before starting.
   S3. Suppose you haven't been on a bike since you got your driver's license. Then (in that case) you will first need to condition your legs, your heart, and your gluteus.
   S4. Suppose you are serious about giving cycling a try. Then (in that case) it is worth shopping for a new bike.

2. Antonym for *if*: *unless*
3. Synonyms: *in case, provided, on condition*

WHILE-CLAUSES

Problems for You to Solve (p. 173)

1. Clause markers which can substitute for *while* (meaning *contrast*) : *whereas, even though, although.*
2. S1.   Anyone who can balance a bike and pedal can take up cycling. *Nevertheless*, no one is ready for long, strenuous rides right at the start.

   S2.   The former comes in the form of track-racing bikes. *However*, the latter is designed for long cycling tours.

   S3.   Sport-touring usually have dropped handlebars and narrow, grooved tires. *However*, all-terrain bikes have rigid, upright handlebars and wide, knobby tires.

   S4.   There is much disagreement among cyclists as among motor-cyclists about the pros and cons of wearing helmets. *Nevertheless*, the facts speak for themselves.

For Your Critical Thinking (p. 173)

In S5 *while* is a time clause marker, which can be substituted for *when*. In S6 and S7 *while* means *contrast*.

NOUN CLAUSES

Problems for You to Solve (p. 174)

S1.   Visit a couple of bike shops to find *it* out exactly.

S2.   Make your choice based on *it*.

S3.   *It* is ride for fitness and fun — you can always try specialized riding once you have more experience.

S4.   Getting the right size will determine *it* — and that will determine *it*.

S5.   A frame that is either too small or too large will make riding awkward, and turn *it* ... .

Problems for You to Solve (p. 175)

S1.   *Object* of the verb *find out.*

S2.   *Object* of the preposition *on.*

S3.   *Subject* complement of *is.*

S4.   *Object* of the verb *determine.*
S5.   *Object* of the verb *turn.*

*ONCE-*CLAUSES

For Your Critical Thinking (p. 175)

In S1 *once* means *at one time* and is used as an *adverb.* In S2 and S3 *once* means *when* and is a *clause marker.*

Sentence and Paragraph Relating

For Your Critical Thinking (p. 175)

1. The first sentence is the topic sentence. The controlling idea (implied) is that cycling is a tool for both enjoyment and exercise.
2. All the sentences in the paragraph tell the reader that the reason for the increasing popularity of cycling among Americans is that it promotes physical fitness, serving as a means of both enjoyment and exercise. Thus the paragraph is *unified under one topic (cohesive).*
3. The transition words *one reason, also,* (used twice), and *and* (in the last sentence) *structurally unify the sentences* into a *coherent* paragraph, relating all the sentences to the supporting statement for the controlling idea, namely, "One reason for its steadily growing popularity is that Americans are discovering both the pleasures and the physical benefits it offers." All the other sentences provide details for this supporting statement.
4. In Par. 1 the writer talks about the positive side of cycling as a pastime. In the second paragraph the writer alerts the readers to a negative aspect, knowledge of which is the first step in learning to ride. The transition word *however* is a device used by the writer to relate these two contrasting ideas and to catch the readers' attention to his or her purpose, namely, explaining the steps involved in learning to ride a bicycle. In Par. 3 the writer warns the readers about the likelihood of experiencing saddle soreness. In Par. 4, there is a sudden switch from "saddle sore" to "buying a bike." These two ideas are being connected to each other by the use of *however.* What the

writer accomplishes by the use of this device is that the readers' attention is drawn to the importance of buying a bicycle — a necessary step in the process of learning how to ride — until which time they do not have to be concerned about getting saddle sore.

5. The sentences that *in fact* helps to relate are : "If your idea of exercise has been stepping out on the porch and stooping over to pick up the morning paper, don't expect cycling to be easy on your body." and "As with any program, the first thing you should do is to check with your doctor before starting, especially if your are over thirty-five. The two ideas are almost the same. *In fact* reaffirms the idea expressed in the sentence that precedes it.

6. In Par. 11 and 12, the author talks about the steps involved in competing in cycling races. In paragraph 13, he states that even though cycling races are exciting, what motivates most learners is not the prospect of participating in cycling races, but the "sheer pleasure of wheeling through neighborhoods and country roads." These two different ideas, expressed in different paragraphs, are structurally related to each other by the use of the transition word *but*.

Vocabulary, Word Forms, and Idioms

FILL-INS (p. 176)

1b. (1) increasing (2) chosen (3) hobby (4) popular (5) find
     (6) helpful (7) enjoyment (8) exercise (9) Like
     (10) great extent (11) Besides (12) proper (13) flexible
     (14) stronger (15) Furthermore (16) active (17) However
     (18) hurt (19) shocking experience (20) since
     (21) activates (22) slowed down
2b. (23) Despite (24) risks (25) involved (26) like
     (27) activity (28) Even though (29) be able
     (30) everybody (31) start off (32) In case (33) go
     (34) bend down (35) difficult (36) As a matter of fact
     (37) strongly advised (38) special (39) consulting
     (40) prior to
3b. (41) In spite of the fact (42) race (43) exciting
     (44) interests (45) absolute (46) provides (47) get rid of
     (48) pressures (49) tensions (50) other (51) interested
     more

Expository Writing

THE PROCESS ESSAY

The Organization of a Process Essay

Application (p. 188)

1. The writer uses the first paragraph and part of the second for introduction. See pp. 330–331, no. 2, no. 3 above.
2. "While anyone who can balance a bike and pedal can take up cycling, no one is ready for long, strenuous rides at the first start." The sentence arouses the reader's curiosity to learn what they should do before they start long, strenuous rides.
3. The purpose is to alert the reader to some risks involved in learning to ride. The writer gives this warning because a reader who wants to recreate the process has to be aware of these risks. (See p. 188, Developmental Paragraphs.)
4. Eight steps:

   Step 1. Check with your doctor before starting to learn, especially if you are over thirty-five.
   Step 2. Don't start off with long rides, which may make you saddle sore.
   Step 3. Shop for a bicycle.
   Step 4. Buy the right one.
   Step 5. Buy a helmet.
   Step 6. Start to ride, slowly increasing speed, time, and distance according to your body's capacity.
   Step 7. Prepare yourself for racing, if you want to.
   Step 8. Most of all, enjoy riding as a pastime which helps you get rid of life's worries and anxieties, at least for a while.

5. Answers may vary according to each student's reaction.
6. The end result the writer wants the reader to get is: learn to ride a bicycle for the sake of enjoying it as a pastime, the byproduct of which is relaxation for the mind and body.
7. Directional: "Starting to Cycle" and "The Best Way to Sell Your Car."
   Instructional: "Adventure on the Colorado" and "The Development of Language in Children."
   The reader can follow the steps explained in the directional essays and get the same end result. The writers follow the organiza-

tional pattern of a directional process essay, describing major steps. Each major step is further explained very clearly. The reader is also warned against possible problems.

Readers may be able to recreate the steps explained in "Adventure on the Colorado" and have the same experience as the writer did. However, the purpose is not to invite the reader to recreate the process but to share the writer's experience and inform the readers of what to expect in case they want to have a similar experience. Therefore, the essay is more instructional than directional.

"The Development of Language in Children" is strictly instructional. Only a child can recreate the process, in which case it is an automatic process, not a deliberate one.

Except for the "Adventure on the Colorado" (which follows a spatial order), all the essays follow a chronological order in taking the reader from one step to the other.

8. Review the answer to no. 7 above.

CHAPTER 8

Vocabulary, Word Forms, and Idioms

FILL-INS (p. 201)

1b. (1) ago (2) considered (3) However, (4) motivate (5) same (6) ancestors (7) chance (8) relax (9) socialize (10) powerful (11) operating (12) influential

2b. (13) last (14) reason (15) influences (16) attitude (17) For example (18) many (19) seems (20) regularly (21) portray

3b. (22) and (23) always (24) represented (25) wealth (26) companionship (27) Although (28) symbol (29) sophisticated (30) sexy

4b. (31) effect (32) judge (33) statistics (34) happen (35) mostly (36) as a result of (37) attributed to (38) Shocking/agonizing/painful (39) accidents (40) many (41) major (42) cause (43) below (44) old (45) drunken (46) plays (47) probability (48) habitual (49) reason (50) possible (51) reason (52) fall asleep (53) putting out (54) Fifty percent (55) walking (56) not (57) just (58) every year (59) make up (60) caused by